THE PRAVARGYA BRĀHMAṆA
OF THE
TAITTIRĪYA ĀRAṆYAKA

THE PRAVARGYA BRĀHMAṆA
OF THE
TAITTIRĪYA ĀRAṆYAKA

an ancient commentary on the Pravargya ritual

Introduction, translation and notes by
JAN E.M. HOUBEN

MOTILAL BANARSIDASS PUBLISHERS PVT. LTD.
DELHI

First Edition: Delhi, 1991

ISBN: 81-208-0868-1

Also available at:
MOTILAL BANARSIDASS
41 U.A., Bungalow Road, Jawahar Nagar, Delhi 110 007
120 Royapettah High Road, Mylapore, Madras 600 004
16 St. Mark's Road, Bangalore 560 001
Ashok Rajpath, Patna 800 004
Chowk, Varanasi 221 001

PRINTED IN INDIA
BY JAINENDRA PRAKASH JAIN AT SHRI JAINENDRA PRESS, A-45 NARAINA INDUSTRIAL AREA, PHASE I, NEW DELHI 110 028 AND PUBLISHED BY NARENDRA PRAKASH JAIN FOR MOTILAL BANARSIDASS PUBLISHERS PVT. LTD., BUNGALOW ROAD, JAWAHAR NAGAR, DELHI 110 007

to my father

Jacobus Hermanus Joseph Houben

CONTENTS

PREFACE

The Taittirīya Āraṇyaka contains several elements from a later origin than the Taittirīya Brāhmaṇa and Saṃhitā. The recognition of this by scholars like A. Weber and A. B. Keith, may have been the reason for their relative neglect of this part of the Taittirīya tradition. However, the mantras and Brāhmaṇa of the Pravargya ritual have found their place in the Āraṇyaka probably not because they originated later, but because of the special character of the Pravargya ritual. The Pravargya is one of the few rituals that has been explicitly referred to in the Ṛgveda (usually under the name "Gharma"). The abstract and spiritual nature of what is probably the main purpose of the ritual - the participants should acquire the lustre of the sun - the simple means by which it can be performed and the way the main implement, the pot which is heated red-hot, is worshipped, give it a special place in the vast assortment of Vedic rites.

For a complete description of the Pravargya according to the Śrauta Sūtras, the reader is referred to van Buitenen's *The Pravargya* (Poona, 1968) and the *Śrautakośa.* The present book gives a translation and discussion of the Pravargya Brāhmaṇa of the Taittirīya tradition. It is, depending on the recension, either the fifth or the eighth chapter of the Taittirīya Āraṇyaka. The text discusses the use of the Pravargya mantras and abounds in Brāhmaṇical explanations of the mantras and acts. It follows the ritual in an older, slightly different version than the Śrauta Sūtras. The translation and introduction intend to make the text accessible to students of comparative cultural history, to Sanskrit students who are not specialists in the field of Vedic ritual (the Sanskrit text has been given with the translation), and to others who might be interested in the subject. Scholarly problems connected with the text and its subject are discussed in notes at the end.

My study at the State University Utrecht, under my Sanskrit teachers, dr. L. van Daalen and dr. T. Goudriaan, and especially under my teacher in Vedic Sanskrit, prof. dr. H. Bodewitz, resulted in the "doctoraalscriptie" (1987) on which the present book is based. To their teaching and continuing inspiration I owe a lot. Without the latter's patience in discussing and criticizing, on the basis of his thorough knowledge of the intricacies of the Vedic ritual, earlier drafts of this work, I would have given up halfway. I am thankful to Dr. G. Kreyenbroek, who helped me find the information I needed about old Iranian rituals. In an indirect way prof. em. J. Gonda contributed to this book, not only through his highly valuable works in the field of Vedic studies, but also because all of my Sanskrit teachers were former students of his. While I alone am responsible for the shortcomings which this book no doubt still has in spite of all efforts to avoid them, it is my pleasant duty to express my thanks to these teachers and also to the following persons. I thank mr. A. J. A. C. Nooteboom, mr. D. O'Brien (London) and ms. L. N. Vallaster (Vancouver) for their advice concerning style and diction, and mr. S. Chu (Vancouver) for his help in drawing the plan of the place of sacrifice (Appendix). In Vancouver I incurred moreover the debt of gratitude to dr. G. Sparham, prof. dr. A. Aklujkar and prof. dr. K. Bryant, for their help and advice concerning the computerized processing of this text. Both for the roman and for the Devanāgarī script I used prof. Bryants' fonts. I am also thankful to mrs. H. Zweerus of the Computer centre of the State University Utrecht, who helped me solve some technical problems in the final stages of the preparation of the manuscript.

Finally, thanks are due to the publishers of Motilal Banarsidass, for accepting this work for publication.

ABBREVIATIONS*

Abbreviations of Sanskrit Texts

AiĀ — Aitareya-Āraṇyaka; ed. and tr. by A. B. Keith (*Anecd. Oxon. A. S.* 9), 1909; ed. (with Sāyaṇa's commentary) ĀSG 38, [3]1959.

AiB — Aitareya-Brāhmaṇa; ed. Th. Aufrecht, Bonn 1879; tr. A. B. Keith in *Ṛigveda Brāhmaṇas* (HOS 25), 1920.

ĀpŚS — Āpastamba-Śrauta-Sūtra belonging to the Taittirīya-Saṃhitā, with the commentary of Rudradatta; ed. R. Garbe (BI 92), 1882-1902 (3 vols.); tr. W. Caland, vol. 1: Quellen der Religionsgeschichte, Göttingen, 1921; vol. 2-3 Amsterdam Academy. Amsterdam 1924-28.

ĀśvŚS — Āśvalāyana-Śrauta-Sūtra; ed. BI 49, 1874. partly tr. (Adhyāyas 1-4) by K. Mylius, see *Altorientalische Forschungen* 14 (1987):108-159 for the tr. of Adhyāya 4 and references to his publications of the first three Adhyāyas.

AV — Atharva-Veda-Saṃhitā (Śaunaka); ed. R. Roth, W. D. Whitney and M. Lindenau, Bonn [3]1966; tr. W. D. Whitney, HOS 7-8, 1905; partly tr. M. Bloomfield, SBE 42, 1879.

BŚS — Baudhāyana-Śrauta-Sūtra; ed. W. Caland, Calcutta, I 1904, II 1907, III 1913. partly ed. and tr.: see *Śrautakośa*.

BhŚS — Bhāradvāja-Śrauta-Sūtra; ed. and tr. C. G. Kashikar. 2 vols. Poona 1964.

GB — Gopatha-Brāhmaṇa; ed. D. Gaastra, Leiden 1919.

HirŚS — Hiraṇyakeśi-Śrauta-Sūtra; (=Satyāṣāḍha-Śrauta-Sūtra); ed. ĀSG 53 (10 vols.), 1907-1932.

JB — Jaiminīya-Brāhmaṇa; ed. Raghu Vira and Lokesh Chandra, Sarasvati Vihāra Series 31, 1954; Second rev. edition: Delhi-Varanasi-Patna, 1986; partly ed. and tr. W. Caland, *Das Jaiminīya-Brāhmaṇa in Auswahl*, Amsterdam Academy 1919; partly tr. H. W. Bodewitz, *Jaiminīya Brāhmaṇa I, 1-65*, (thesis Utrecht), Leiden 1973; *The Jyotiṣṭoma Ritual. Jaiminīya Brāhmaṇa I, 66-364.* Leiden, (in press).

JUB — Jaiminīya-Upaniṣad-Brāhmaṇa; ed. and tr. H. Oertel, *JAOS* 16 (1896):79-260.

KaṭhĀ — Kaṭha-Āraṇyaka (also called: Kaṭha-Brāhmaṇa); citations follow Witzel's edition. Ed. L. von Schroeder in *Die Tübinger Kaṭha-Handschriften und ihre Beziehung zum Taittirīya-Āraṇyaka* (*Sitzungsberichte Akad. Wien, phil.-hist. Classe*, 137), 1898; ed. and tr. M. Witzel (thesis Erlangen), 1972, and Kathmandu 1974. Cp. introduction, note 73.

---

* This list of abbreviations contains bibliographical information about the main works referred to in this book. For more detailed bibliographical information about works upto 1983, L. Renou's and R. N. Dandekar's excellent Vedic Bibliographies should be consulted.

KauṣĀ	Kauṣitaki-Āraṇyaka (=Śāṅkhāyana-Āraṇyaka); ed. ĀSG 90 (1922); tr. A. B. Keith, London 1908.
KauṣB	Kauṣītaki-Brāhmaṇa (=Śāṅkhāyana-Brāhmaṇa); ed. B. Lindner, Jena 1887; tr. A. B. Keith in *Ṛigveda Brāhmaṇas* (HOS 25), 1920.
KS	Kāṭhaka-Saṃhitā; ed. L. von Schroeder, Leipzig 1900-1910 (3 vols.).
MS	Maitrāyaṇī-Saṃhitā; ed. L. von Schroeder, Leipzig 1881-1886.
MŚS	Mānava-Śrauta-Sūtra; ed. F. Knauer, Petersburg 1900-1903; ed. and tr. J. M. van Gelder, New Delhi, 1961-1963, Reprint: Sri Satguru Publications, Delhi 1985.
ṚV	Ṛg-Veda-Saṃhitā; ed. F. M. Müller, saṃhitā and pada texts (2 vols) [3]Varanasi 1965; tr. K. F. Geldner, HOS 33-35, 1951; partly tr. L. Renou in *Études Védiques et Pāṇinéennes* (see under Renou, *ÉVP*).
ṚVKhil	Ṛg-Veda-Khilāni; ed. J. Scheftelowitz in *Die Apokryphen des Ṛgveda (Khilāni)*, (*Indische Forschungen* 1), Breslau 1906.
ŚvetU	Śvetāśvatara-Upaniṣad; ed. and tr. R. Hauschild, Leipzig 1927.
ŚB	Śatapatha Brāhmaṇa (Mādhyandina-Śākhā); ed. A. Weber, London 1855. tr. J. Eggeling, SBE 12, 26, 41, 43, 44 (1882-1900).
TĀ	Taittirīya-Āraṇyaka; (a) ed. with Sāyaṇa's commentary by Rajendralal Mitra (BI), Calcutta, 1872. Abbreviated as C. (b) ed. with Sāyana's commentary by K. V. Abhyankarshastri and G. A. Joshishastri, (ĀSG 36, 2 vols), Poona 1897, repr. [3]1967. Abbreviated as P. (c) ed. with the commentary of Bhaṭṭa Bhāskara Miśra by A. Mahadeva Sastri and K. Rangacarya; Government Oriental Series, Bibliotheca Sanskrita Nos. 26, 27 and 29, Mysore, 1900-1902; reprint New Delhi 1985. Abbreviated as M.
TB	Taittirīya-Brāhmaṇa; ed. with Sāyaṇa's commentary by N. Sastri Godabole, (ĀSG 37, 3 vols), Poona 1934-1938, repr. [3]1979.
TS	Taittirīya-Saṃhitā; ed. A. Weber, *IS* 11-12, 1871-1872; ed. with the commentary of Madhava Acharya by E. Röer et.al. (BI, 10 vols.), 1854-1899; repr. [2]1980-1981.; tr. A. B. Keith, HOS 18-19, 1914.
VaikhŚS	Vaikhānasa-Śrauta-Sūtra; ed. W. Caland, (BI 265) Calcutta 1941.
VS	Vājasaneyi-Saṃhitā; ed. A. Weber, London 1852.

Abbreviated titles (secondary and oft-cited literature)

Bodewitz, *Agnihotra*	H. W. Bodewitz, *Daily Evening and Morning Offering (Agnihotra) according to the Brāhmaṇas*, Leiden, 1978.
Caland, '*Wunschopfer*'	W. Caland, *Altindische Zauberei. Darstellung der altindischen 'Wunschopfer'*. Verhandelingen der Kon. Ak. van Wetensch. te Amsterdam, Afd. Letterkunde, Nieuwe Reeks, 10, no 1. Amsterdam, 1908.

Caland-Henry, *Agniṣṭoma*	W. Caland and V. Henry, *L'Agniṣṭoma, description complète de la forme normale du Sacrifice de Soma dans le culte Védique.* Paris, 1906-1907.
Gonda, *Aspects*	J. Gonda, *Aspects of Early Viṣṇuism.* [2]Delhi-Varanasi-Patna, 1969.
Gonda, *Change and Continuity*	J. Gonda, *Change and Continuity in Indian Religion.* The Hague, 1965.
Gonda, *Eye and Gaze*	J. Gonda, *Eye and Gaze in the Veda.* Kon. Ned. Ak. van Wetensch., Afd. Letterkunde, Nieuwe Reeks, deel 75, no. 1. Amsterdam, London, 1969.
Gonda, *Prajāpati and the Year*	J. Gonda, *Prajāpati and the Year.* Kon. Ned. Ak. van Wetensch., Afd. Letterkunde, Nieuwe Reeks, deel 123, Amsterdam, Oxford, New York, 1984
Gonda, *Religionen*	J. Gonda, *Die Religionen Indiens* 1: *Veda und älterer Hinduismus.* Stuttgart, 1960, [2]1978.
Gonda, *Select.*	J. Gonda, *Selected Studies.* Leiden, 1975, vol. 2: Word Studies; vol. 3: Grammatical and Philological Studies; vol. 4: History of Ancient Indian Religion.
Gonda, *Vision*	J. Gonda, *The Vision of the Vedic Poets.* The Hague, 1963.
Gonda, *Vedic Literature*	J. Gonda, *Vedic Literature.* (*History of Indian Literature*, vol. 1, fasc. 1) Wiesbaden, 1975.
Gonda, "Pravargya Mantras"	J. Gonda, "A Propos of the Mantras in the Pravargya Section of the Ṛgvedic Brāhmaṇas," *IIJ* 21 (1979):235-271.
Hauer, *Yogapraxis*	J. W. Hauer, *Die Anfänge der Yoga-Praxis*, Stuttgart, 1922.
Heesterman, "Severed Head"	Heesterman, "The Case of the Severed Head" in: *Essays in Indian Ritual, Kingship and Society*, Chicago, 1985.
Hillebrandt, *Ritual-literatur*	A. Hillebrandt, *Ritualliteratur. Vedische Opfer und Zauber*, Strassburg, 1897.
Hillebrandt, *Vedische Mythologie*	A. Hillebrandt, *Vedische Mythologie*, 2 vol. [2]Breslau, 1927-1929.
Kashikar, "Apropos"	C. G. Kashikar, "Apropos of the Pravargya ", *Centre of Advanced Sanskrit Studies*, Number 1 (Publ. of the Centre of Advanced Study in Sanskrit), Poona 1973:1-10.
Kashikar, "Avāntaradīkṣā"	C. G. Kashikar, "The Avāntaradīkṣā of Pravargya", *BDCRI*, vol. 35, no. 3-4, Poona 1976:66-72.
Kashikar, "Mahāvīra"	C. G. Kashikar, "The Concept of Mahāvīra in the Pravargya", *Golden Jubilee Volume, Vaidika Saṃśodhana Maṇḍala*, Poona 1982:136-139.
Keith, *Religion*	A. B. Keith, *Religion and Philosophy of the Veda.* Cambridge Mass. 1925.
Kramrisch, "Mahāvīravessel"	S. Kramrisch, "The Mahāvīravessel and the plant Pūtika", *JAOS* 95/2: 222-235; reprinted as the third chapter of: *Persephone's Quest: Entheogens and the Origin of Religion*, Yale University Press 1986.

Krick, *Feuergründung*:	H. Krick, *Das Ritual der Feuergründung*. Vienna Acad. 1982.
Kuiper, "Basic Concept"	F. B. J. Kuiper, "The Basic Concept of Vedic Religion", *History of Religions* 15 (1975): 107-120. Also in: F. B. J. Kuiper, *Ancient Indian Cosmogony*. essays selected and introduced by John Irwin, New Delhi, 1983:9-22.
Kuiper, "The Bliss of Aša"	F. B. J. Kuiper, "The Bliss of Aša", *IIJ* 8/2(1964): 96-129. Also in: F. B. J. Kuiper, *Ancient Indian Cosmogony*, essays selected and introduced by John Irwin, New Delhi, 1983:56-89.
Kuiper, "Was the Pūtīka a mushroom?"	F. B. J. Kuiper, "Was the Pūtīka a mushroom?" In: *Amṛtadhārā. Prof. R. N. Dandekar felicitation volume*, ed. S. D. Joshi, Delhi, 1984.
Lüders, *Varuṇa*	H. Lüders, *Varuṇa*, Göttingen, 2 vol., 1951-1959.
Malamoud, *Svādhyāya*	C. Malamoud, *Le Svādhyāya, récitation personnelle du Veda; Taittirīya-Āraṇyaka livre II*. Paris, Institut de Civilisation Indienne, 1977.
Minard, *Énigmes*	A. Minard, *Trois Énigmes sur les Cent Chemins. Recherches sur le Śatapatha-Brāhmaṇa*. 2 vol., Paris 1949-1956.
Oldenberg, *Die Religion*	H. Oldenberg, *Die Religion des Veda*. Berlin, ^{3}1923.
Oldenberg, *Vorw.Wiss.*	H. Oldenberg, *Vorwissenschaftliche Wissenschaft. Die Weltanschauung der Brāhmaṇa-Texte*. Göttingen, 1919.
Rau, *Altertumskunde*	W. Rau, *Zur vedischen Altertumskunde*. Abh. der Akademie der Wiss. und Lit., geistes- und sozialwiss. Klasse (Mainz) 1983, no. 1.
Rau, *Meaning of púr*	W. Rau, *The Meaning of púr in Vedic Literature*. Abh. der Marburger Gelehrten Gesellschaft, 1973, no. 1, München, 1976.
Rau, *Metallgeräte*	W. Rau, *Metalle und Metallgeräte im vedischen Indien*, Abh. der Akademie der Wiss. und Lit., geistes- und sozialwiss.Klasse (Mainz) 1973, no. 8.
Rau, *Staat*	W. Rau, *Staat und Gesellschaft im alten Indien*. Wiesbaden 1957.
Rau, *Töpferei*	W. Rau, *Töpferei und Tongeschirr im vedischen Indien*, Abh. der Akademie der Wiss. und Lit., geistes- und sozialwiss. Klasse (Mainz) 1972, no. 10.
Renou, *Écoles Védiques*	L. Renou, *Les écoles védiques et la formation du Veda*. Paris 1947.
Renou, *ÉVP*	L. Renou, *Études Védiques et Paṇinéennes*, 1-17, Paris 1955-1969.
Rönnow, "Zur Erklärung des Pravargya etc."	K. Rönnow, "Zur Erklärung des Pravargya , des Agnicayana und der Sautrāmaṇī", *Monde Oriental* 23 (1929):113-173.
Sen, "Verbforms"	N. Sen, "Some Remarkable Words and Verbforms from the Taittirīya Āraṇyaka". *BDCRI* 35 (1975):145-153.
Śrautakośa	*Śrautakośa. Encyclopaedia of Vedic Sacrificial Ritual.* Volume 2 (Agniṣṭoma with Pravargya), Sanskrit Section part 1 (Based on the Saṃhitās, the Brāhmaṇas, the Āraṇyakas and the Baudhāyanaśrautasūtra), Poona, 1970.

	Volume 2 (Agniṣṭoma with Pravargya), English Section part 1 (Based on the Śrautasūtras belonging to the various Vedic Schools), Poona, 1973.
Staal, *Agni*	*Agni, the Vedic ritual of the Fire Altar*, 2 vol., Asian Humanities Press, Berkeley, 1983. Vol. 1: ed. by F. Staal in collaboration with C. V. Somayajipad and M. Itti Ravi Nambudiri; Vol. 2: ed. by F. Staal with the assistance of Pamela MacFarland.
Thite, *Sacrifice*	G. V. Thite, *Sacrifice in the Brāhmaṇa Texts*. Poona, 1975.
van Buitenen, *Pravargya*	J. A. B. van Buitenen, *The Pravargya. An Ancient Indian Iconic Ritual*. Poona, 1968.
Zysk, *Religious Healing*	K. G. Zysk, *Religious Healing in the Veda*. (Transactions of the American Philosophical Society, vol. 75, part 7) Philadelphia, 1985.

Other abbreviations

ALB	*Adyar Library Bulletin*, Adyar Madras.
ĀSG	Ānandāśrama-Saṃskṛta-Granthāvali, Poona.
BDCRI	*Bulletin of the Deccan College Research Institute*, Poona.
HOS	Harvard Oriental Series, Harvard University Press, Cambridge, Massachusetts; London, England.
IIJ	*Indo-Iranian Journal*, Dordrecht-Boston.
IS	*Indische Studien*, Leipzig.
SBE	Sacred Books of the East, London.
BI	Bibliotheca Indica, Calcutta.

transl (translated) and *übers* (übersetzt) after an abbreviated title of a Vedic text indicates (one of) the translation(s) mentioned under that abbreviation.

S	Sāyaṇa's commentary on the Taittirīya-Āraṇyaka. See under TĀ, (a) and (b).
Bh	Bhaṭṭa-Bhāskara Miśra's commentary on the Taittirīya-Āraṇyaka. See under TĀ, (c).
C, P, M	See under TĀ (a), (b) and (c).

part I: INTRODUCTION

INTRODUCTION

1 The Pravargya Ritual

The oldest portions of the wonderfully complex structure of Vedic texts are interlaced with numerous references to ritual acts and ceremonies. The exact contents of the ritual acts and ceremonies referred to are often no longer recoverable. Among these references mention is made of a probably simple hot-milk offering, *gharmá*,[1] to the Aśvins, the twin-gods connected with dawn and sunrise. A Gharma offering to the Aśvins is one of the two main constituents[2] of the Pravargya ritual[3] as described by later

---

1 (a) Cf. Hillebrandt, *Ritualliteratur*:15.

(b) The oldest references we have are those in the Ṛgveda. A Ṛgvedic hymn that received much attention in connection with the Gharma offering, is the so-called frog-hymn (ṚV 7, 103). (See Hillebrandt, *Ritualliteratur*:134f; H. Lüders, *Varuṇa* 2:363-4; van Buitenen, *Pravargya*:31-33; C. Kashikar "Apropos of the Pravargya":7; see also Gonda, *Vedic Literature*:143). Important references are further in ṚV 1, 119, 2; 1, 164, 26-27 (perhaps 28-29; for 43 see section 4 below); 1, 180, 4; 3, 53, 14; 5, 19, 4; 5, 30, 15; 5, 43, 7; 5, 73, 6; 5, 76, 1; 7, 70, 2; 8, 9, 7; 8, 87, 2; 8, 89, 7; 10, 181, 3. For verses that were most probably actually *used* in a Pravargya ceremony in its earliest forms see Gonda, "A propos of the Mantras in the Pravargya section of the ṚgVedic Brāhmaṇas":236-271, esp. 262. It may be questioned, however, whether it is probable that in the earliest forms of the Pravargya, the vessel and its preparation did not play an important role (see section 4 below). In the ṚV khilasūktas and in the AtharvaVeda, there are several references to the Gharma. Special mention deserve: verse 2 of the so-called Brahma-jajñānam hymn (ṚVKhil 3, 22, 2; AV 4, 1, 2, forming part of the first recitation by the Hotṛ, ṚVKhil 3, 22, 1-4; van Buitenen, *Pravargya*:67); AV 7, 73, called the Gharma-sūkta (in a different order in the Paippalāda version 20, 11 and 20, 12, 1; according to Vaitānasūtra 14, 5a it should be recited by the Brahmán-priest during the offering of the Gharma beverage); ṚVKhil 1, 2, 10; 1, 11, 1; AV 8, 8, 17; 4, 11, 5 and 6; 4, 22, 4; 9, 1, 8.

2 The fact that these two constituents can be distinguished does not imply that they necessarily have a separate origin. In section 4 of this Introduction I will argue that already in Ṛgvedic times the two main constituents of what is called Pravargya in the later texts, formed one single rite. In later texts, *gharmá* may stand for the ceremony as a whole.

3 The term Pravargya (*pravargyà-*, to be placed [sc. on the fire], from *pra-vṛj-*) refers to the ceremony as a whole, and to the main implement, the vessel that is to be heated on the fire and from which the offering to the Aśvins is made. The term is met

texts, the Brāhmaṇas, Āraṇyakas and Śrauta Sūtras. The other constituent is the ceremonial preparation, sacrificial use and solemn disposal of a special vessel, which has several names: Head of Makha, Pravargya, Gharma, Mahāvīra. This is mainly performed by the Adhvaryu, the priest connected with the Yajurveda. The earliest elaborate sources on this constituent specifically, are the Yajurveda texts Taittirīya Āraṇyaka Book 5, Kaṭha-Āraṇyaka Book 2 and 3 and Śatapatha Brāhmaṇa Book 14.[4]

2 Short Description of the Rite

It seems that the Gharma was originally an independent early morning rite. But the Gharma or Pravargya as described in the Brāhmaṇas, Āraṇyakas and Sūtras, is an optional performance in the context of elaborate Soma sacrifices. It takes place either on the Upasad days before

---

with for the first time in the Brāhmaṇa and Āraṇyaka sources of this ceremony. For a complete description of the Pravargya, based on the Śrauta Sūtras see van Buitenen, *Pravargya* (1968); some of his conclusions are criticized by C. G. Kashikar: "Apropos of the Pravargya" (1973), and "The Avāntaradīkṣa of Pravargya" (1976). In "The Concept of Mahāvīra in the Pravargya" (1982) the same author discusses, without entering into a discussion with van Buitenen, the mythological story connected with the Pravargya rite as found in different sources (see section 3.4). The Pravargya in the Agniṣṭoma is described in *Śrautakośa* Volume 2, Sanskrit section part 1 and English section part I. G. U. Thite gives a short description and an interpretation of the rite in *Sacrifice in the Brahmana-Texts*:125ff. Pictures of the Pravargya performed during the Agnicayana in Kerala, South India, 1975, can be seen in Staal, *Agni* 1:368-377. Here we also find a short description and several plans of the place of sacrifice. See also *Agni* 1:217, 231, 233 (the Pravargya vessel and other implements) and *Agni* 1:545-6 (the disposal of the Pravargya implements). For Bhandari, "Pravargya Mahāvīra and Idols," *Journal of the Asiatic Society of Bombay*, vol.52/53 1977-78 (1981): 25-31 see note 33 below. Older literature on the Pravargya: Hillebrandt, *Ritualliteratur*:134ff; Oldenberg, *Die Religion*: 446ff; Keith, *TStransl*, Introduction, p. cxxiiiff; Keith, *Religion*:332f; Lüders, *Varuṇa* II:359-368; Gonda, *Religionen* I:153.

4 For a discussion of the Brāhmaṇa and Āraṇyaka sources of this rite see sections 5 and 6 below and the references mentioned in the notes to those sections.

the pressing days (twice on each day), or on the pressing day (only once). The outlines of this Pravargya ritual are as follows:

a. First, the preparation of the vessels: after an offering of clarified butter to Savitṛ, the Adhvaryu collects clay and several other ingredients and mixes these. They are formed into one main vessel,[5] two spare vessels and several minor clay implements. The vessels are dried in the sun, polished and fumigated with the smoke of burning horse-dung. Next, they are baked in a fire pit. Afterwards the vessels are cooled down by pouring goat's milk over them. During the preparation it is mainly the Adhvaryu who plays an active role.

b. On the day of the Pravargya performance, there are recitations of the Adhvaryu, the Brahmán and the Hotṛ. The main vessel is taken and held with the tongs over the Āhavanīya (some sources: Gārhapatya) fire and anointed with clarified butter to the accompaniment of a sāman,[6] sung by the Prastotṛ. The vessel is placed on a golden (others: a silver) disk that lies on a special mound. The vessel is further anointed with clarified butter and heated. It is surrounded with coals and enclosing sticks and the vessel is covered with a golden disk. The fire is fanned with three fans. The vessel becomes red-hot. The participants (except the wife of the

---

5 This Pravargya-vessel was "a flat-bottomed cooking vessel, constructed from three strips of clay without using the potter's wheel, between 0.24m and 0.60m in diameter, in the middle contracted like an hour-glass, with a girdle (or?) a collar and above a nose-shaped spout, about 0.06m long " (transl. from W. Rau, *Töpferei*:21). Cf. note 36 and 38 to the translation; and Rau, "Vedic texts on the manufacture of pottery," in *Journal of the Oriental Inst. of Baroda* 23 (3), (1974): 137-142.

6 A sāman is a ritual song, a melody sung on the text of mostly Ṛgvedic verses. The songs are collected in the Sāmaveda. See Gonda, *Vedic Literature*, note 18 on p. 314-315; Wayne Howard, *Sāmavedic Chant*, New Haven 1977. For the problems connected with the place of the Sāmaveda in the Pravargya Ritual, see J. A. B. van Buitenen, *Pravargya*, chapter 9 (also J. A. B. van Buitenen, "The Sāmaveda in the Pravargya Ritual," *Mélanges d'Indianisme à la Mémoire de Louis Renou*. Paris, É. de Boccard, 1968); the Sāmaveda does not take a primary position in the Pravargya. But to say, as van Buitenen does, that it was not a Sāmavedic rite is probably not justifiable; see the discussion in Kashikar, "Apropos":8-10.

sacrificer) look reverentially at the vessel and recite a certain group of formulas. The wife pronounces the last formula of this group.

c. The cow and the goat are milked. Their milk is poured into the hot Pravargya vessel. It is taken to the Āhavanīya fire where the Gharma offering to the Aśvins is made. The vessel is made to overflow in all directions. The remnants are used for an Agnihotra offering and eventually the participants partake of the milk. After this, the vessel and other implements are placed back on the throne.

d. After the last Pravargya performance, the implements are solemnly disposed of, normally at the Uttaravedi. The vessels and other implements can be laid down in the form of a man or in the shape of the orb of the sun. Several sāmans are sung by all participants (including the wife).

The sacrifice is performed on behalf of the sacrificer (*yájamāna*), by the Adhvaryu and his assistant the Pratiprasthātṛ (belonging to the Yajurveda), the Hotṛ (belonging to the Ṛgveda), the Prastotṛ (belonging to the Sāmaveda), the Agnīdh and the Brahmán (belonging to the Atharvaveda or to any Veda). Our text, Taittirīya Āraṇyaka 5, is primarily concerned with the Yajurvedic office of the Adhvaryu and his assistant. While the Hotṛ and the Prastotṛ take care of most of the recitations and chants, the Adhvaryu is the practical organizer of the sacrifice: he collects and prepares the materials, conducts the activities, and summons the Hotṛ and Prastotṛ to recite and sing.[7] The Adhvaryu also has his own texts to be recited. These are mainly prose formulas, but contain metrical portions too. A few passages are to be chanted. The Brahmán is mainly a silent witness. His permission must be asked to start

[7] Cf. KaṭhĀ 2, 49+: "The sacrifice is the chariot of the Yajus. This is yoked by the Adhvaryu at the sacrifice (*adhvará*). That is why the Adhvaryu is called Adhvaryu. The Adhvaryu is he who leads all this forward. The Adhvaryu summons the other priests saying 'Do this, do this.'"

important parts of the sacrifice.[8] The sacrificer invites all the priests and bears the expenses.

3 *Interpretation of the Pravargya* [9]

While the Śrauta Sūtras give a more or less technical description of the rites discussed, they presuppose the Brāhmaṇa and Āraṇyaka literature in which interpretations and explanations of the ritual acts are given. The mantras to be employed are indicated with a few words, or sometimes given in full (when they do not occur in the Saṃhitās). In this branch of the Vedic literature it becomes clear that the meaning or interpretation of every minute detail of the ritual was of the utmost importance for the participants. Sometimes, knowledge of the meaning of ritual acts seems to have been even more important than the actual performance of the acts.[10]

---

8 For the function of this priest see note 110 to the translation; the Agnīdh is in practice more connected with the function of the Adhvaryu, than with that of the Brahmán, see Oldenberg, *Die Religion*:384, note 4, 389; cf. Krick, *Feuergründung*:272, note 676.

9 The works mentioned in note 3 above discuss also the interpretation of the Pravargya (with the exception of the *Śrautakośa* and Staal's *Agni*). See moreover Rönnow, "Zur Erklärung des Pravargya etc."; and Heesterman, "The Case of the Severed Head" in: *Essays in Indian Ritual, Kingship and Society*, Chicago 1985.

10 The right effect of a rite accrues only to him *yá evā́ṃ véda*, who knows the right implications of the ritual acts in the microcosmic and macrocosmic spheres. ŚB 13, 6, 1, 1 promises the results of the performance of the Puruṣamedha to him "who even (only) knows this": he "overpasses all beings, and becomes everything here." And, as Weber observed (*IS* 10 (1868): 110), in ŚB 11, 2, 7, 11 the mere knowledge of certain ritual views or formulas ("die blosse Kunde gewisser ritueller Anschauungen oder Sprüche") gives among other things *brahmavarcasá* (see note 31 to the translation) to the knower.

The essential meaningfulness[11] of Vedic ritual does not imply that all ancient authorities completely agreed with each other on all details of a rite. Indeed, to a considerable extent we owe the elaborateness of the Brāhmaṇas to the differences in the interpretation of ritual acts by different authorities and the discussions that took place. The rites discussed in the Brāhmaṇas are almost exclusively solemn services. It is not strange that the need for a systematic discussion first arose here. While these complicated and often expensive rites were held to be of a great importance, their performers were no doubt not very numerous. In some cases the performances were rather exceptional. Uncertainties about the performances could easily arise in such a situation, and with that, the need for a systematic discussion. It is not improbable that, alongside these solemn services, there was a repertoire of daily house rites and customs, widely spread among the Vedic people, that was so firmly established that there was no need to discuss elements of this

---

11 According to F. Staal, Vedic ritual is essentially meaningless (e.g. "The Meaninglessness of Ritual," *Numen* , 26, fasc. 1). To leave out meaning in this way may be convenient in a technical (if you wish: syntactical) description of ritual. But from the point of view of the early performers of these rites, it certainly does not represent the complete reality adequately The resulting model is not sufficiently rich because important factors are not taken into account.

The idea of the meaninglessness of ritual is not new. Besides Kautsa (referred to in the Nirukta), we may mention Śaṅkara. In Śaṅkaras Advaita Vedānta, we find that there is a meaninglessness (*naiṣkiṃcanya*) of the ritual; but nevertheless ritual is not without value: by performing rituals, a person becomes purified and fit for the realisation of the knowledge of the Absolute (Brahman). But if someone desires to know Brahman (if he has *brahma-jijñāsa*) he does not necessarily need to perform Vedic rituals first (see C. Malamoud in the introduction to his translation of TĀ 2, *Svādhyāya*:61-67). However, what is important here is not whether from some philosophical point of view the ritual and perhaps even every "worldly" action is meaningless or not. We must find and answer to the question whether the ritual was meaningful for the performers themselves and then we should look not only at the time when the ritual was completely fossilized (as is done by Staal in the above mentioned article, p. 3, 4), but, if possible, also at the time when creative, motivated changes took place, i.e. the time when the Brāhmaṇas took shape. Doing this, we will see that the rites were generally considered to be quite meaningful.

unproblematic basic language of rite and custom.[12] The influences of cultural renewals and confrontations became more powerful only in a later epoch: the need to discuss these house rites as well grew, and the Gṛhya Sūtras took concrete shape. The problematic cases in the interpretation of elements and aspects of the Śrauta rituals (the solemn services) are most important in order to understand the reasoning of the Brahmanical authors and their contemporaries. They may perhaps even give us an idea of the underlying unproblematic basic language of rite and custom as it existed in their days, viewed, it is true, through the eyes of those authors. In this context a detailed study of the Brāhmaṇa and Āraṇyaka texts, which discuss these rites, is of the utmost importance.

In a modern discussion of the interpretation of ancient rites like the Pravargya, we have to distinguish first between (a) the complete rite as it was performed and experienced by the ancient participants; (b) the rite as we find it in the Brāhmaṇas and Āraṇyakas; and (c) the interpretations of modern scholars. It is clear that our conclusions regarding the first aspect of the Pravargya can be only very tentative.[13] A further distinction is to be made within b. The interpretations by the author of the Brāhmaṇa or

---

12 Both language and ritual may be considered to be systems of "signs expressing ideas" (F. de Saussure, *Cours de Linguistique Générale*:33). Cf. S. Al-George, in "L'Inde Antique et les Origines du Structuralisme," (*Actes du Xième Congres International de Linguistes* 1970, II:238): "L'Acte rituel est un acte symbolique et, comme tel un acte d'expression rattachable à un système sémiologique, ainsi que l'a qualifié Ferdinand de Saussure." ("The ritual act is a symbolic act and, as such, an expressive act that can be related to a semiological system as qualified by Ferdinand de Saussure.")

13 The impossibility of a complete explanation of a ritual performance can be compared to some extent with the impossibility of explaining performing arts like dancing. Compare Isidore Duncan's saying (quoted by F. Staal in the article mentioned in note 11): "If I could tell you what it meant, there would be no point in dancing it." This saying obviously indicates a meaningfulness of the performance, rather than its meaninglessness (as Staal suggests). The full meaning of a ritual and of an artistic performance can only be expressed by the performance itself. An analysis of the performance may increase our ability to appreciate it, but can never express the full meaning as a whole.

Āraṇyaka may differ in important respects from the interpretations by those who established the rituals discussed, and introduced the mantras. The latter interpretations should become clear from a study of the general structure of the rite. In the case of the Pravargya we will see that the interpretation of one Brāhmaṇa author seems to correspond less with the "original" interpretation than that of other authors. Lastly, it may be asked to what extent the way in which the mantras are used in the rite, corresponds with the original intention of the poets who created those mantras.[14]

In this introduction, there is no room to give a complete explanation of the Pravargya from all these points of view, or to discuss completely all relevant interpretations of other scholars (the reader is referred to the works mentioned in notes 3 and 9 to this introduction). Having given the outlines of the Pravargya rite (in sections 1 and 2) and having mentioned some general principles that should not be lost sight of in the interpretation, I prefer now to point out, on the basis of the Brāhmaṇa and Āraṇyaka sources and the content of the mantras,[15] some aspects of this rite that have not received enough attention from previous scholars.

3.1 The Pravargya and the Sun

All Yajurveda Brāhmaṇa and Āraṇyaka sources agree in connecting the Pravargya ceremony with the sun. The rite and the most important object, the vessel, are frequently identified with the sun. Although by way of certain (sometimes optional) acts several concrete, exterior aims could be pursued, the main purpose of this rite was rather to bring about some more or less abstract results in the participants. Modern interpreters generally agree that the ritual of the Pravargya was considered to be "ein

---

14 Cf. Gonda, "Pravargya Mantras":236.

15 In this latter field we find an important contribution in Gonda's article "Pravargya Mantras," see under Abbreviations.

Mittel, dem Opferer Anteil an den Sonnenglut zu verleihen."[16] "Die Hitze des Gluttranks stellt die Sonnenhitze dar; das Opfer soll diese sichern, stärken, vor allem aber sie dem Opferer zugute kommen lassen."[17] There is less consensus on the question as to whether the rite was expected to have some magical effects on the sun or other (personified) natural phenomena. According to Oldenberg, the Pravargya was performed to strengthen the sun, so that it may come safely through the rainy season. According to Lüders, who sometimes seems to have got trapped in his own interpretational theories, the Pravargya had to strengthen not the sun but the "celestial fluid," represented by the hot milk in the heated vessel. This would have been necessary in the dry and hot times before the rainy season. Van Buitenen (*Pravargya*:33) did not agree with Lüders because "both the ritual itself as well as the special *dīkṣā* for it show conspicuously the incompatibility of Pravargya and moisture." Kashikar, without adding new arguments, chooses for Lüders' explanation ("Apropos":6-8).

From a study of the TĀ 5 it appears that, in the eyes of its author, the Pravargya was mainly directed to the sun.[18] It aimed at giving the participants the power and lustre of the sun. At the same time several elements were built into the rite to protect them against the detrimental effects of too great an absorption of "solar energy." We get a similar picture of a rite that is directed to the sun from the texts that are most

---

16 "a means to give the sacrificer a share in the glow of the sun" (Gonda, *Religionen*, 1:153).

17 "The heat of the hot beverage represents the heat of the sun; the sacrifice should secure it, strengthen it, but, above all, the sacrifice should let it benefit the sacrificer" (Oldenberg, *Die Religion*:448).

18 It was realized by the Vedic people that the sun played an important role in the production of rain, and in this sense rain was one of the side-issues of the rite (see note 96 to the translation). For him who wanted to stress this point, there was a special option (TĀ 5, 10, 6). But the lustre and heat of the sun, and, consequently, the avoidance of rain, rainclouds and moisture during the performance are the most important characteristics of the Pravargya. Other purposes of the Pravargya that are, like the rain-magic, not specific for this rite, are the furtherance of fertility (TĀ 5, 6, 12 end) and the getting rid of the enemy "who hates us and whom we hate" (e.g. TĀ 5, 8, 7; 5, 10, 5).

closely parallel: ŚB 14 and KaṭhĀ 2 and 3. The most striking difference between the KaṭhĀ and the other two texts is that in the former the sun, called "Rudra Mahāvīra," is represented mainly in its dangerous and fearful aspects.

While KauṣB 8, 3-7 agrees with the other sources in frequently identifying the Pravargya vessel and sacrifice with the sun,[19] the other Ṛgvedic Brāhmaṇa, AiB, stands isolated[20] in never explicitly connecting the vessel or the rite with this heavenly body. Instead, the Pravargya is explained as a *devamithuna* , a "divine pairing": Agni or the sacrifice is the *devayoni* , the "divine womb," from which the sacrificer is reborn. The passage (AiB 1, 22) runs as follows: "The Gharma (sacrifice) is a divine pairing; the Gharma (vessel) is the member, the two tongs the testicles, the supporting vessel the bowl of the buttocks, the milk the seed; this seed is poured in Agni as the divine womb, for the sake of procreation. . . . He is born from the divine womb, the fire, out of the oblations." The theme of Agni or the sacrifice as *devayoni* , the "divine womb," from which the sacrificer is (re)born, is a favourite one to the author of this Brāhmaṇa.[21] But in the context of the Pravargya an explanation along these lines seems not to be able to account for important points in this performance. The explanation as found in other sources, where the Pravargya is connected with the sun and gives its lustre and power to the participants, is, as we will see, much more consistent with the rite as a whole.

Turning now to the mantras used in the Pravargya, we will see that there are important connections with the sun here, a fact that corresponds with the frequent identifications with the sun in the Yajurveda Brāhmaṇas and Āraṇyakas. The relationship with the sun is not as explicit as in those explanatory texts. But a connection with the sun cannot be

---

19 E.g. in the phrase "The Mahāvīra is he yonder that gives heat."

20 Leaving apart the very short reference to the Pravargya in PB 7, 5, 6, only GB 2, 2, 6 follows AiB in this respect (and in many other respects); GB 2, 2, 6 has AiB 1, 18 and the end of 1, 22 almost verbatim.

21 Cf. AiB 2, 3; 2, 14; 3, 19; 6, 9 and 6, 29.

denied in cases like: "you are sun(-light) (*súvar*), give me sun(-light)" (TĀ 4, 8, 4(22f)), and "Agni (the Pravargya vessel) comes together with Agni (the sun)" (TĀ 4, 7, 1(3a)). The Gandharva mantras,[22] praising the Pravargya as the celestial Gandharva, are most probably introduced into the rite because of the connection and sometimes even identification of the Gandharva with the sun. However, many mantras that are connected with the sun can only be interpreted in the context of the well-known imagery of the sun as the "light of inner vision." When the Pravargya vessel on the fire is red-hot, there is a long recitation by the Hotṛ, which starts with ṚV 10, 177.[23] There are no serious difficulties in following Gonda in his remark that this hymn "deals with the inner light of the visionary illumination and perception," and that its stanzas "may have served to destroy spiritual ignorance."[24] The third and last stanza of this hymn is used as the first of the Avakāśa mantras,[25] which are to be recited by the sacrificer together with all the priests after the fanning, while looking reverentially at the glowing vessel (TĀ 5, 6, 4). In some of the subsequent Avakāśa mantras the Pravargya is praised as "lord of the whole mind," as the "father of hymns (*matí*-s),"[26] as the "thought (*máti*) of the inspired poets." In one of the above-mentioned Gandharva

22 TĀ 4, 11, 5(13)ff; see note 141 to the translation.

23 "The inspired ones see the bird (i.e. the light of insight and inspiration) with their heart; the inspired poets see it in the midst of the ocean while tracing the track of the rays. The bird, the Gandharva, bears the word in his mind and speaks it within the womb; the inspired seers guard this inspired thought which is bright-like-lightning, and is of the nature of the light of heaven at the abode of ṛta. I saw the herdsman wandering hither and thither on his pathways, without lying down. He envelops himself in those (waters) that converge and in those that spread out; he revolves in all beings" (Gonda, *Vision*:28, 31, 32, 178, 277, 281). Our Āraṇyaka interprets the last verse, recited as the first of the Avakāśa mantras, in a macrocosmic context as the sun and in a microcosmic context as prāṇa (TĀ 5, 6, 4).

24 Gonda, "Pravargya Mantras":238; cf. Geldner, *ṚVübers*, 3:389, introductory note to the hymn; and Gonda, *Vision*:91.

25 See note 79 to the translation.

26 See note 77 to the translation.

mantras, the Gandharva-Sun is expected to "stimulate or promote 'visions' and to assist or favour them."[27] The first mantra uttered by the Hotṛ, the first verse of the Brahma-jajñānam hymn, is often and not without reason connected with the sun, that rises in the east. Still, Gonda's more abstract translation is very defensible: "the seer (Seer) has unveiled the brahman that had, of old, first come into existence from the well-shining boundary; he has revealed its fundamental (and) highest places, the womb of the existent and of the non-existent" (*Vision*:357). In reference to this verse, Gonda suggests that the "boundary refers to the borderland between the phenomenal and the transcendent which is momentarily crossed by the seer when the light of vision comes to him." (*Vision*:357). In the peace-recitation that concludes each performance, there is, by way of the (personified physical) sun, a reference to the imagery of the sun of inner light arising from the ocean in the heart: "The one that arises from the wide ocean, shining wide from the middle of the water, may he . . . sun and seer, purify me with thought."[28] We can also compare TĀ 4, 11, 6(17): "You are Thought, with the ocean as birthplace." It may be noted that, according to F. B. J. Kuiper, "The Bliss of Aša":125, "The Ṛigvedic seer gets his vision with or in his heart. This heart is equated to the cosmic mountain and its subterranean ocean."

Apart from the mantras referring to the sun, we also find several mantras (and chants based on mantras) referring to the preparation and consumption of the Soma beverage. These are mainly employed during the milking of the cow and the goat, and during the offering proper. If we interpret these mantras in terms of Lüders' "celestial fluid" and connect them with the rains of the monsoon, we run the risk of floundering. An interpretation in the direction indicated by Gonda ("Pravargya Mantras":254-5), is more consistent with the entire rite. The Soma mantras contrast with but do not necessarily contradict the connection of the Pravargya with the (spiritual) sun. In the next section, I will make a

27 TĀ 4, 11, 8(19d); Gonda, *Vision*:91.

28 TĀ 4, 42; van Buitenen, *Pravargya*:123.

few observations on the important but complicated relation between Soma and this rite.

The connection between the Pravargya and the sun can be maintained if the mantras used in this rite are studied more closely. However, this connection with the sun should be considered to exist primarily in the context of a cultivation of spiritual experiences or even, to quote the words F. B. J. Kuiper used in a comparable context, of "an old Vedic tradition of meditative practices" ("The Bliss of Aša":125). All this fits in very well with the special "mystery" character of this rite: its mantras were studied while special observances were to be followed;[29] it is connected with the mysterious *mádhu*, that was proclaimed by Dadhyañc to the Aśvins;[30] it is called (or included in what is called) Āraṇya Svādhyāya in MŚS 4, 8, 1; and KaṭhĀ 3, 229+ makes mention of the *pravargyopaniṣád*, the "Geheimlehre" of the Pravargya; the Taittirīyas and the Kaṭhas have placed the Pravargya sections in their Āraṇyakas; according to the author of the ŚB, the Pravargya should not be taught "to any and every one, since that would be sinful . . . ; but one may teach it to one who is known to him, and who has studied sacred writ, and who may be dear to him, but not to any and every one" (Eggeling, *ŚBtransl* 14, 1, 1, 26). Nor should the Pravargya be *performed* for any and every one, "lest he should do everything for every one, for the Pravargya is everything; but let him perform it for him who is known, or to whoever

---

29 TĀ 5, 8, 13; L.Renou, *Écoles Védiques*:149: "C'est le rite Pravargya qui ouvre le «mystère» *(rahasya)* ou, comme on dit aussi dans ces traditions, le *śukriya(vrata).*" ("It is the Pravargya rite that opens the «mystery» (*rahasya),* or, as is also said in these traditions, the *śukriya(vrata).*"); cf. below, section 3.3.

30 This connection is not a "novel association" by the author of the ŚB (thus van Buitenen, *Pravargya*:21, 22). It is not correct that no mantras referring to Dadhyañc are used in the Pravargya (*Pravargya*:18): the Kaṭhas prescribe a mantra, KaṭhĀ 3, 226 (approximately = ṚV 1, 116, 12), that refers to the *mádhu* proclaimed by the mythical Dadhyañc to the Aśvins. In Bṛhad-Āraṇyaka-Upaniṣad (BĀU) 2, 5, 1-19, *mádhu* is explained as a mystical "sweet" doctrine. The simplistic interpretation that Dadhyañc declared to the Aśvins the knowledge of how to use honey in the ritual (Keith, *Religion* 1:225) does not seem very attractive.

may be dear to him, or who has studied sacred writ" (J. Eggeling, *ŚBtransl* 14, 2, 2, 46).

3.2 The Pravargya and Soma

In the Śrauta rituals, the Pravargya is only described as an optional, introductory rite for the Agniṣṭoma, i.e. for the regular Soma sacrifice. The central part is formed by the offering of a heated milk-mixture, the Gharma, to the Aśvins. Afterwards, the concelebrants of the rite also partake of the beverage. The relation of this rite with its "big brother", the Agniṣṭoma is somewhat complicated. The vessel in which the milk is to be heated receives, like the Soma stalks, a wooden throne. The Pravargya throne is called "Emperor's Throne", a more dignified name than Soma's "King's Throne". The importance attached to both the Soma and the Gharma beverage, already in the earliest sources and coming clearly to the fore in the ritual, made the ritualists of some circles discuss whether the throne for the Emperor Gharma should be higher or that for King Soma (ĀpŚS 15, 5, 7). The story of Makha in the first anuvāka of TĀ 5 presents the Pravargya as the "Head of the Sacrifice," without which the Agniṣṭoma does not yield the desired results. And yet, a sacrificer's first Agniṣṭoma must not include the Pravargya, probably because there must first be a "body" before the "head" of the sacrifice can be attached to it. KB 8, 3 makes an exception for the sacrificer who is himself a "learned Brahman": he is allowed to perform the Pravargya even at his first sacrifice.

Some aspects of the relation between the Pravargya and the Soma sacrifice can perhaps be explained by stating that there are elements in the Pravargya that are to give this rite a higher status by stressing its similarity or even superiority to the Soma sacrifice, the latter being the most important sacrifice in Vedic ritual from the times of the Ṛgveda onwards.[31] But we will see below that the relation is both more intimate and more complicated than this.

In the Soma sacrifice, the Soma is object and instrument of the sacrifice (respectively the Soma as god and the Soma beverage as oblation to the gods); Soma is moreover a "secondary instrument" in the form of the Soma-stalks, which contain the basis of the Soma beverage. Likewise, in the Pravargya ritual, the Gharma is object and instrument of the sacrifice (respectively the Gharma as god and the Gharma beverage as oblation to the gods); Gharma is moreover a "secondary instrument," inasmuch as the vessel in which the Gharma will be heated is also called Gharma. Both the Gharma or Pravargya vessels and the Soma stalks receive a wooden throne. The mantras that praise the Gharma as object and instrument of worship exhibit several similarities with Soma mantras.

Several aspects of the Pravargya, which were considered by van Buitenen as indications of a Pūjā-character of the rite, can be much better explained in connection with their similarities with the Soma sacrifice and its mantras.[32] Moreover, van Buitenen's interpretation of the vessel as an anthropomorphic image, connected with the supposed Pūjā-character of the rite, is not very convincing.[33] Like in other Vedic rites, the symbolism in the Pravargya is rather abstract. Only during the disposal of the Pravargya there is, as one of the options, the disposal of the implements in the form of a man (Mahāvīra), who is by no means represented realistically.

---

31 Cf. Thite, *Sacrifice*:49-54, 128.

32 See van Buitenen, *Pravargya*:23-28; and Kashikar, "Apropos":4-6.

33 Cf. Rau, *Töpferei*:72: "Was pp. 9-12 und 59-62 besagter Arbeit [sc. van Buitenen, *Pravargya*] über die Form des *mahāvīra* vermutet wird, dürfte sich kaum halten lassen." ("What has been surmised on pp.9-12 and 59-62 of the above mentioned work [sc. van Buitenen, *Pravargya*] about the shape of the *mahāvīra*, would be hardly tenable"). By the same token, the ancient descriptions of the Pravargya do not warrant the conclusions of Bandhari, "Pravargya Mahāvīra and Idols", *Journal of the Asiatic Society of Bombay*, vol.52/53 1977-78 (1981):25-31.

Apart from being a form of worship, the Soma sacrifice has a magical aspect, in its function as a rain-bringing rite. This aspect is, however, not the main object of the rite but rather a side-issue, as was already recognized by Oldenberg (*Die Religion*:456).[34] But there were "magical" effects on another level that were probably far more important. In the Soma mantras, much attention is paid to the relation of the Soma pressing, with what is going on at this other level. The drops of Soma, pressed from the stalks and purified through sieves, are treated in the hymns as if they are somehow parallel to the inspired thoughts that arise and are purified in the minds and hearts of the Vedic poets. In a publication devoted to the study of the Vedic poets and the creative processes in which their hymns were produced, Gonda observes, in connection with the ritual Soma hymns, that "the god who, as the material soma, undergoes in the course of sacrificial ceremonies, a process of clarification, and who, at the same time, is the inspirer of thoughts, is believed to be the power presiding over clarification and to bring about that process with regard to the inspired thoughts which, while being received by the 'poet' in his heart, are transformed into liturgical words which in their turn are to accompany oblations of the soma juice and to make these effective" (Gonda, *Vision*:279).

While in the Pravargya no Soma is pressed, several verses in praise of the Soma have found an important place in the Pravargya, and more than once a sāman is built on a verse from the Soma Pavamāna hymn cycle. Some may consider this to be a clear example of borrowing mantras from a different rite in such a way that the original meaning of the mantra is neglected or strained in its new application. But it has been rightly observed that e.g. ṚV 9, 83 from the ninth or Soma Maṇḍala, was already in early times connected with the Pravargya (Gonda "Pravargya Mantras":254). ṚV 9, 73, forming part of the Hotṛ's recitation during the fanning of the Pravargya vessel, is not used in other rites. ṚV 8, 9, 4 and 7 call the Gharma offering to the Aśvins "Soma". Note that, apart from the Soma sacrifice, the Gharma milk offering to the Aśvins is perhaps the

34 See also e.g. Keith, *TStransl*:cxx.

only rite rather frequently and explicitly referred to in the Ṛgveda. The mysterious Soma and the rather trivial milk-and-ghee mixture of the Gharma, both being characterized as "sweet" (*mádhu*), are treated in these hymns as having similar properties to a considerable extent.

Whatever the biological identity of the Soma plant may appear to be,[35] it should not be overlooked that the oldest Vedic texts consider the mantras and chants indispensable "ingredients" in the preparation of the Soma beverage.[36] We see that in an actual ritual performance connected with the Soma beverage (like the 1975 Agnicayana performance documented by F. Staal), a most important place is taken by the well-recited mantras and properly sung sāmans. In the Pravargya, the physical

---

35 Although the problem of the identity of the Soma was recognized by European scholars from the beginning, Wasson was probably the first to take the Soma-experiences described in the ṚV seriously (R. G. Wasson, *Soma, Divinc Mushroom of Immortality*, The Hague-New York, 1968). On the basis of his knowledge of plants and their possible effects on the nervous system, he arrived at the conclusion that Soma must have been the Fly Agaric (Amanita muscaria). The reactions of specialists were mixed. It was especially J. Brough who discussed Wasson's identification of the Soma-plant thoroughly. In "Soma and *Amanita muscaria*", *Bulletin of the School of Oriental and African Studies*, 34 (1971):331-362 and "Problems of the «Soma-mushroom» Theory", *Indologica Taurinensia* 1 (1973):21-32, he showed that there is not much textual evidence to support his argument. Nevertheless, many scholars still recognize Wasson's hypothesis as a very acceptable one (e.g. Gonda, *Religionen*, (second ed.)1:362, note 82; Staal, *Agni* 1:105-113; R. Stuhrman in *IIJ* 28 (1985):85-93).

As early as in the times of the Brāhmaṇas and Srauta Sūtras, many substitutes were mentioned for the Soma, among other things the Pūtīka plant. In the Pravargya ceremony this plant is added to the clay from which the vessels are formed. Critics have mentioned the fact that none of the substitutes for Soma were mushrooms as one of the weak points of Wasson's Soma-mushroom theory. Mostly they are creepers. Kramrisch's identification of this Pūtīka with a mushroom called Putka with the Santals in: "The Mahāvīra and the Plant Pūtika", has therefore been welcomed as an important fortification of this theory. However, from the text that is translated here (referred to by Kramrisch) it is clear that the Pūtīka, though probably not a creeper, can hardly have been a mushroom. See note 25 to the translation and the TĀ paragraph to which it refers.

36 cf. ṚV 7, 26, 1: *ná sóma índram ásuto mamāda, nā́brahmāṇo maghávānaṃ sutā́saḥ.* "The unpressed Soma has never intoxicated Indra, *nor the pressed juices unaccompanied by sacred hymns*".

ingredient of the inebriating Soma juice, pressed from the mysterious stalks, is missing. Instead, we have a milk-and-ghee mixture, that in itself will have few psychotropic effects. But the less material ingredients are present. Perhaps, they were thought to bring about in the properly prepared participants experiences similar to those brought about - no doubt in a more intense way - by consuming the Soma beverage. Note that, in the normal case when the Pravargya forms part of the Agniṣṭoma, the sacrificer has started to follow certain observances (comprising restrictions in speaking and eating) on the day before the performances, and that the priests, if they were good Brahmins, followed their own rules of life. For the Avāntaradīkṣā as a preparation on the Pravargya see section 3.3 below. Be that as it may, what Gonda proposed very cautiously, while discussing the occurrence of the Soma hymn ṚV 9, 73 among the Pravargya-mantras, seems to be entirely acceptable, sc. "that those who introduced the *sūkta* into the *pravargya* litany, while regarding the heating of the Mahāvīra and the clarification of the soma as parallels, wished to bring about by means of its recitation an analogous psychical process" (Gonda, "Pravargya Mantras":255).

Considered this way, the relation that exists between the Pravargya and Soma does not contradict the Pravargya's connection with the sun, but rather complements it.

3.3 The Pravargya and the Intermediate Initiation (avāntaradīkṣā)

A remarkable aspect of the Pravargya is that it is connected with special rules or observances to be followed by those who wish to study its mantras. The observances belong to the Avāntaradīkṣā or Intermediate Initiation. For a description and discussion mainly based on the Śrauta Sūtra sources see van Buitenen, *Pravargya:*137-141 and 38-41. Improvements in the understanding of this rite have been brought forward by C. G. Kashikar: "The Avāntaradīkṣā of Pravargya" (*BDCRI*, 35.3-4 (1976): 66-72).[37] The Avāntaradīkṣā that is to be followed when the Pravargya mantras are learned (Avāntaradīkṣā$_p$) should be distinguished from the part of the Dīkṣā[38] belonging to the Soma sacrifice that has the same name. This latter Avāntaradīkṣā (Avāntaradīkṣā$_s$) takes place immediately before the actual Soma pressing. While during the Dīkṣā the sacrificer is, in the symbolism of the Brāhmaṇas, identified with an embryo that should be reborn in the sacrifice, he and his wife have to follow certain observances: they restrain their speech, they consume only certain things like milk, gruel, ghee in restricted quantities. The Dīkṣā may last a few days but also a month or a whole year, "until the sacrificer has become lean." During the Avāntaradīkṣā$_s$ the observances become a little more severe; only hot food is consumed, the sacrificer tightens his girdle more tightly. The Dīkṣā and Avāntaradīkṣā$_s$ of the

---

37 In spite of the efforts in this field of (especially) van Buitenen and Kashikar, there are still important problems in the exact interpretation of the Avāntaradīkṣā. Neither van Buitenen nor Kashikar made use of the KaṭhĀ that contains important fragments on the Avāntaradīkṣā (KaṭhĀ 3, 155+; 3, 198-207; 3, 219+). The problem of the interpretation of TĀ 5, 8, 13 in relation to the Avāntaradīkṣā was not observed by previous scholars. See below, and note 130 to the translation. For the KaṭhĀ see note 73.

38 See in general Gonda, *Change and Continuity*:315-377; cf. Staal, *Agni* 1:331-333. For the etymology of the word: Minard, *Énigmes*, 2:263-4. For the Dīkṣā of the Soma sacrifice see: *Śrautakośa*, vol. 2, Sanskrit:27-43; 518-522; vol. 2, English pt.1:67-100. For the Avāntaradīkṣā of the Soma sacrifice see: *Śrautakośa*, vol. 2, Sanskrit:530 (under: "*14.ātithyeṣṭyādi*"); vol. 2, English pt.1:151-162.

Soma sacrifice are an immediate preparation of the sacrificer for the sacrifice.[39]

The Avāntaradīkṣā$_p$ connected with the Pravargya ceremony, on the other hand, is undergone by the Veda student, the Brahmacārin, when he has arrived at the point where the Pravargya mantras are to be studied. This Avāntaradīkṣā$_p$ takes place outside the immediate context of a sacrifice. In this respect Kashikar was right when he stated that it was not the priest or the sacrificer who followed the observances of this Avāntaradīkṣā$_p$, but the pupil who desired to study the Pravargya mantras and their Brāhmaṇa by the side of his teacher.[40] The study of different portions of the Veda is connected with different *vratá*-s, observances or rules of life. The Pravargya mantras and Brāhmaṇa form part of the so-called Saumya Kāṇḍa, the study of which is connected with the Śukriyavrata.[41] When the Pravargya is to be studied the pupil adopts,

---

39 Dīkṣā and tapas ("ascesis") are often mentioned together, see Gonda, *Religionen* 1:109; *Change and Continuity*:340ff. Is *gharmásya vraténa* in AV 4, 11, 6d (*gharmásya vraténa tápasā*) a reference to an early form of the Avāntaradīkṣā$_p$? If so, we have here an early text-place in which the Avāntaradīkṣā$_p$ and tapas are mentioned in one breath.

40 The observances were no doubt, as far as possible and useful, also followed by the teacher, see ŚB 14, 1, 1, 29. KaṭhĀ 3, 199ff, probably still referring to the Avāntaradīkṣā$_p$, uses the dual: "They both put long life etc. in themselves". Van Buitenen suggests (*Pravargya*:39) that it was possibly the professional priest who underwent the year-long initiation as a specific preparation to the Pravargya sacrifice, which does not seem very attractive. About the possibility that it was originally also the sacrificer who underwent the Avāntaradīkṣā$_p$ see below. Yet, to translate the Avāntaradīkṣā$_p$ portions of the Śrauta Sūtras (the texts in which this possibility is not specifically mentioned) in such a way that it is the sacrificer who undergoes the initiation and follows the observances, is certainly not recommendable. This is done by Dandekar in the *Śrautakośa*, vol.2, English Section, part 1:18-28. Caland translates with "Schüler" ("student"), which as a general translation is more acceptable than Dandekar's "sacrificer" (Caland *ĀpŚSübers*:463-467).

41 The Śukriyavrata is described in the Gṛhyasūtras of the Taittirīyas, e.g. BaudhGS 3, 2, 3f; BharGS 3, 6f. See note 153 to the translation. For the Saumya Kāṇḍa see section 5 below.

within the already adopted Śukriyavrata, another *vratá* that is for some reason not called Avāntaravrata but Avāntaradīkṣā.[42]

In the text that has been translated here (TĀ 5), there is only a short reference to the observances that are to be followed by one studying the Pravargya mantras. The passage is found in TĀ 5, 8, 13 and immediately followed by a mythical passage that explains the relation of the observances with the recitation of the mantras. The observances as they are found in our text are less elaborate than those that are prescribed by the Śrauta Sūtras for the Avāntaradīkṣā$_{p}$.Problematic is, that in this passage the author of the TĀ does not seem to address the Brahmacārin.[43] It is therefore not impossible that the commentator Sāyaṇa is right when he takes the sacrificer (*yájamāna*) as the one who follows these observances that are meant for "one who undertakes the study of the Pravargya."[44] In that case, the Pravargya observances mentioned in TĀ 5, 8, 13 become similar to the Agniṣṭoma Dīkṣā and Avāntaradīkṣā$_{s}$ in that they are all followed by the sacrificer. As it is, several formulae and other elements are held in common. If the prescribed period of one year can be compressed into a few days that symbolically represent the whole year (cf. ŚB 14, 1, 1, 28), the similarity with the Dīkṣā and Avāntaradīkṣā$_{s}$ for the Agniṣṭoma is still greater. In KaṭhĀ 2, 198+, the Avāntaradīkṣā$_{p}$ is compared with the Dīkṣā in a way that is very similar to the comparison of the Dīkṣā and Avāntaradīkṣā$_{s}$ in TS 6, 2, 2, 7. If these observances, connected with the study of the Pravargya mantras and to be followed by the pupil when he learns these mantras, could be followed by the sacrificer too, they would indeed be worthy of the name "Avāntaradīkṣā" (rather than "Avāntaravrata").[45] It may be surmised that the observances of TĀ 5, 8, 13 were to be followed by those sacrificers (e.g. Rājanyas) who

---

42 Kashikar, "Avāntaradīkṣā".

43 See note 130 to the translation.

44 *pravargyādhyāyenānuṣṭhānaṃ kurvatā puruṣeṇa pūrvoktam etad vrataṃ caraṇīyam* (Sāyaṇa on TĀ 5, 8, 13).

45 See also note 11 to the translation.

had not yet studied the Pravargya mantras during their Brahmacārin-time.

Our passage, TĀ 5, 8, 13, is cited by almost all Śrauta Sūtras (e.g. BŚS 9,12; ĀpŚS 15, 12, 13). But, curiously enough, this does not take place in the context of the discussion of the Avāntaradīkṣā$_p$. And, more curious still, it is cited in such a way that one interprets the passage as prescribing observances to be followed by the sacrificer *after* the performance of the Pravargya sacrifice.[46] In the Brāhmaṇa and Āraṇyaka sources as far as available, however, no mention is made of observances to be followed *after* the completion of the Pravargya. The Indian commentators Sāyaṇa and Bhaṭṭa-Bhāskara Miśra, do not mention an interpretation according to which the observances should be followed *after* the sacrifice.[47] It is clear that the authors of the Śrauta Sūtras reinterpreted TĀ 5, 8, 13; but it is not clear whether they reinterpreted it to support an old, existing practice, or whether the reinterpretation reflected a new development in the rite.[48]

Finally, in the Avāntaradīkṣā$_p$ there are again several elements that show the general connection of the Pravargya with the sun. The one who undergoes the Avāntaradīkṣā$_p$ should not use an umbrella to protect himself against the sun, according to the ŚB he should not even cover himself with a garment, "lest he should be concealed from that (sun)" (ŚB

46 Baudhāyana introduces the citation with *pravargyam bhakṣayitvā*, Bharadvāja and Āpastamba with *tena pravṛjya.*

47 *pravargyānuṣṭhāyī* (S) and *pravargyam bhakṣayitā* (Bh) rather express simultaneity of the observances and the Pravargya performance. This may be understood as follows: the word *pravargya* of these commentators refers to a Pravargya performance that includes a special form of the Avāntaradīkṣā$_p$, immediately preceding the actual performance and undergone by the sacrificer. S, whose commentary is the most elaborate, clearly connects the observances both with the study of the mantras and with the sacrificer. But even he, though thoroughly acquainted with the Śrauta Sūtras, does not indicate that in these texts the TĀ passage has been interpreted in a way that differs considerably from his own interpretation.

48 A similar rule was to be followed by the sacrificer after the piling of the fire altar: *nā́gníṃ citvā́ rāmā́m úpeyād* (TS 5, 6, 8, 3e). Cf. Weber, *IS* 10 (1868): 74; 83, 84, n. 3.

14, 1, 1, 33). The pupil spends the first night blindfolded, not sleeping and in complete silence. The next morning, he is made to look at a few objects, among other things the sun, a fire, a piece of gold and a stark naked woman (*mahānagnā́*). While the Mahānagnā is, with van Buitenen, "symbolic of the fecundity which the Pravargya seeks to further," the fire and the gold clearly represent the sun. During the rest of the year he should not use clay vessels, because "die Erdsubstanz ist mit den Toten in fortwährende Berührung."[49] Now, he should not look at or speak to anything or anyone, thus "he puts brilliant energy into himself" (KaṭhĀ 3, 199+). On the moon-phase days he has to fast and abstain from sleeping. As long as he is engaged in the study of the Pravargya, he should not study other things. He should not study (recite) when wet, or in cloudy weather, or in the shade. He eats food preferably in sunlight; in the night the food should be illuminated by fire.

Summarizing, it may be said that in the Avāntaradīkṣā$_p$ the pupil "does not only go through a year of technical studies; he accumulates during this year the personal power of tapas, daily strengthened by the sun with which he entertains such a special relation" (van Buitenen, *Pravargya*:41).

---

49 "clay and earth are in continuous contact with the dead", Oldenberg, *Die Religion*: 418. In another context it has been said: "Wenn er es mit etwas Tönernem bedeckte, würden die Väter (d.h. die Verstorbenen) die Gottheit sein der es gehört." ("If he would cover it with something made of clay, the Fathers (i.e. the Deceased) would be the deity to which it belongs.") Oldenberg, *Die Religion*: 419. The injunction not to use clay vessels cannot be explained by the "very special significance" ascribed in the Pravargya to "clay vessels, the most important of which, the Mahāvīra, represents the sun." (van Buitenen, *Pravargya*:40). Clay is used because other materials appeared not to be suitable for a vessel that should be heated red hot. See note 164 to the translation for the "excuse" by which the use of clay is made acceptable by the author of the Pravargya Brāhmaṇa of the Taittirīyas.

3.4 *The Pravargya myth*

In the symbolical explanation of the relation of this Pravargya to other sacrifices, especially its relation to the Agniṣṭoma or regular Soma sacrifice, it is once again the sun that plays an important role, although at first sight this is not clear in the TĀ-version. ŚB and TĀ introduce here the story of the personified sacrifice (Makha-Viṣṇu) who loses his head.[50] This myth should be placed in the context of the sacrificial symbolism of the reconstruction of Prajāpati: "the main object of sacrificial performances generally is the reconstruction of Prajāpati, the personified universe, and (the divine body of) the Sacrificer" (Eggeling, *SBE* 44, p. xlvii). We can follow Eggeling further when he states that the sun may be considered to be the head of the universe (while the universe is identical with Prajāpati, who is also identified with the sacrifice). The Pravargya vessel, the counterpart of the sun, is the head of Makha-Viṣṇu (sacrifice personified) and the sacrificer; and "this ceremony is thus performed in order to complete the universe and sacrifice, as well as the divine body of the Sacrificer, by supplying them with their head, their crowning-piece, so to speak" (Eggeling, *SBE* 44, p. xlviii).

In the TĀ-version of the myth (anuvāka 1), the sacrifice, personified as Makha Vaiṣṇava, is beheaded and its trunk is divided threefold into the morning, midday and evening pressing. This threefold sacrifice is not effective and needs to be completed with a fourth element: its head. The Aśvins, the physicians of the gods, know how to do this. This head is the Pravargya ceremony, which has to make the regular Soma sacrifice complete. Whereas the ŚB-version identifies in this myth both the Pravargya that has to complete the sacrifice, and the sacrifice as a whole with the sun (ŚB 14, 1, 1, 10; 27; 28; 31 and 6; 32 respectively), the connection with the sun is not immediately clear in the TĀ-version. Explicit identifications of the Pravargya and the sun start not before anuvāka 4 of the TĀ. However, an indirect identification may already be

---

50 For bibliographic references see the introductory note to the first anuvāka (p. 45). For Makha (Vaiṣṇava)/Viṣṇu see note 5 to the translation.

read into the passage of the myth which has the cut-off head of Makha Vaiṣṇava proceed along the sky. It is the head that will be called the Pravargya later on, and this Pravargya will be identified with the sun.

The closest parallel to the myth in the TĀ is ŚB 14, 1, 1. Other versions, PB 7, 5, 6; JB 3, 126 (in the story of Cyavana), MS 4, 5, 9 and AiB 1, 18 are very short. The JB section refers to the sun explicitly: "the head which was cut off, that is yonder Āditya (the sun), but it is also the Pravargya." The story in the PB and that in the MS are not connected with the sun, the story in the MS not even with the Pravargya. The AiB section on the Pravargya (1, 18) has the sacrifice crushed (and not beheaded) and afterwards gathered together by the Aśvins. As we would expect (see above, p. 12), the Pravargya is not connected with the sun in the AiB myth. The same is true for GB 2, 2, 6, which follows AiB 1, 18 closely. KauṣB 8, 3, which is parallel to the AiB Pravargya section, has no myth, but does identify the Mahāvīra with the sun. The Pravargya Brāhmaṇa in the KaṭhĀ does not begin with a story like that at the beginning of the ŚB and TĀ versions. It has only isolated references to the story, which is, moreover, characterized by a remarkable difference: it is not Makha Vaiṣṇava (TĀ) or Viṣṇu (ŚB) who is beheaded by his own bowstring, but Rudra (KaṭhĀ 3, 207+) or the sacrifice (KaṭhĀ 2, 115+).[51] It is clear that in all these cases the myth has to express the place and importance of the Pravargya ceremony vis-à-vis the regular Soma sacrifice. We cannot maintain that "to ascribe to it any symbolic sense would doubtless be a mistake" (Keith, *Religion*:112).

In the light of these myths, the Pravargya (or Mahāvīra) vessel may be considered as an (aniconic) representation of the head of the sacrifice, rather than, with Kashikar, "Mahāvīra":139, as a "headless human body which had become void of sap." In the macrocosmic sphere, the head of the sacrifice is the sun.

---

51 Note in this connection that the twin gods that are intimately connected with the Pravargya, the Aśvins, are also closely related to Rudra, see e.g. Geldner, *ṚVÜbers.* 4:43 under "die Aśvins und die andere Götter."

Although the KaṭhĀ does not start with a Pravargya myth like those in the TĀ and ŚB, it does contain dispersed elements of that myth. The most important KaṭhĀ passages in this connection are KaṭhĀ 3, 207+ and 2, 115. Here it is the head of Rudra, severed from its trunk by the bowstring, that is called Pravargya. Instead of the phrases in the TĀ "yonder Āditya (the sun) is actually the Pravargya" and in the ŚB "that (sun) is the Pravargya," the Kaṭhas have: "yonder Āditya (the sun) is actually Rudra Mahāvīra." The solar character of Rudra in this Āraṇyaka of the Kaṭhas is noteworthy. Rudra's cut-off head and the Pravargya are also connected in TĀ 1, 5, 5, i.e. in one of the two anuvākas of the TĀ that have been ascribed to the Kaṭhas. The sun is sometimes called Rudra Mahāvīra in those anuvākas.

Because the mantras of the different versions of the Pravargya are to a great extent similar, the question arises whether the connection with the Viṣṇu/Vaiṣṇava myth or that with the Rudra myth is more original. The mantras with "Makha," harmonizing well with the TĀ and ŚB version of the myth, also occur in the Kaṭha Pravargya mantra collection, but they seem to be out of context there: the Kaṭhas have not given important Brāhmaṇa explanations for them. The KaṭhĀ explains Makha as sacrifice, but does not give him a place in the myth. On the other hand, all versions, except that of the Vājasaneyins, have one mantra in praise of the Pravargya vessel, that only fits the Rudra myth: KaṭhĀ 2, 92 = TĀ 4, 5, 7(17) (= ṚV 2, 33, 10). Whether one of the two myths was more original and if so which one, we cannot decide, but as from the moment that they both existed there must have been an exchange. On the basis of the existing material the Viṣṇu/Vaiṣṇava myth seems to have emerged from this exchange as more important.

4 The Age of the Pravargya Ritual

If we distinguish for a moment between a milk-offering-constituent and a preparation-of-the-vessel-constituent in the Pravargya ritual, we can say that the great antiquity of the former element is well established by the frequent references to the Gharma offering in the Ṛgveda (see note 1(b)). According to van Buitenen the two constituents are of a different origin: "While the Vedic Gharma offering may well have been poured out for the Aśvins as an independent little rite, and while the Mahāvīra ceremonial of creating, worshiping and disposing of the clay artifact may well have been a non-Vedic rite in origin, the two rites combined are exclusively known in the context of the Agniṣṭoma" (*Pravargya*:6). In the Pravargya ritual as described in the Śrauta Sūtras this twofold origin is, according to van Buitenen, still clearly discernible (*Pravargya*:23-28). Kashikar, however, basing himself on the same Śrauta Sūtra descriptions of the rite, holds that there is "no reason for regarding the Pravargya as a coalescence of two distinct rites: it is a unitary rite" ("Apropos":6). Gonda does not follow Kashikar and holds that there has been a Ṛgvedic hot milk rite, in which "the Mahāvīra vessel played no part."[52] The references in verses of the Ṛgveda (and in those of the Khila Sūktas) to the Gharma seem to be, according to Gonda, "not to the Mahāvīra of the elaborate *pravargya* ritual of the Sūtras and Brāhmaṇas but to the vessel in which the milk to be offered to the Aśvins was boiled and to its contents, the hot milk" (Gonda, "Pravargya Mantras":262). According to Gonda, the Mahāvīra vessel may originally have been the subject of a separate rite (Gonda, "Pravargya Mantras":261).

However, the fact that the ceremonial preparation of the vessel belonged to the Adhvaryu's office does not imply that this part of the rite did not exist in the Vedic ritual in the time of the Ṛgveda, nor that it was separate from the milk offering. If we were to assume that the preparation took place in roughly the same way as in the time of the Śrauta Sūtras, we should not be surprised to find few references to this part of the rite in the Ṛgveda, because it did not belong to the Hotṛ's office.

---

52 Gonda, 1979, "Pravargya Mantras":261. Our text, TĀ 5, prefers to call the vessel "Pravargya." I also prefer that name, rather than "Mahāvīra" ("Mighty Hero"), because the latter might create the erroneous impression that the vessel was mainly looked upon as an anthropomorphic image.

Still, there seems to be a rather clear reference to the preparation of the clay vessel by the Adhvaryu in one Ṛgvedic verse: verse 43 of ṚV 1, 164[53] has: "from afar I saw the smoke of dung" (ṚV 1, 164, 43a). This may well refer to the fumigation of the unbaked clay vessels with the smoke of horse-dung by the Adhvaryu (van Buitenen, *Pravargya*:60, §10). The next pāda, which puzzled several scholars, may refer to the place where this takes place, the Gārhapatya fire, from the point of view of another officiant[54] or of the sacrificer,[55] standing at the eastern door and reciting the verse while watching the fumigation of the vessels in the Prācīnavaṃśa. When looked at through the eastern door, the location of the Gārhapatya may be described as "in the middle (i.e. not north or south of a line drawn from the eastern door through the Āhavanīya), on the farther side of this nearer (fire, sc. the Āhavanīya)" (43b). The devatā of pāda c is according to the Anukramaṇī "Soma", but the *ukṣā́ṇaṃ pṛ́śnim* that is cooked in this pāda can be consistently interpreted as the milk-and-ghee-mixture (having a spotted appearance) that will be heated as the Gharma. Pāda d places the ritual in a primeval age: "those were the first

---

53 *śakamáyaṃ dhūmám ārā́d apaśyaṃ viṣūvátā pará enā́vareṇa / ukṣā́ṇaṃ pṛ́śnim apacanta vīrā́s tā́ni dhármāṇi prathamā́ny āsan.* Several verses of this hymn refer to the Pravargya ceremony; some verses are actually used in this rite as we know it from the Śrauta Sūtras. The sacrificial setting of the entire hymn is clear from the beginning. From some verses (e.g. 1, 164, 5-7 and 21) we get the impression that the subject is someone who is newly accepted in the circle of Vedic priests. It is probably rather hazardous to draw conclusions concerning the relative age of a hymn within the Ṛgvedic corpus on the basis of an alleged philosophical or popular or hieratical character of a hymn (cf. Gonda, *Vedic Literature*: 26-29). But even if it is assumed that ṚV 1, 164 is a relatively late hymn (V. Arnold, *Vedic Metre in its Historical Development*, Cambridge University Press 1905:269, 273), it represents most probably an older stage than the Pravargya sections of the Taittirīyas, so that the following argumentation will not be affected.

54 E.g. the Hotṛ, whose presence at this stage of the Pravargya rite is not yet required, but who, by the time that the baked vessels are going to be used in the ceremony, will enter through the eastern door of the Prācīnavaṃśa (van Buitenen, *Pravargya*:64, §4).

55 Sāyaṇa, while he takes in 26-27 the Hotṛ as the speaker, ascribes verse 43 to the *yájamāna*. 1, 164, 26-27 are actually recited by the Hotṛ during the Pravargya according to the Śrauta Sūtras (van Buitenen, *Pravargya*:96).

ordinances." Thus, this interpretation offers a very reasonable solution to one of the riddles of this "riddle-hymn," a solution that is moreover in accordance with the intimate connection with the Pravargya of other verses of this hymn. Previous scholars were side-tracked because they interpreted *śakamáyaṃ dhūmám* for some reason as smoke from *cow*-dung and/or connected it with the *śakadhū́ma* of AV 6, 128 (the "weather prophet").[56]

If this interpretation of ṚV 1, 164, 43 is correct, there is some positive evidence that as early as in Ṛgvedic times the Pravargya was a unitary rite, comprising both the manufacturing of a clay vessel and the offering of hot milk from it to the Aśvins.[57] There were, however, originally options in which other materials than clay were used for the Gharma vessel. This, at least, appears from one place where the Gharma is called *ayasmáya*, "metal" (ṚV 5, 11, 5), and seems to be reflected in ŚB 14, 2, 2, 54.[58]

This ancient form of the Pravargya was probably not necessarily connected with a Soma sacrifice. While the TĀ and ŚB start the Pravargya Brāhmaṇa with a myth that explains the Pravargya as an important part, the "Head," of the Agniṣṭoma sacrifice (see 3.4), the first

---

56 See Geldner, *ṚVübers*, 1, 235; C. Kunhan Raja, *Asya Vamasya Hymn*, Madras 1956:73-74; V. S. Agrawala, *Vision in Long Darkness*, Varanasi 1963:161; Renou, *ÉVP* 16:88; W. N. Brown, *India and Indology (papers Brown)*, Delhi 1978:73 (in a paper reprinted from *JAOS* 88:199-218, "Agni, Sun, Sacrifice and Vāc: A sacerdotal Ode by Dīrghatamas. Rigveda 1, 164"); The interpretation of *śakamáyaṃ dhūmám* as smoke from *cow*-dung may be traced back to Sāyaṇa, who explains *śakamáyaṃ* as *śakṛnmayaṃ śuṣkagomayasambhūtam.*

57 If the Pravargya as known from the Śrauta Sūtras corresponds in its broad outlines to a Ṛgvedic rite, the interesting question arises whether there was, like in the case of the Soma/Haoma sacrifice, an Iranian counterpart to this rite. But, while the Ṛgvedic name of the hot vessel and its contents, *gharmá*, has an Iranian parallel (*garəma*), I could not discover a ceremony similar to the Gharma/Pravargya ceremony. The Parsis do have rites in which goat's milk and ghee form the oblations, but there seems to be no rite in which the preparation or even only the heating of a vessel plays any role (cf. J. J. Modi, *Religious Customs and Ceremonies of the Parsees*, Bombay (1922): 295, 299, 321, 359).

58 See note 164 to the translation.

parts of the Kaṭha Āraṇyaka contain only a description of the Pravargya without reference to the Agniṣṭoma. The original status of the Pravargya as an independent rite seems to be reflected here. The Pravargya as belonging to the Soma sacrifice, is referred to only in the third and (as it seems) last chapter of the Kaṭha-Āraṇyaka[59].

5 Taittirīya Āraṇyaka 5 and its relation to the Taittirīya Brāhmaṇa and Saṃhitā

The Brāhmaṇa of the Pravargya ceremony of the Taittirīya śākhā of the Yajurveda is prapāṭhaka or book 5 of the Taittirīya Āraṇyaka,[60] divided into 12 anuvākas (chapters) and 108 daśatis or decades of lines. The Pravargya mantras are TĀ 4. Much of the TĀ is probably comparatively old, though many parts show signs of a late (secondary) redaction.[61] As far as linguistic and stylistic peculiarities are concerned, the TĀ Pravargya portions follow the TS.[62] For example, the form *ajakṣīréṇa* in TĀ 5, 3, 9 is as it appears in the TS, where there is a "clear tendency to shorten the long

59 Another indication of an originally independent Pravargya, is discussed in note 11 to the tanslation.

60 Thus according to the Āndhra recension (see below) to which Sāyaṇa's commentary is attached. In the Drāviḍa recension the same Prapāṭhaka comes eighth. Bhaṭṭa-Bhāskara's commentary follows the latter recension. On the Taittirīya Āraṇyaka in general see: Rajendralala Mitra's introduction to his edition of the text (Calcutta, 1872, see under TĀ (b)); Keith, *TStransl*, Introduction, p. lxxviii-lxxxv; Gonda, *Vedic Literature*:429-430.

61 For a survey of the contents of the Āraṇyaka and its relation to the Saṃhitā and Brāhmaṇa, see Keith, *TStransl*, Introduction, p. lxxviii-lxxxv. N. Sen ("Verbforms", 1975) suggests three major stages of development of the books of the Āraṇyaka to be distinguished: the oldest group is formed by books 2-6 (so it includes the Pravargya sections); the second stage is represented by books 1 and 7-9; the last stage is book 10 (Mahānārāyaṇa-Upaniṣad).

62 For a discussion of the language and style of the TS see Keith, *TStransl*, Introd uction, p. cxl-clix.

vowels of the first parts of words in composition" (Keith, *TStransl.*, Intr.p.cxliv). Further, there are several formulas held in common with the TS. For instance, the rare formula *pū́rvam evóditám, úttareṇābhí gr̥ṇāti,* occurring several times in our text (TĀ 5, 6, 6; 8, 3; 9, 10) is also in TS 5, 1, 4, 4.

In his study of the use of verse-repetitions in the Taittirīya Saṃhitā, Brāhmaṇa and Āraṇyaka (in *Proceedings of the All-India Oriental Conference*, 28th session, Karnatak University, nov. 1976: 233-244), C. G. Kashikar arrives, as far as the Āraṇyaka is concerned, at the conclusion that "the entire *Taittirīya Āraṇyaka* was compiled at a much later date" than the Saṃhitā. The "compilers of the *Taittirīya* texts have generally recorded as *pratīkapāṭha* a verse at its second and subsequent occurrences," although "there are a number of exceptions to this rule which cannot be looked upon as mere accidents of the tradition." However, the facts that have been collected to form the basis of this conclusion are the following: there is variation in the order of contents of the TĀ: the Āndhra tradition (with Sāyaṇa's commentary) has ten prapāṭhakas, the Drāviḍa tradition eight prapāṭhakas in a different order. There seems to have existed even a third, Karṇāṭaka tradition.[63] There are exceptions to the rule that the complete citations precede a *pratīkapāṭha*, but this would be, in the view of the absence of a fixed order of its contents, of no great significance. In TĀ 1, 27, 6 occurs a *pratīka*, but the corresponding complete verse is not present in the TS nor in the TB. A complete citation is found in the Āpastamba Mantrapāṭha (2, 4, 3). This would indicate, according to Kashikar, that this part of the Āraṇyaka is not older than this comparatively late text (*Proc. All-India Or. Conf.*, 28th session, (1976): 243).

---

63 See on the arrangement of the text in several manuscripts also K. Madhava Krishna Sarma, "A Note on the Text of the Taittirīya Āraṇyaka", *ALB* 3, part 2 (1939): 68-72.

Now the above mentioned points, looked at carefully, permit only of the much weaker conclusion that the order of contents was not fixed for a long time and perhaps had never been fixed. There is no reason to assume a "comparatively late composition" (*Proc. All-India Or. Conf.*, 28 (1976): 242) of the whole Āraṇyaka.[64] That the order was not fixed is reflected in the existence of the two recensions of the TĀ that are current today. There are also different orders for studying or reading the Taittirīya texts according to the Gṛhya Sūtras. First, there is the reading in which the text follows the order generally known: the text is divided into Saṃhitā, Brāhmaṇa and Āraṇyaka. This is called the Sārasvatapāṭha. Second, there is the division of the Taittirīya Yajurveda into five Kāṇḍas: the Prājāpatya, Saumya, Āgneya, Vaiśvadeva and Svāyambhuva Kāṇḍa.

---

64 (a) The opinion of the Sūtra authors on the relations between Saṃhitā, Brāhmaṇa and Āraṇyaka are of some importance in addition to the internal etxtual evidence. Their works are the earliest sources after the main Taittirīya Yajurveda texts themselves. In an earlier article (see note 68), Kashikar arrives at the conclusion that, in general, the Saṃhitā, Brāhmaṇa and Āraṇyaka enjoyed equal authority from the part of the authors of the Taittirīya Śrauta Sūtras.

(b) Keith contradicts himself in his introduction to the translation of TS: "The Pravargya sections (*Āraṇyaka*, iv and v) seem also to be a later addition, as the parallel to the Mantras is found only in the Khila book of the *Maitrāyaṇī* (iv 9), and there is no parallel to the Brāhmaṇa at all therein. This is supported by the fact that the *Vājasaneyi* has the Mantras in books xxxvi-xxxix, a supplement, and the *Çatapatha Brāhmaṇa* treats the Pravargya in its last book, together with the Upanishad, both in the Mādhyandina and also apparently once in the Kāṇva recension." (p. lxxxi-lxxxii). But that this place of the Pravargya sections need not be due to their being a late addition, appears from Keith's own words, some 40 pages further on: The Pravargya "seems in the Yajurveda tradition to have been held of too great secrecy and importance to be included in the ordinary teaching of the school rather than to be later in time or in development, *for there are no clear traces of lateness in either the Mantra or the Brāhmaṇa portions of the texts.*" (p. cxxiv-cxxv, my emphasis).

(c) For some more pieces of evidence that point to a comparitively late *final* redaction (*after* Patañjali's Mahābhāṣya) of the Yajurveda and other Vedic texts that contain old material, see J. Bronkhorst in *Kratylos*, 32 (1987):55-56.

In this latter division of the so-called Ārṣeyapāṭha, the Pravargya mantras and Brāhmaṇa form part of the second or Saumyakāṇḍa.[65] Part of the evidence, presented by Kashikar, would point at a contradictory conclusion, viz. that the Āraṇyaka has *preceded* the Taittirīya Brāhmaṇa: two Pravargya mantras, cited in their complete form in the TĀ (in 4, 3 and 4, 42), are cited in *pratīka*-form in the TB. The *pratīka* citation in TĀ 1, 27, 6 may well have been preceded by a complete citation of the verse (which is ṚV 1, 89, 9) in a (lost or not yet found) Kaṭha text. The traditional attribution of the first two prapāṭhakas of the Taittirīya Āraṇyaka to this śākhā is well founded.[66] This leaves open the possibility that an important part of the Āraṇyaka is not later, or not much later, than the Saṃhitā and Brāhmaṇa, with as perhaps the only exceptions the Upaniṣadic portions.[67] The continuity between the Āraṇyaka and the Saṃhitā and Brāhmaṇa appears also from the authors of the Sūtras and of the Kāṇḍānukrama: they refer to the mantra and Brāhmaṇa portions of the Taittirīya texts without making a distinction between TS, TB and TĀ.[68] Like the texts of the TS and TB, the Pravargya portions of the TĀ seem to have taken form

---

65 See Kashikar, "Avāntaradīkṣā":66-67; Baudhāyana Gṛhya Sūtra 3, 1; 3, 2, 4-3, 34; and Āgniveśya Gṛhya Sūtra 1, 2, 1.

66 See Weber, *Indische Studien* 13 (1873): 269; Gonda, *Vedic Literature*:350.

67 Cf. Weber, *Indische Studien* 1 (1850): 77 and Sen, "Verbforms".

68 Brāhmaṇa portions of any of these texts are quoted as *brāhmaṇa*. In his article "The Taittirīya-Brāhmaṇa in Relation to the Sūtrakāras", *Pratidānam*, (ed. J. C. Heesterman et al.), Mouton, The Hague-Paris 1968:398-408, C. G. Kashikar examines the way in which the Taittirīya Sūtra authors cite the mantras from TS and TB (either *pratīkena* or in *sakalapāṭha*) and arrives at the conclusion that "the Saṃhitā, Brāhmaṇa and Āraṇyaka in their present form generally enjoyed equal authority among the Taittirīyas".

in the Madhyadeśa. In later times we find the important Taittirīya schools especially in South-India.[69]

Mention should be made at this place of W. Rau's observation that the TĀ is rather frequently cited in Patañjali's Vyākaraṇa Mahābhāṣya: "Andererseits erstaunt es, das sprachlich wahrhaftig verlotterte TĀ so oft zitiert zu finden. Könnte es erst nach dem 2. Jahrhundert v. Chr. bis zu seinem jetzigem Gestalt verwahrlost sein?"[70] It should be noted, however, that only certain parts of the Āraṇyaka can be considered to be "linguistically tumbled down." That the accentuation of the Āraṇyaka is at times very irregular was already noted by Weber (*IS* 10 (1868): 440, note 1).[71] But there are also parts where the accentuation corresponds to the regular accentuation of the TS, as described by Weber (*IS* 13 (1873):

---

69 All Yajurveda Saṃhitās had their origin probably in this same Madhyadeśa (Renou, *Écoles Védiques:*194ff). The place of Kurukṣetra is roughly known, but the location of Khāṇḍava, Tūrghna and Parīṇah cannot be further determined (MacDonell & Keith, *Vedic Index*:1:169; 2:135; hypotheses about Parīṇah: Ram Gopal, *Proc.All-India Or.Conf.* 1976 (1978): 249; and Krick, *Feuergründung*:499). In the times when the Śrauta, Gṛhya and Dharma Sūtras were written, we find the important Taittirīya schools (Baudhāyana, Bharadvāja, Āpastamba) in South-India, below the river Godāvarī. The Maitrāyaṇīyas and Vājasaneyins of that time can be located in North India (E. Brucker, *Die Spätvedische Kulturepoche nach den Quellen der Śrauta-, Gṛhya- und Dharmasūtras*, Wiesbaden 1980:67, 68, 70; K. Mylius in *Mitteilungen des Instituts für Orientforschung der deutschen Akademie der Wiss. Berlin* 17, no. 3:369-382). For Śrauta traditions in contemporary India see C. G. Kashikar and A. Parpola, "Śrauta Traditions in Recent Times" in Staal, *Agni*:2:193-251; and Witzel "Materialien zu den vedischen Schulen" in *Studien zur Indologie und Iranistik*, Heft 7 (1981): 108-132; Heft 8/9 (1982/3): 171-240; Heft 10 (1985): 231-237.

70 "On the other hand, it is surprising to find that the TĀ, which is linguistically quite tumbled down, is cited so often. Perhaps it started to be neglected into its present state not before the 2nd century B.C.?" W. Rau, *Die vedischen Zitate im Vyākaraṇa-Mahābhāṣya* (Abh. d. Akademie der Wiss. und Lit., geistes- und soz. wissensch. Klasse, Mainz), Jahrgang 1985, no. 4:103.

71 For the irregular accentuation of TĀ 2 see Malamoud's notes at the text in his *Svādhyāya*.

1-128). The two prapāṭhakas that deal with the Pravargya belong to those parts.

Because the order of the Yajurveda was not fixed for a long time, it remains very difficult to draw conclusions regarding the relative age of different parts of what we now call the Taittirīya Saṃhitā, Brāhmaṇa and Āraṇyaka. Textual evidence tends to point to contradictory conclusions. But because the Pravargya is such an old rite, clearly referred to in the Ṛgveda (perhaps even the preparation of the clay vessel is referred to), it seems reasonable to assume that the Taittirīyas had to pay attention to this rite at an early date. The Pravargya must have formed part of the Kṛṣṇa Yajurveda recensions in the earliest times, and was on certain grounds placed in the Āraṇya sections.[72]

6 Taittirīya Āraṇyaka 5 and its relation to other texts

Let us now briefly consider the relation of TĀ 5 with the parallel texts. From the Kaṭha śākhā we have important fragments of both the mantras and the Brāhmaṇa of the Pravargya.[73] The Maitrāyanīyas have preserved

---

72 The following statement of L. Renou was therefore based on erroneous judgements: "Enfin le Pravargya, portion essentielle du Yajus Blanc «récent» . . . n'a guère de correspondant dans les Saṃhitā Noires: il a fallu du temps pour qu'un tel rite fasse son chemin jusque dans le plus haut Recueil." ("Finally, the Pravargya, an essential portion of the 'recent' White Yajus . . . has hardly anything corresponding to it in the Black Saṃhitās: some time was needed for such a rite to make its way up to the highest collection", Renou, *Écoles Védiques*:140f). Cf. Witzel's remarks in the introduction to his critical edition of the Kaṭha Āraṇyaka, p. II-IV.

73 These fragments were already edited (though imperfectly) in 1898 by L. von Schroeder, under the unrevealing title "Die Tübinger Kaṭha-Handschriften und ihre Beziehungen zum Taittirīya-Āraṇyaka", *Sitzungsberichte der Phil.-hist. Classe der kaiserl. Ak. der Wissenschaften* 137 (1897) no. 4; Caland's translation of the Pravargya praśna of ĀpŚS contains many references to the Kaṭhas. Yet van Buitenen does not mention the Kaṭha texts in the Introduction to his description of the Pravargya, in which he aims at an interpretation of this rite on the basis of the old sources. In his articles

only the mantras: MS 4, 9. The Vājasaneyins have the mantras (VS 37-39) and a corresponding Brāhmaṇa (ŚB 14,[74] in the Kāṇva recension to be found in book 16). Sources from Brāhmaṇas attached to other Vedas than the Yajurveda are AiB 1, 18-22 and KauṣB 8, 3-7.[75] Shorter references to the Pravargya are found in PB 7, 5, 6;[76] JB 3, 126;[77] and lastly GB 2, 2, 6 (almost equal to AiB 1, 18 and 22).

The most important parallel texts are Kaṭha Āraṇyaka 2 and 3 and Śatapatha Brāhmaṇa 14. The fact that the Pravargya mantras and Brāhmaṇa are placed in the Āraṇyakas of the Taittirīyas and of the Kaṭhas, and with the Vājasaneyins in the last portions of the VS and ŚB, should be explained by an intentional ordering of the text at some stage,[78] rather than by their being later additions. As has been argued above, there are reasons to assume that they formed part of the different recensions in the earliest times. The relation between the three texts would be, in that case, approximately parallel to the relation between the main texts of the Taittirīyas, the Kaṭhas and the Vājasaneyins. With regard to the Saṃhitās, the Kaṭhas (and the Maitrāyaṇīyas) and the Taittirīya, belonging to the Kṛṣṇa Yajurveda, can be taken together as against the Vājasaneyins, who belong to the Śukla Yajurveda. While the differences in geographical, linguistic, religious, and cultural background of the Yajurveda schools

---

"Apropos" and "Avāntaradīkṣā", Kashikar made no use of the KaṭhĀ. At present, there is a new textcritical edition with German translation and commentary by M. Witzel (see under Abbreviations, KaṭhĀ). (According to Kashikar, "Mahāvīra":137 note 4, a Devanāgarī edition with English translation will appear as Nepal Research Publications, no.2.)

74 Translated by J. Eggeling, *SBE* vol. 44, 1900.

75 Translated by Keith, *Ṛigveda Brāhmaṇas*, Harvard Oriental Series 25, London 1920.

76 Translated by Caland, Calcutta 1931.

77 Caland, *Das Jaiminīya-Brāhmaṇa in Auswahl*, Amsterdam 1919:251-257. Here the Pravargya myth is closely parallel to the one in ŚB 14, 1. It forms part of the story of Cyavana.

78 Cf. Keith, *TStransl*, Introduction, p. cxxiv-cxxv, cited in note 64(b) above; and van Buitenen, *Pravargya*:38, n. 118.

were generally not very great,[79] the Taittirīyas seem to be more recent than the other Kṛṣṇa Yajurveda schools,[80] and the Vājasaneyins more recent than the Taittirīyas.[81]

M. Witzel mentions some compositional and linguistic arguments on the basis of which he assumes that the KaṭhĀ is the oldest and the ŚB Pravargya section the most recent. But it must be pointed out here, that several linguistically problematic or complicated mantras of the Taittirīyas are much simpler in their Kaṭha version, or contain what could be considered as later forms.[82] In the case of *dhármāsi sudhárma*[83] the Kaṭhas stand apart with what seems to be a complete recast of the mantra. That the KaṭhĀ contains old material may be concluded from its discussion of the Pravargya without reference to a Soma sacrifice in the first chapters. Whether or not the KaṭhĀ is actually older than the other two texts - the linguistic material is so limited, that on that basis no far reaching conclusions can be drawn - it contrasts in several respects with the other two texts.

The earliest elaborate sources on the Pravargya rite apart from the TĀ and the other two texts, are the Śrauta Sūtras. From the Kaṭhas no Śrauta Sūtra is known to us. Most of the Yajurveda Sūtras belong to the Taittirīya school, and, as far as the Pravargya is concerned, they frequently refer to the TĀ. Of these, Baudhāyana follows the Āraṇyaka most closely. The description of the Pravargya rite in the Kātyāyana Śrauta Sūtra, the only Śrauta Sūtra of the Śukla Yajurveda, is rather succinct in comparison with the elaborate descriptions of Baudhāyana, Bhāradvāja and Āpastamba. While the TĀ Pravargya sections are often referred to in the Śrauta Sūtras, there are now and then several differences in the details of performance between the TĀ Pravargya ritual and that of

79 They all took shape in the Madhyadeśa, where they were not isolated from each other. See note 69.

80 Renou, *Écoles Védiques:*144-5.

81 Eggeling, *ŚBtransl* I:xxvii; Renou, *Écoles Védiques:*138, note 3).

82 Cf. note 24, 28 and 134(a) to the translation.

83 TĀ 4, 10, 2(3a); VS 38, 14fg; see note 120 to the translation.

the Śrauta Sūtras. In one case there even seems to be a complete reinterpretation of a TĀ-passage.[84]

7 About the Text and Translation

For the convenience of the reader, the Sanskrit text has been given along with the translation. There are three editions of the TĀ: C, P and M (see Abbreviations, under TĀ). None of them can be called really critical. In general they are quite similar, as far as the Pravargya mantras and Brāhmaṇa are concerned. I follow edition M, which seems to have the fewest cases of faulty or unclear printing. The text has been reproduced as precisely as possible as it appears in this edition, except for the following:

a) Sandhi. Unusual sandhis used in this edition (-थ्स-, -अस् स-, -ट्थ् स-) have been replaced by the more commonly used (-त्स-, -अ: स-, -ट् स-).

b) Avagraha. All three editions, M, C and P, make use of the single and double avagraha, to indicate *pariśliṣṭa-sandhi* with *a* and *ā*, but none of them is entirely consistent. The use of the avagraha in those cases has the theoretical disadvantage that it suggests that the sandhi results from an absorption of the second vowel by the first (Malamoud, *Svādhyāya*:92). The avagraha has been used by me only to mark the disappearance of an initial short *a* after *e* and *o*, in accordance with modern usage (as e.g. in the *Śrautakośa*, Sanskrit section; cf. Whitney, Sanskrit Grammar:9, §16a and b).

c) Word division. Wherever sandhi permits the division of words, there is no reason not to show this in the text, since the "partial word division now in use in printed Devanāgarī texts is a make-shift" (F. B. J. Kuiper in his preface to *Gopālakelicandrikā* (Verhand. der Kon. Nederl. Akademie van Wetensch., Afd. Letterkunde, N. R., deel 134. Amsterdam-Oxford-New York, 1987), p. 6. It may seem that this make-shift is enforced by the character of the Indian script (Kuiper, loc. cit.), but in fact Devanāgarī has all instruments to separate syllables, words and word groups at whichever

---

84 See section 3.3 above, and note 11 and 130 to the translation.

place the author, editor or scribe wishes. In a few cases in the text, the accent shows that what is given as two words, actually form one single word. In those cases I combined those two parts. After all, these irregular separations may very well originate from the editors or from late manuscripts used by them, since early manuscripts usually give no word divisions at all.

d) Punctuation. The daṇḍas are exactly reproduced from edition M. Commas, question marks and quotation marks have been added by me. In the case of quotations of words or mantras spoken, the sandhi with the following *íti* has of course been maintained. In case this sandhi resulted in a single vowel, the end quotes appear after this vowel and before the *ti* of *íti*. Moreover, if the Brāhmaṇa cites only a part of the mantra, and if the rest has been translated in the translation, the additional parts have been added within brackets in the text too. The traditional division in daśatis has been indicated by a number between double daṇḍas at the end of each daśati. The translation follows this division, as far as possible, and the numbers have been given between parentheses at the beginning of each daśati.

Variants appearing in the other two editions that are not obvious printing errors, have been mentioned in notes. The list of words at the end of each anuvāka, and at the end of the book, do not need to be included here. They have an important function in the transmission of the text: they should preserve the authenticity and prevent interpolations and omissions.

Like most previous scholars, I will refer in the notes to edition C: the first number indicates the prapāṭhaka, the second the anuvāka, the third the daśati; in the case of the Pravargya mantras there is a fourth number (between parentheses), which is the number a specific part of the text has in this edition. This part may consist of one or more mantras, or of a few pādas, a single pāda or less, depending on how the commentator (in this case Sāyaṇa) has divided the text in his commentary. In edition P the division is similar to the division in C, but the numbers are absent. In edition M specific parts are numbered too, but the division follows that of the commentator Bhaṭṭa-Bhāskara. Unfortunately, there is considerable confusion in the way the Pravargya sections are referred to by different scholars. Usually three numbers are given, and the last number refers in some cases to the daśati, and in other cases to the number a specific passage or mantra has in edition C. To facilitate reference to the three editions, a concordance has been added (appendix 2).

The rest of a mantra has been translated (within square brackets: [ ]), if this prapāṭhaka of the Āraṇyaka presents only the *pratīka.* In this way a more complete picture of the ritual will arise. Moreover, the exposition of the Āraṇyaka frequently presupposes the complete mantra. Only in the cases where the addition of the other pādas of a mantra would interrupt and obscure the exposition, these pādas are given in a note. The mantras in the translation are printed in *italics.* The sequence of mantras cited in this book of the Taittirīya Āraṇyaka (the Brāhmaṇa of the Pravargya ritual) follows with a few exceptions that of the preceding book TĀ 4 (the collection of mantras of the Pravargya ritual). Therefore they can be found easily if one knows in what chapter(s) of the preceding book the mantras of a certain chapter are. This will be indicated in the introductory note at the beginning of each chapter.

References to the broad outlines of the ritual are given within parentheses ( ) in the translation. These references are based, a) on the context in the text, b) on the commentators Bh and S, and the old Śrauta Sūtras BŚS, BhŚS and ĀpŚS, as far as they do not contradict the TĀ text. More detailed references and discussions not directly necessary for an understanding of the text and translation, are given in the notes at the end. If quotations and citations are not from an English source, they have been translated into English. For a detailed description of the sacrificial acts the reader is referred to the description of van Buitenen, *Pravargya*, and to the relevant passages in the *Śrautakośa* (see notes to each anuvāka).

part II: TEXT AND TRANSLATION

Anuvāka 1

The Pravargya as the head of the Sacrifice

This anuvāka contains the mythological story of the origin and purpose, the *purākalpa*, of the Pravargya ceremony in the form of the story of Makha. See Introduction section 3.4 and Hillebrandt, *Vedische Mythologie*:4154; Keith, *Religion*:112; Rönnow, "Zur Erklärung des Pravargya etc.":113ff, esp. 127; Eggeling, *SBE* 44, p. xlvi-l; van Buitenen, *Pravargya*:16ff; Gonda, *Aspects*:167ff; Kashikar, "Mahāvīra"; and Heesterman, "The Case of the Severed Head" in: *Essays in Indian Ritual, Kingship and Society*, Chicago 1985. In the introduction of the TĀ edition C (p. 27-28), a translation of this anuvāka is quoted from Muir, *Sanskrit Texts* IV, p.112.

हरिः ॐ ।
"शं नस् तन् नो मा हासीत् ।"
ॐ शान्तिः शान्तिः शान्तिः ॥ ॐ ॥

देवा वै सत्रम् आसत । ऋद्धिपरिमितं यशस्कामाः । तेऽब्रुवन् । "यं नः प्रथमं यश ऋच्छात् । सर्वेषां नस् तत् सहासद्" इति । तेषां कुरुक्षेत्रं वेदिर् आसीत् । तस्यै खाण्डवो दक्षिणार्ध आसीत् । तूर्घ्नम् उत्तरार्धः । परीणज् जघनार्धः । मरव उत्करः ॥१॥

Hari Om!
"Good fortune to us . . . may it leave us not!"[1]
Om peace, peace, peace. Om!

(1) The gods, indeed, desirous of glory, held a sacrificial session, ending (only) with success.[2] They said: "If glory reaches one of us first, let it be in common to us all." For them, Kurukṣetra[3] was the altar-space, Khāṇḍava was its southern part, Tūrghna the northern part, Parīṇah the rear part. The desert regions were the rubbish-heap.

तेषाँ मखं वैष्णवं यशं आर्च्छत् । तन् न्य् अंकामयत । तेनापांक्रामत् । तं देवा अन्व् आंयन् । यशोंऽवरुरुंत्समानाः । तस्यान्वागंतस्य । सव्याद् धनुर् अजांयत । दक्षिंणाद् इषंवः । तस्मांद् इषुधन्वं पुण्यंजन्म । यज्ञजंन्मा हि ॥२॥ तम् एकं सन्तंम् बहवों नाभ्य् अंधृष्णुवन् । तस्माद् एकंम् इषुधन्विनंम् । बहवोंऽनिषुधन्वा नाभि धृंष्णुवन्ति । सोंऽस्मयत । "एकँ मा सन्तँ बहवो नाभ्य् अंधर्षिषुर्" इतिं । तस्यं सिष्मियाणस्य तेजोऽपांक्रामत् । तद् देवा ओषंधीषु न्य् अंमृजुः । ते श्यामाकां अभवन् । स्मयाका वै नामैते ॥३॥ तत् स्मयाकांनां स्मयाकत्वम् । तस्मांद् दीक्षितेनांपिगृह्यं स्मेतव्यंम् । तेजंसो धृत्यैं ।

स धनुंः प्रतिष्कभ्यांतिष्ठत् । ता उंपदीकां अब्रुवन् "वरँ वृणामहै । अथं व इमं रंन्धयाम । यत्र क्वं च खनांम । तद् अपोंऽभि तृणदामे"तिं । तस्मांद् उपदीका यत्र क्वं च खनंन्ति । तद् अपोंऽभि तृंन्दन्ति ॥४॥ वारेंवृतं ह्य् आंसाम् । तस्य ज्याम् अप्य्

(2) Amongst them, it was Makha Vaiṣṇava whom glory reached first. He desired that (glory) for himself.[4] He slipped off with that (glory). Him the gods followed, because they wished to gain the glory. When he was followed, a bow came forth from his left hand, arrows from his right hand. Therefore, arrow and bow are of pure origin, for they are born from the sacrifice.[5] (3) Him, though he was alone, many (gods) could not overpower. Therefore, many without arrow and bow cannot overpower someone who has arrow and bow. He smiled (*a-smayata*). "Me, though I was alone, the many (gods) did not overpower." Brilliant energy withdrew from him who was smiling. This (brilliant energy) the gods rubbed upon some herbs. These became the Śyāmākas. These are actually Smayākas (*smayate*: he smiles) by name. (4) That is why Smayākas are called Smayākas. Therefore, an initiate should smile (only) after covering the mouth, to preserve his brilliant energy.

He stood leaning on his bow. The white ants[6] there said: "Let us choose a boon, then we will make this (Makha Vaiṣṇava or the sacrifice personified) subject to you. May we, wherever we dig, strike water on that place." Therefore, wherever the white ants dig, there they strike water, (5)

आदन् । तस्य धनुर् विप्रवमाणः शिर उद् अवर्तयत् । तद् द्यावापृथिवी अनु प्रावर्तत ।
यत् प्रावर्तत । तत् प्रवर्ग्यस्य प्रवर्ग्यत्वम् । यद् "घ्राः ४" इत्य् अपतत् । तद् घर्मस्य
घर्मत्वम् । "महतो वीर्यम् अपप्तद्" इति । तन् महावीरस्य महावीरत्वम् ॥५॥ यद्
अस्याः समभरन् । तत् सम्राजः सम्राट्त्वम् ।

तः स्तृतं देवतास् त्रेधा व्य् अगृह्णत । अग्निः प्रातःसवनम् । इन्द्रो माध्यंदिनः
सवनम् । विश्वे देवास् तृतीयसवनम् । तेनापशीर्ष्णा यज्ञेन यजमानाः । नाशिषो
ऽवारुन्धत । न सुवर्गं लोकम् अभ्य् अजयन् ।

ते देवा अश्विनाव् अब्रुवन् ॥६॥ "भिषजौ वै स्थः । इदं यज्ञस्य शिरः प्रति धत्तम्"
इति । ताव् अब्रूतां "वरं वृणावहै । ग्रह एव नाव् अत्रापि गृह्यताम्" इति । ताभ्याम्
एतम् आश्विनम् अगृह्णन् । ताव् एतद् यज्ञस्य शिरः प्रत्य् अधत्ताम् । यत् प्रवर्ग्यः । तेन
सशीर्ष्णा यज्ञेन यजमानाः । अवाशिषोऽरुन्धत । अभि सुवर्गं लोकम् अजयन् ।

for it was chosen by them in the choice of the boon. They ate off (a part of) his bowstring. Stretching up, the bow caused his head to fly off. It proceeded along heaven and earth. That it proceeded (*prāvartata*), that is why the Pravargya is called Pravargya. That it flew off with the sound "ghraaaam," that is why the Gharma is called Gharma. "The life-energy (*vīryà*) of the mighty one (*mahatáḥ*) flew away"[7] (the gods said). That is why the Mahāvīra is called Mahāvīra. (6) That they collected (*sam-abharan*) him from this (earth), that is why the Saṃrāṭ is called Saṃrāṭ.

The gods took threefold hold of him who was spread out. Agni (took) the morning pressing, Indra the midday pressing, the All-gods the third pressing. Offering that headless sacrifice, they gained no blessings, they did not conquer the celestial world.

Those gods said to the two Aśvins: (7) "You, indeed, are the physicians. Put this head of the sacrifice back (on the body)." The two said: "Let us choose a boon: a ladleful[8] must be taken for us too in this (sacrifice)" For them they took that ladleful for the Aśvins. The two put back that head of the sacrifice, the Pravargya. Offering that sacrifice united with its head, they gained blessings, they conquered the celestial world.

यत् प्रंवर्ग्यं प्रवृणक्तिं । यज्ञस्यैव तच् छिरः प्रतिं दधाति । तेन सशीर्ष्णा यज्ञेन यजंमानः । अवाशिषों रुन्धे । अभि सुंवर्गं लोकं जंयति ।
तस्मांद् एष आंश्विनप्रंवया इव । यत् प्रंवर्ग्यः ॥७॥

If one places the Pravargya vessel on the fire, then one puts back the head of the sacrifice. Offering that sacrifice united with its head, one gains blessings, one conquers the celestial world.

Therefore (because they put the head of the sacrifice on the body), this Pravargya is strong (in its mantras and sacrificial acts) for the Aśvins, as it were.

Anuvāka 2

Collection of the materials for the Pravargya Ritual

The mantras of this anuvāka are TĀ 4, 2, 1 - 4, 2, 5(16). For a description of the ritual actions see: *Śrautakośa* vol. 2, Sanskrit part 1:514-515; English part 1:28-30; 32-33; 35-36; 38-39; 41-42; 44-45; 46-47; van Buitenen, *Pravargya*: I, §1-§6.

सावित्रं जुहोति प्रसूत्यै । चतुर्गृहीतेन जुहोति । चतुष्पादः पशवः । पशून् एवाव रुन्धे । चतस्रो दिशः । दिक्ष्व् एव प्रति तिष्ठति ।

छन्दांसि देवेभ्योऽपाक्रामन् । "न वोऽभागानि हव्यं वक्ष्याम" इति । तेभ्य एतच् चतुर्गृहीतम् अधारयन् । पुरोनुवाक्यायै याज्यायै ॥१॥ देवतायै वषट्काराय । यच् चतुर्गृहीतं जुहोति । छन्दांस्य् एव तत् प्रीणाति । तान्य् अस्य प्रीतानि देवेभ्यो हव्यं वहन्ति ।

ब्रह्मवादिनो वदन्ति । "होतव्यं दीक्षितस्य गृहा३इ न होतव्या३म्" इति । हविर् वै दीक्षितः । यज् जुहुयात् । हविष्कृतं यजमानम् अग्नौ प्र दध्यात् । यन् न

(1) (The Adhvaryu) offers the oblation for Savitṛ (the Stimulator),[9] for stimulation. He offers with the (clarified butter) of which four (spoonfuls) are taken (into the ladle). Cattle are four-footed. He gains cattle. There are four quarters. He stands firm in the quarters.

The metres went away from the gods.[10] (They said:) "We, having no share, will not convey your oblation." For these (metres) they (the gods) destined the (clarified butter) of which four (spoonfuls) are taken (into the ladle), for the puronuvākyā, the yājyā, (2) the devatā and the vaṣaṭkāra. When (the Adhvaryu) offers with the (clarified butter) of which four (spoonfuls) are taken (into the ladle), then he propitiates the meters. They, propitiated (by him), convey his oblation to the gods.

The expounders of the Veda say: "Is the (above-mentioned) oblation to be made in the house of a (sacrificer who has been) initiated, or is it not to be made?"[11] The oblation is actually the initiate.[12] If he would make an oblation, he would put the sacrificer, who has been made to be

जुहुयात् ॥२॥ यज्ञपरुर् अन्तर् इयात् । यजुर् एव वदेत् । न हविष्कृतं यजमानम् अग्नौ प्रदधाति । न यज्ञपरुर् अन्तर् एति ।

गायत्री छन्दाꣳस्य् अत्य् अमन्यत । तस्यै वषट्कारोऽभ्यय्य शिरोऽच्छिनत् । तस्यै द्वेधा रसः परापतत् । पृथिवीम् अर्धः प्राविशत् । पशून् अर्धः । यः पृथिवीं प्राविशत् ॥३॥ स खदिरोऽभवत् । यः पशून् । सोऽजाम् । यत् खादिर्य् अभ्रिर् भवति । छन्दसाम् एव रसेन यज्ञस्य शिरः सं भरति ।

यद् औदुम्बरी । ऊर्ग् वा उदुम्बरः । ऊर्जैव यज्ञस्य शिरः सं भरति । यद् वैणवी । तेजो वै वेणुः ॥४॥ तेजसैव यज्ञस्य शिरः सं भरति । यद् वैकङ्कती । भा एवाव रुन्धे ।

"देवस्य त्वा सवितुः प्रसव" इत्य् अभ्रिम् आ दत्ते प्रसूत्यै । "अश्विनोर् बाहुभ्याम्" इत्य् आह । अश्विनौ हि देवानाम् अध्वर्यू आस्ताम् । "पूष्णो

the oblation, in the fire. If he would make no oblation, (3) he would omit a part of the sacrifice. He should say only the yajus-formula.[13] (Thus) he does not put the sacrificer, made to be the oblation, in the fire; (and) he does not omit a part of the sacrifice.

Gāyatrī valued the (other) metres less than herself. Vaṣaṭ-kāra approached (her) and cut off her head.[14] A twofold essence escaped from her. One half entered the earth, one half (entered) the cattle. That (essence) which (entered) the earth (4) became the Khadira. That (essence) which (entered) the cattle became the she-goat. If the shovel is made of Khadira wood, he collects the head of the sacrifice (the Pravargya vessel) with the essence of the metres.

If it is made of Udumbara wood - the Udumbara is actually food - he collects the head of the sacrifice with food. If it is made of bamboo - bamboo is actually brilliant energy - (5) he collects the head of the sacrifice with brilliant energy. If it is made of Vikaṅkata wood he wins splendour.

With *"You, at the impulse of the god Savitṛ"* he takes the shovel, for stimulation.[15] *"With the arms of the Aśvins,"* he says, for the two Aśvins

हस्तांभ्याम्" इत्य् आह यत्यैं । वज्रं इव वा एषा । यद् अभ्रिः । "अभ्रिर् असि नारिर् असी"त्य् आह शान्त्यैं ॥५॥ "अध्वरकृद् देवेभ्य" इत्य् आंह । यज्ञो वा अंध्वरः । "यज्ञकृद् देवेभ्य" इति वावैतद् आंह ।

"उत् तिष्ठ ब्रह्मणस्पत" इत्य् आंह ["देवयन्तंस् त्वेमहे"] । ब्रह्मंणैव यज्ञस्य शिरोऽच्छैंति । "प्रैतु ब्रह्मंणस्पतिर्" इत्य् आंह । प्रेत्यैव यज्ञस्य शिरोऽच्छैंति । "प्र देव्य् एंतु सूनृते"त्य् आंह । यज्ञो वै सूनृतां । "अच्छां वीरं नर्यं पङ्क्तिरांधसम्"इत्य् आंह ॥६॥ पाङ्क्तो हि यज्ञः । "देवा यज्ञं नंयन्तु न" इत्य् आंह । देवान् एव यंज्ञनियंः कुरुते । "देवीं द्यावापृथिवी अनुं मे मंꣳसाथाम्" इत्य् आंह । आभ्याम् एवानुंमतो यज्ञस्य शिरः सं भंरति । "ऋध्यासंम् अद्य मखस्य शिर" इत्य् आंह । यज्ञो वै मखः । "ऋध्यासंम् अद्य यज्ञस्य शिर" इतिं वावैतद् आंह । "मखायं त्वा मखस्यं त्वा

were the Adhvaryus of the gods. *"With the hands of Pūṣan,"* he says, for guidance. The shovel is actually like a *vájra.*[16] *"You are an Abhri (shovel), you are a Nārī (wife),"* he says for appeasement.[17] (6) *"(You are) the maker of the adhvara for the gods,"* he says. The *adhvara* is actually the sacrifice. So he actually says here: "(You are) the maker of the sacrifice for the gods."

"Rise up, lord of the bráhman [we who love the gods beseech you],"[18] he says. With the bráhman-formula he approaches the head of the sacrifice. *"May the lord of the bráhman proceed,"* he says. Proceeding he approaches the head of the sacrifice. *"May the goddess Sūnṛtā*[19] *proceed,"* he says. Sūnṛtā is actually the sacrifice. *"Towards the hero, manly, with fivefold munificence,"*[20] he says, (7) for the sacrifice is fivefold. *"May the gods conduct the sacrifice for us,"* he says. The gods he makes the conductors of the sacrifice. *"O you two goddesses, o Heaven and Earth, give me your permission,"* he says. With the permission of these two he collects the head of the sacrifice. *"Today, may I realize the head of Makha,"* he says. Makha is actually the sacrifice. So he actually says here: "Today, may I realize the head of the sacrifice." *"For Makha (I*

शीर्ष्णे" इत्य् आह । निर्दिश्यैवैनद् धरति ॥७॥ त्रिर् हरति । त्रय इमे लोकाः । एभ्य एव लोकेभ्यो यज्ञस्य शिरः सं भरति । तूष्णीं चतुर्थꣳ हरति । अपरिमिताद् एव यज्ञस्य शिरः सं भरति । मृत्खनाद् अग्रे हरति । तस्मान् मृत्खनः करुण्यतमः । "इयत्य् अग्र आसीर्" इत्य् आह । अस्याम् एवाछम्बट्कारं यज्ञस्य शिरः सं भरति ।

ऊर्जं वा एतꣳ रसं पृथिव्या उपदीका उद् दिहन्ति ॥८॥ यद् वल्मीकम् । यद् वल्मीकवपा संभारो भवति। ऊर्जम् एव रसं पृथिव्या अव रुन्धे । अथो श्रोत्रम् एव । श्रोत्रꣳ ह्य् एतत् पृथिव्याः । यद् वल्मीकः । अबधिरो भवति । य एवं वेद ।

इन्द्रो वृत्राय वज्रम् उद अयच्छत् । स यत्रयत्र पराक्रमत ॥९॥ तन् नाध्रियत । स पूतीकस्तम्बे पराक्रमत । सोऽध्रियत । सोऽब्रवीत् । "ऊतिं वै मेऽधा" इति । तद् ऊतीकानाम् ऊतीकत्वम् । यद् ऊतीका भवन्ति । यज्ञायैवोतिं दधति ।

take) you, for the head of Makha (I throw) you (down on the black antelope skin),"[21] he says. Proclaiming this he takes the (clay). (8) He takes three times. Three are these worlds. From these worlds he collects the head of the sacrifice. The fourth (part) he takes in silence. From the unbounded he collects the head of the sacrifice.[22] From the clay-pit he takes first. Therefore, the clay-pit is most pitiful. *"So big you were in the beginning,"*[23] he says. On (the earth) he collects the head of the sacrifice, so that it does not get lost.

As food the white ants indeed heap up that essence of the earth: (9) the ant-hill. If (material from) the ant-hill is (added to the clay as) a requisite,[24] he gains the essence of the earth, food. And the faculty of hearing (he gains) too. Because that ant-hill is the faculty of hearing of the earth. He does not become deaf, who knows thus.

Indra raised his *vájra* against Vṛtra. (Standing) in whatever place he attacked him, (10) there he did not stand firm. He attacked him (standing) in a bunch of Pūtīka plants.[25] He stood firm. He said: "You, indeed, gave me help (*ūti*)." That is why the Ūtīkas are called Ūtīkas. If there are Ūtīka plants (added to the clay), they give help to the sacrifice.

"अग्निजा असि प्रजापते रेत" इत्य् आह । य एव रसः पशून् प्राविशत् ॥१०॥ तम् एवाव रुन्धे ।

पञ्चैते संभारा भवन्ति । पाङ्क्तो यज्ञः । यावान् एव यज्ञः । तस्य शिरः सं भरति । यद् ग्राम्याणां पशूनां चर्मणा संभरेत् । ग्राम्यान् पशूञ् छुचार्पयेत् । कृष्णाजिनेन सं भरति । आरण्यान् एव पशूञ् छुचार्पयति । तस्मात् समावत् पशूनां प्रजायमानानाम् ॥११॥ आरण्याः पशवः कनीयांसः । शुचा ह्य् ऋताः ।

लोमतः सं भरति । अतो ह्य् अस्य मेध्यम् । परिगृह्या यन्ति । रक्षसाम् अपहत्यै । बहवो हरन्ति । अपचितिम् एवास्मिन् दधति । उद्धते सिकतोपोप्ते परिश्रिते नि दधति शान्त्यै ।

मदन्तीभिर् उप सृजति ॥१२॥ तेज एवास्मिन् दधाति । "मधु त्वा मधुला करोत्व्" इत्य् आह । ब्रह्मणैवास्मिन् तेजो दधाति । यद् ग्राम्याणां पात्राणां कपालैः

"You are born of Agni, (you are) the seed of Prajāpati,"[26] he says. The very essence that entered the cattle, (11) that he wins.

These requisites are five. The sacrifice is fivefold. He collects the head of the entire extent of the sacrifice. If he would procure (the ingredients) with the hide of domestic animals, he would afflict the domestic animals with suffering. He procures (the ingredients) with a black antelope skin. Only wild animals he afflicts with suffering. Therefore, of animals that are born similar in size, (12) wild animals are smallest (at maturity), for they are afflicted with suffering.

On the hairy side he procures (the ingredients), for on this side is what is fit for sacrifice of it. They come (to the place of sacrifice) after having wrapped this (hide) round (the ingredients), for keeping back the Rakṣases. Many take (the hide with the ingredients). They pay reverence to it.[27] They put it down on uprooted earth, covered with sand and fenced in, for appeasement.

He mixes it with boiling water. (13) Brilliant energy he puts in it. *"The sweet must make you sweet,"*[28] he says. With the bráhman-formula he puts brilliant energy in it. If he would mix it with the potsherds from

सः सृजेत् । ग्राम्याणि पात्राणि शुचार्पयेत् । अर्मकपालैः सः संजति । एतानि वा अंनुपजीवनीयानि । तान्य् एव शुचार्पयति । शर्कराभिः सः संजति धृत्यैं । अथों शंत्वायं । अजलोमैः सः संजति । एषा वा अग्नेः प्रिया तनूः । यद् अजा । प्रिययैवैनं तनुवा सः संजति । अथो तेजंसा । कृष्णाजिनस्य लोमंभिः सः संजति । यज्ञो वै कृष्णाजिनम् । यज्ञेनैव यज्ञः सः संजति ॥१३॥

pots of (inhabited) villages, he would afflict the pots of (inhabited) villages with suffering. He mixes it with potsherds of a ruined village.[29] These certainly do not serve for livelihood. These he afflicts with suffering. He mixes it with gravel,[30] for firmness. And also for auspiciousness. He mixes it with the hairs of a she-goat. This she-goat is actually a beloved form of Agni. He mixes it with a beloved form. And also with brilliant energy. He mixes it with the hairs of a black antelope skin. The black antelope skin is actually the sacrifice. He mixes the sacrifice with the sacrifice.

Anuvāka 3

The preparation of the Pravargya vessel

This section discusses the preparation of the main Pravargya vessel, together with two spare ones. According to the Śrauta Sūtras some other clay utensils are prepared now too. The mantras of this section are TĀ 4, 2, 5(17) - end, and 4,3. For a description of the ritual actions see: Śrautakośa vol. 2, Sanskrit part 1:515-516; English part 1:30-31; 33-35; 36-38; 40-41; 42-47; van Buitenen's description: I, §7-§14. A German translation of this Anuvāka is given by Rau, *Töpferei*:60-62.

परिश्रिते करोति । ब्रह्मवर्चसस्य परिगृहीत्यै । न कुर्वन्न् अभि प्रांण्यात् । यत्
कुर्वन्न् अंभिप्राण्यात् । प्राणाञ्न् छुचार्पयेत् । अपहाय प्राणिंति । प्राणानां गोपीथायं ।
न प्रंवर्ग्यं चादित्यं चान्तर् एंयात् । यद् अंन्तरेयात् । दुश्चर्मा स्यात् ॥१॥ तस्मान्
नान्तराय्यंम् । आत्मनों गोपीथायं । वेणुंना करोति । तेजो वै वेणुंः । तेजंः प्रवर्ग्यंः ।
तेजंसैव तेजः सम् अंर्धयति ।

"मखस्य शिरोऽसी"त्य् आंह । यज्ञो वै मखः । तस्यैतच् छिरंः । यत् प्रंवर्ग्यः ॥२॥
तस्मांद् एवम् आंह । "यज्ञस्यं पदे स्थ" इत्य् आंह । यज्ञस्य ह्य् एंते पदे । अथो
प्रतिष्ठित्यै । "गायत्रेणं त्वा छन्दंसा करोमी"त्य् आंह ।"त्रैष्टुंभेन त्वा छन्दंसा

(1) He prepares (the Pravargya vessel) in a place that is fenced off, for taking completely hold of the lustre of spiritual knowledge (*bráhman*).[31] Let him not breathe (*ná prāṇyāt*) towards (the Pravargya vessel), while preparing it. If he would breathe towards it, while preparing it, he would afflict the life-breaths (*prāṇá*-s)[32] with suffering.[33] He breathes avoiding it, for protection of the life-breaths. Let him not come in between the sun and, the Pravargya vessel. If he would come between them, he would get a bad skin. (2) Therefore, he should not come in between, for the protection of himself. He prepares it with a bamboo-stick. Bamboo is actually brilliant energy. The Pravargya is brilliant energy. With brilliant energy he brings brilliant energy to fulfilment.

"*You are the head of Makha,*" he says. Makha is actually the sacrifice. Thereof this Pravargya is the head. (3) Therefore he says thus. "***You are the two feet of the sacrifice,***" he says, for these are the two feet of the sacrifice. And also (he says this) for a firm stand. "*With the gāyatrī-*

करोमि । जागंतेन त्वा छन्दंसा करोमि"] । छन्दोंभिर् एवैनँ करोति । त्र्युंद्धिं करोति
। त्रयं इमे लोकाः । एषां लोकानाम् आप्त्यैं । छन्दोंभिः करोति ॥३॥ वीर्यँ वै छन्-
दाꣳसि । वीर्यँणैवेनँ करोति । यजुंषा बिलँ करोति, व्यावृंत्त्यै । इयंन्तं करोति । प्रजा-
पंतिना यज्ञमुखेन संमितम् । इयंन्तं करोति । यज्ञपरुषा संमितम् । इयंन्तं करोति ।
एतावद् वै पुरुंषे वीर्यम् । वीर्यसंमितम् ॥४॥ अपंरिमितं करोति ।
अपंरिमितस्यावंरुद्ध्यै । परिग्रीवं कंरोति, धृत्यैं ।

"सूर्यस्य हरंसा श्रायें"त्य् आंह । यथायजुर् एवैतत् । अश्वशकेनं धूपयति ।
प्राजापत्यो वा अश्वंः, सयोनित्वायं । "वृष्णो अश्वंस्य निष्पद् असी"त्य् आंह
["वरुंणस् त्वा धृतव्रंत आधूंपयतु । मित्रावरुंणयोर् ध्रुवेण धर्मणा"] । असौ वा
आंदित्यो वृषाश्वंः । तस्य छन्दाꣳसि निष्पत् ॥५॥ छन्दोंभिर् एवैनँ धूपयति ।

metre I prepare you. [With the triṣṭubh-metre I prepare you. With the jagatī-metre I prepare you]," he says. With the metres he prepares it. He prepares it with three layers. Three are these worlds. (He prepares it with three layers) for reaching these worlds. He prepares it with the metres. (4) The metres are actually life-energy. With life-energy he prepares it. He makes a bowl with a yajus-formula,[31] for making a distinction.[32] So big he makes it,[33] corresponding to Prajāpati, to the mouth of the sacrifice.[34] So big he makes it, corresponding to a part of the sacrifice. So big he makes it; indeed, so much life-energy there is in man. It corresponds to the life-energy. (5) (But other authorities say:) he makes it unmeasured, for gaining the unmeasured. He makes it with a neck all around[35] for holding.

"With the flame of the sun be baked," he says. This is exactly like the yajus-formula (expresses). He fumigates it with the dung of a (male) horse. The horse actually belongs to Prajāpati: (it serves) to connect it with its place of origin.[36] *"You are the excrements of the Male Horse. [Let Varuṇa, whose vows are maintained, fumigate you with the stable law of Mitra and Varuṇa.],"* he says. The Male Horse is actually yonder Āditya (the sun). The metres are its excrements. (6) With the metres he fumigates it.

"अर्चिषे त्वा, शोचिषे त्वे"त्य् आह ["ज्योतिषे त्वा । तपसे त्वा"]। तेज
एवास्मिन् दधाति । वारुणोऽभीद्धः । मैत्रियोपैति, शान्त्यै ।

"सिद्ध्यै त्वे"त्य् आह । यथायजुर् एवैतत् । "देवस् त्वा सवितोद् वपत्व्" इत्य्
आह ["सुपाणिः स्वङ्गुरिः । सुबाहुर् उत शक्त्या"] । सवितृप्रसूत एवैनं ब्रह्मणा
देवताभिर् उद् वपति । "अपद्यमानः पृथिव्याम्, आशा दिश आपृणे"त्य् आह ॥६॥
तस्माद् अग्निः सर्वा दिशोऽनु वि भाति[37] । "उत् तिष्ठ बृहन् भवोर्ध्वस् तिष्ठ ध्रुवस्
त्वम्" इत्य् आह, प्रतिष्ठित्यै ।

ईश्वरो वा एषोऽन्धो भवितोः । यः प्रवर्ग्यम् अन्वीक्षते । "सूर्यस्य त्वा चक्षुषान्व्
ईक्ष" इत्य् आह । चक्षुषो गोपीथाय । "ऋजवे त्वा, साधवे त्वा, सुक्षित्यै त्वा, भूत्यै
त्वे"त्य् आह । इयं वा ऋजुः । अन्तरिक्षꣳ साधु । असौ सुक्षितिः ॥७॥ दिशो भूतिः ।
इमान् एवास्मै लोकान् कल्पयति । अथो प्रतिष्ठित्यै ।

(Baking the vessels in a fire pit:) *"For fire you, for the flame you, [for light you, for heat you],"* he says. He puts brilliant energy in it.[38] It belongs to Varuṇa when it is surrounded by flames. With a verse dedicated to Mitra he approaches, for appeasement.[39]

(Taking the vessels out of the fire pit:) *"For success you,"* he says. This is exactly like the yajus-formula (expresses). *"May the god Savitṛ take you out, [(the god) with good hands, with good fingers, with good arms, and with his power],"* he says. Only instigated by Savitṛ he takes it out, with the bráhman-formula, together with the gods. *"Without falling down on the earth, fill the regions and the quarters,"* he says. (7) Therefore, (as) Agni (he, the Pravargya) shines brightly in all quarters. *"Rise up, be great, stand upright, you, be stable,"* he says for firmness.

He who looks at the Pravargya may indeed become blind. *"I look with the eyesight of the sun,"* he says, for the protection of his eyesight. *"For the straight one you, for the good one you, for secure dwelling you, for prosperitity you,"* he says. The straight is actually this (earth). The good is the intermediate space. The secure dwelling is yonder (sun). (8) The quarters are prosperity. For him he forms these very worlds. And also (he says this) for firmness.

“इदम् अहम् अमुम् आमुष्यायणं विशा पशुभिर् ब्रह्मवर्चसेन पर्यूहामी”त्य् आह । विशैवैनं पशुभिर् ब्रह्मवर्चसेन पर्यूहति । “विशे”ति राजन्यस्य ब्रूयात् । विशैवैनं पर्यूहति । “पशुभिर्” इति वैश्यस्य । पशुभिर् एवैनं पर्यूहति ।

असुर्यं पात्रम् अनाच्छृण्णम् ॥८॥ आ च्छृणत्ति । देवत्राकः । अजक्षीरेणा च्छृणत्ति । परमं वा एतत् पयः । यद् अजक्षीरम् । परमेणैवैनं पयसा च्छृणत्ति । यजुषा व्यावृत्त्यै । छन्दोभिर् आ च्छृणत्ति । छन्दोभिर् वा एष क्रियते । छन्दोभिर् एव छन्दांस्य् आ च्छृणत्ति । “छृन्धि वाचम्” इत्य् आह । वाचम् एवाव रुन्धे । “छृन्ध्य् ऊर्जम्” इत्य् आह । ऊर्जम् एवाव रुन्धे । “छृन्धि हविर्” इत्य् आह । हविर् एवाकः ।

“देव पुरश्चर[40] सघ्यासं त्वे”त्य् आह । यथायजुर् एवैतत् ॥९॥

“Now I surround so-and-so, descendant of so-and-so, with people, with cattle, with the lustre of spiritual knowledge,” he says. With people, with cattle, with the lustre of spiritual knowledge he surrounds him. Let him say *“With people”* for a Kṣatriya. Only with people he surrounds him. (Let him say:) *“With cattle”* for a Vaiśya. Only with cattle he surrounds him.

The vessel belongs to the Asuras when nothing is poured over it.[41] (9) He pours (milk) over it. He brings it among the gods. He pours goat's milk over it. Goat's milk, indeed, is the most excellent milk. The most excellent he pours over it. (He pours) with a yajus-formula[42], for making a distinction. He pours with the metres. With metres this one is actually prepared. He pours the metres over the metres. *“Flow over on speech,”* he says. He gains speech. *Flow over on food,”* he says. He gains food. *“Flow over on the oblation,”* he says. He makes an oblation.

(With the following formula the Pravargya vessel and the other utensils, cooled down by the milk, are wrapped in the skin of a black antelope and hung up till the Pravargya will be put up and heated) *“O god, o leader, may I be able to bear you,”* he says. This is exactly like the yajus-formula (expresses).

Anuvāka 4

Putting up and heating the Pravargya vessel

This is the first of the anuvākas discussing the regular performances of the Pravargya (anuvākas 4-8). These take place during one or more days. The mantras of this section are TĀ 4, 5. For a description of the ritual actions see: *Śrautakośa* vol. 2, Sanskrit part 1:531-532; English part 1:167-189; van Buitenen, *Pravargya*: II, §6-§19.

"ब्रह्मन् प्रचंरिष्यामो, होतंर् घर्मम् अभि ष्टुही"त्य् आंह । एष वा एतर्हि बृहस्पतिः । यद् ब्रह्मा । तस्मां एव प्रंतिप्रोच्य प्रचंरति । आत्मनोऽनांर्त्यै । "यमायं त्वा मखाय त्वे"त्य् आंह ["सूर्यस्य हरंसे त्वा"] । एता वा एतस्यं देवतांः । ताभिंर् एवैनंꣳ सम् अंर्धयति । मदंन्तीभिः प्रोक्षंति । तेजं एवास्मिंन् दधाति ॥१॥ अभिपूर्वं प्रोक्षंति । अभिपूर्वम् एवास्मिन् तेजों दधाति । त्रिः प्रोक्षंति । त्र्यांवृद् धि यज्ञः । अथों मेध्यत्वायं । होतान्व् आंह । रक्षंसाम् अपंहत्यै । अनंवानम् । प्राणानाꣳ सन्तंत्यै । त्रिष्टुभंः सतीर् गांयत्रीर् इवान्व् आंह ॥२॥ गायत्रो हि प्राणः । प्राणम् एव यजंमाने दधाति । सन्तंतम् अन्व् आंह । प्राणानांम् अन्नाद्यंस्य सन्तंत्यै । अथो रक्षंसाम् अपंहत्यै

(1) *"O Brahmán, we shall go forward; o Hotṛ, praise the Gharma,"*[46] he says. The Brahmán priest is now actually Bṛhaspati. He goes forward after having said (this mantra) to him, to prevent injury to himself. *"For Yama you, for Makha you, [for the flame of the sun you],"* he says. These are indeed the gods who belong to this (Pravargya). With these he brings this to fulfilment.[47] He sprinkles with boiling water. Brilliant energy he puts in it. (2) He sprinkles in due order.[48] In due order he puts brilliant energy in it. He sprinkles three times, for the sacrifice has three series. And also (he sprinkles three times) to make it fit for the sacrifice. The Hotṛ recites,[49] in order to ward off the Rakṣases. (He recites) without taking breath (between the verses).[50] For the continuity of the life-breaths. Although they are triṣṭubh-verses, he recites them as if they were gāyatrī-verses, (3) for the prāṇa belongs to the gāyatrī-metre. He puts prāṇa in the sacrificer. He recites uninterruptedly. For the continuity of the life-breaths, of food. And also (he recites uninterruptedly) to ward off

। यत् परिमिता अनुब्रूयात् । परिमितम् अवं रुन्धीत । अपरिमिता अन्व् आंह । अपरिमितस्यावरुद्ध्यै ।

शिरो वा एतद् यज्ञस्यं ॥३॥ यत् प्रवर्ग्यः । ऊर्ग् मुञ्जाः । यन् मौञ्जो वेदो भवंति । ऊर्जैव यज्ञस्य शिरः सम् अर्धयति । प्राणाहुतीर् जुंहोति । प्राणान् एव यजमाने दधाति । सप्त जुंहोति । सप्त वै शीर्षण्याः प्राणाः । प्राणान् एवास्मिन् दधाति । "देवस् त्वां सविता मध्वांनक्त्व्" इत्य् आंह ॥४॥ तेजसैवैनम् अनक्ति । "पृथिवीं तपसस् त्रायस्वे"ति हिरंण्यम् उपास्यति । अस्या अनतिदाहाय । शिरो वा एतद् यज्ञस्यं । यत् प्रवर्ग्यः । अग्निः सर्वा देवताः । प्रलवान् आदीप्योपास्यति । देवतास्व एव यज्ञस्य शिरः प्रतिदधाति । अप्रतिशीर्णाग्रं भवति । एतद्बर्हिर् ह्य् एषः ॥५॥ "अर्चिर् असि शोचिर् असी"त्य् आंह ["ज्योतिर् असि तपोऽसि"] । तेजं एवास्मिन् ब्रह्मवर्चसं दधाति । "सꣳ सीदस्व महाꣳ असी"त्य् आंह । महान् ह्य् एषः ।

the Rakṣases. If he would recite a limited number (of verses), he would gain a limited (world). He recites an unlimited number (of verses), for gaining the unlimited.

(He wipes with a bunch of Muñja-grass, called veda:) That Pravargya is actually the head of the sacrifice. (4) Muñja-grass is food. If the veda-bunch is made of Muñja-grass, he brings the head of the sacrifice to fulfilment with food. He offers the Prāṇāhutis. He puts the prāṇas in the sacrificer. He offers seven. Seven, indeed, are the prāṇas of the head.[51] He puts the prāṇas in him. *"Let the god Savitṛ anoint you with the sweet,"* he says. (5) He anoints him with brilliant energy.[52] With *"Protect the earth from heat,"* he puts the golden disk (on the mound), to prevent excessive burning of the earth. The Pravargya is actually the head of the sacrifice. Agni is all the gods. He lights the (Muñja-) stalks and puts them (on the disk). Near the gods he puts back the head of the sacrifice. That (bunch) has a top that is not crushed, for this (Pravargya) has this (Muñja-grass) as the sacred grass. (6) *"You are fire, you are a flame [you are light, you are heat],"* he says. He puts brilliant energy, the lustre of spiritual knowledge, in it.[53] *"Sit down (on the burning grass), you are great,"*[54] he says, for this one is great.

ब्रह्मवादिनो वदन्ति । "एते वाव त ऋत्विजः । ये दर्शपूर्णमासयोः । अथ कथा होता यजमानायाशिषो ना शास्त ?" इति । पुरस्तादाशीः खलु वा अन्यो यज्ञः । उपरिष्टादाशीर् अन्यः ॥६॥

"अनाधृष्या पुरस्ताद्" इति यद् एतानि यजूꣳष्य् आह । शीर्षत एव यज्ञस्य यजमान आशिषोऽवं रुन्धे । आयुः पुरस्ताद् आह । प्रजां दक्षिणतः । प्राणं पश्चात् । श्रोत्रम् उत्तरतः । विधृतिम् उपरिष्टात् । प्राणान् एवास्मैं समीचो दधाति । ईश्वरो वा एष दिशोऽनून्मंदितोः । यं दिशोऽनु व्यास्थापयन्ति ॥७॥ "मनोर् अश्वासि भूरिपुत्रे"तीमाम् अभि मृशति ["विश्वाभ्यो मा नाष्ट्राभ्यः पाहि"] । इयं वै मनोर् अश्वा भूरिपुत्रा । अस्याम् एव प्रति तिष्ठत्य्, अनुन्मादाय । "सूपसदा मे भूया, मा मां हिꣳसीर्"इत्य् आहाहिꣳसायै ।

"चितः स्थ, परिचित" इत्य् आह । अपचितिम् एवास्मिन् दधाति । शिरो वा

The expounders of the Veda say: "Here, indeed, are the same priests as in the new and full moon sacrifices. Then, how is it that the Hotṛ does not ask for the blessings for the sacrificer?" Indeed, one (kind of) sacrifice has the prayers for blessings before, the other has the prayers for blessings after (the chief action).[55]

(7) When the sacrificer says these yajus-formulas (beginning with): *"(You are) an invincible (quarter) in the east,"*[56] he obtains what he wishes already at the beginning of the sacrifice. (The prayer for) life he says in the east, progeny in the south, breath in the west, hearing in the north, separated maintenance above. (The sacrificer) puts the combined life-breaths in him(-self). If people make someone[57] go round in different directions, he may indeed get confused in regard to the successive quarters. (Therefore, the following mantra is prescribed:) (8) With: *"You are Manu's mare, with numerous foals [protect me from all dangers],"* he touches this (earth). Manu's mare, with numerous foals is actually this (earth). On her he stands firm, to prevent confusion. *"May you be of good approach for me, may you not harm me,"* he says to prevent harm.

(He puts coals from the Gārhapatya fire around the vessel:) *"Be a pile, a surrounding pile,"* he says. He pays reverence to this one. The

एतद् यज्ञस्य । यत् प्रवर्ग्यः । असौ खलु वा आदित्यः प्रवर्ग्यः । तस्य मरुतो रश्मयः ॥८॥ "स्वाहा मरुद्भिः परि श्रयस्वे"त्य् आह । अमुम् एवादित्यꣳ रश्मिभिः पर्य् ऊहति । तस्माद् असाव् आदित्योऽमुष्मिन् लोके रश्मिभिः पर्यूढः । तस्माद् राजा विशा पर्यूढः । तस्माद् ग्रामणीः संजातैः पर्यूढः ।

अग्नेः सृष्टस्य यतः । विकङ्कतं भा आर्छत् । यद् वैकङ्कताः परिधयो भवन्ति । भा एवाव रुन्धे । द्वादश भवन्ति ॥९॥ द्वादश मासाः संवत्सरः । संवत्सरम् एवाव रुन्धे । "अस्ति त्रयोदशो मास" इत्य् आहुः । यत् त्रयोदशः परिधिर् भवति । तेनैव त्रयोदशं मासम् अव रुन्धे । "अन्तरिक्षस्यान्तर्धिर् असी"त्य् आह, व्यावृत्त्यै । "दिवं तपसस् त्रायस्वे"त्य् उपरिष्टाद् धिरण्यम् अधि नि दधाति । अमुष्या अनतिदाहाय । अथो आभ्याम् एवैनम् उभयतः परि गृह्णाति । "अर्हन् बिभर्षि सायकानि धन्वे"त्य् आह

Pravargya is actually the head of the sacrifice. Indeed, yonder Āditya (the sun) is the Pravargya. The Maruts[59] are its rays. (9) *"Svāhā! Surround with the Maruts,"* he says. He piles yonder Āditya (the sun) with rays. Hence in yonder world yonder Āditya (the sun) is surrounded with rays. Hence the king is surrounded with people. Hence the leader of a community is surrounded by his men.

When Agni was created and went forth,[60] his splendour came to the Vikaṅkata-tree. (Therefore,) if the enclosing sticks are made of Vikaṅkata-wood, he gains splendour. They are twelve. (10) Twelve months are a year. He gains the year. "There is a thirteenth month,"[61] they say. If there is a thirteenth enclosing stick, he gains the thirteenth month with it. *"You are the concealment of the firmament,"*[62] he says, for making a distinction. With: *"Protect heaven from heat,"* he puts the golden (disk) down, on top (of the Pravargya vessel), to prevent excessive burning of yonder (world). And also, with these two (the silver disk below, the golden disk on top) he encloses this (Pravargya vessel) from both sides. *"Worthily you carry the arrows and the bow, [worthily the worshipful and brilliant golden amulet, worthily you have this universe, born from the waters, at your*

[“अर्हन् निष्कं यजतं विश्वरूपम् । अर्हन्न् इदं दयसे विश्वम् अब्भुवम् । न वा ओजीयो रुद्र त्वद् अस्ति”] ॥१०॥ स्तौत्य् एवैनम् एतत् ।

“गायत्रम् असि, त्रैष्टुभम् असि, जागतम् असी”ति धवित्राण्य् आ दत्ते । छन्दोभिर् एवैनान्य् आ दत्ते । “मधु मध्व्”इति धूनोति [“मधु”] । प्राणो वै मधु । प्राणम् एव यजमाने दधाति । त्रिः परि यन्ति । त्रिवृद् धि प्राणः । त्रिः परि यन्ति । त्र्यावृद् धि यज्ञः ॥११॥ अथो रक्षसाम् अपहत्यै । त्रिः पुनः परि यन्ति । षट् सं पद्यन्ते । षड् वा ऋतवः । ऋतुष्व् एव प्रति तिष्ठन्ति ।

यो वै घर्मस्य प्रियां तनुवम् आक्रामति । दुश्चर्मा वै स भवति । एष ह वा अस्य प्रियां तनुवम् आ क्रामति । यस् त्रिः परीत्य चतुर्थं पर्य् एति । एताꣳ ह वा अस्योग्रदेवो राजनिर् आ चक्राम ॥ १२॥ ततो वै स दुश्चर्माभवत् । तस्मात् त्रिः परीत्य न चतुर्थं परीयात् । आत्मनो गोपीथाय ।

disposal; indeed, there is nothing stronger than you, o Rudra],"[63] he says. (11) Thus he praises this (Pravargya vessel).

With: *"You belong to the gāyatrī, you belong to the triṣṭubh, you belong to the jagatī,"* he takes the (three) fans. With the metres he takes these. With: *"Sweet, sweet, [sweet],"* he fans. The sweet is actually prāṇa. He puts prāṇa in the sacrificer. They circumambulate three times (sunwise), for prāṇa is threefold. They circumambulate three times, for the sacrifice has three series. (12) And also (they circumambulate three times) to ward off the Rakṣases. They circumambulate again three times (but in the opposite direction). That makes six. There are, indeed, six seasons. They stand firm in the seasons.

He who treads upon the Gharma's own body, certainly gets a bad skin. He actually treads upon the Gharma's own body, who, after having circumambulated three times, goes around a fourth time. Ugradeva Rājani[64] actually trod upon that (body) of it. (13) Thereupon, he indeed got a bad skin.[65] Therefore, after having circumambulated three times, let him not go around a fourth time, for the protection of himself.

प्रा॒णा वै ध॒वित्रा॑णि । अव्य॑तिषङ्ग॑ धून्वन्ति । प्रा॒णाना॒म् अव्य॑तिषङ्गा॒य, क्लृप्त्यै॑।
वि॒नि॒षद्य॑ धून्वन्ति । दि॒क्ष्व् ए॑व प्रति॑ तिष्ठन्ति । ऊ॒र्ध्वं धू॑न्वन्ति । सु॒व॒र्गस्य॑ लो॒कस्य॒
सम॑ष्ट्यै । स॒र्वतो॑ धून्वन्ति । तस्मा॑द् अ॒यꣳ स॒र्वत॑: पवते ॥१३॥

The fans are actually the prāṇas. They fan[66] without entanglement (of the fans), in order that the prāṇas do not become entangled (but) become well-ordered. Sitting down apart (around it, facing different directions) they fan. They are firmly established in the quarters. They fan upwards, to reach the celestial world. They fan in all directions. Therefore, this (wind) blows in all directions.

Anuvāka 5
Praising the installed Pravargya vessel

The mantras of this small anuvāka are TĀ 4, 6. For a description of the ritual actions see: *Śrautakośa* vol. 2, Sanskrit part 1:532; English part 1:169; 172; 176; 179; 182; 185; 187; van Buitenen, *Pravargya*: II, §21-§22.

"अग्निष् ट्वा वसुभिः पुरस्ताद् रोचयतु गायत्रेण छन्दसे"त्य् आह । अग्निर् एवैनं वसुभिः पुरस्ताद् रोचयति गायत्रेण छन्दसा । "स मा रुचितो रोचये"त्य् आह । आशिषम् एवैताम् आ शास्ते ।

"इन्द्रस् त्वा रुद्रैर् दक्षिणतो रोचयतु त्रैष्टुभेन छन्दसे"त्य् आह । इन्द्र एवैनं रुद्रैर् दक्षिणतो रोचयति त्रैष्टुभेन छन्दसा । "स मा रुचितो रोचये"त्य् आह । आशिषम् एवैताम् आ शास्ते ।

"वरुणस् त्वादित्यैः पश्चाद् रोचयतु जागतेन छन्दसे"त्य् आह । वरुण एवैनम् आदित्यैः पश्चाद् रोचयति जागतेन छन्दसा ॥१॥ "स मा रुचितो रोचये"त्य् आह । आशिषम् एवैताम् आ शास्ते ।

"द्युतानस् त्वा मारुतो मरुद्भिर् उत्तरतो रोचयत्व् आनुष्टुभेन छन्दसे"त्य्

(1). *"Let Agni, together with the Vasus, make you shine in the east, with the gāyatrī-metre,"* he says. Agni, together with the Vasus, makes him shine in the east, with the gāyatrī-metre. *"Shining, make me shine!"* he says. This prayer he prays.

"Let Indra, together with the Rudras, make you shine in the south, with the triṣṭubh-metre," he says. Indra, together with the Rudras, makes him shine in the south, with the triṣṭubh-metre. *"Shining, make me shine!"* he says. This prayer he prays.

"Let Varuṇa, together with the Ādityas, make you shine in the west, with the jagatī-metre," he says. Varuṇa, together with the Ādityas, makes him shine in the west, with the jagatī-metre. (2) *"Shining, make me shine!"* he says. This prayer he prays.

"Let Dyutāna Māruta,[67] *together with the Maruts, make you shine in the north, with the anuṣṭubh-metre,"* he says. Dyutāna Māruta, together

आह । द्युतान एवैनं मारुतो मरुद्भिर् उत्तरतो रोचयत्य् आनुष्टुभेन छन्दसा । "स मा रुचितो रोचये"त्य् आह । आशिषम् एवैताम् आ शास्ते ।

"बृहस्पतिस् त्वा विश्वैर् देवैर् उपरिष्टाद् रोचयतु पाङ्क्तेन छन्दसे"त्य् आह । बृहस्पतिर् एवैनं विश्वैर् देवैर् उपरिष्टाद् रोचयति पाङ्क्तेन छन्दसा । "स मा रुचितो रोचये"त्य् आह । आशिषम् एवैताम् आ शास्ते ॥२॥

"रोचितस् त्वं देव घर्म देवेष्व् असी"त्य्[68] आह । रोचितो ह्य् एष देवेषु । "रोचिषीयाहं मनुष्येष्व्"इत्य् आह । रोचत एवैष मनुष्येषु । "सम्राड् घर्म रुचितस् त्वं देवेष्व् आयुष्मा३ँ स् तेजस्वी ब्रह्मवर्चस्य् असी"त्य् आह । रुचितो ह्य् एष देवेष्व् आयुष्मा३ँ स् तेजस्वी ब्रह्मवर्चसी । "रुचितोऽहं मनुष्येष्व् आयुष्मा३ँ स् तेजस्वी ब्रह्मवर्चसी भूयासम्" इत्य् आह । रुचित एवैष मनुष्येष्व् आयुष्मा३ँ स् तेजस्वी ब्रह्मवर्चसी भवति । "रुग् असि, रुचं मयि धेहि मयि रुग्" इत्य् आह । आशिषम् एवैताम् आ शास्ते ।

with the Maruts, makes him shine in the north, with the anuṣṭubh-metre. *"Shining, make me shine!"* he says. This prayer he prays.

"Let Bṛhaspati, together with the All-gods, make you shine from above, with the Paṅkti-metre," he says. Bṛhaspati, together with the All-gods, makes him shine from above, with the Paṅkti-metre. *"Shining, make me shine!"* he says. This prayer he prays.

(3) *"You are shining, o god Gharma, among the gods,"* he says, for he is shining among the gods. *"May I be shining among men!"* he says. He shines among men. *"Sovereign king Gharma, you are shining among the gods, long-lived, full of brilliant energy, having the lustre of spiritual knowledge,"* he says, for he is shining among the gods, long-lived, full of brilliant energy, having the lustre of spiritual knowledge. *"May I be shining among men, long-lived, full of brilliant energy, having the lustre of spiritual knowledge,"* he says. He becomes shining among men, long-lived, full of brilliant energy, having the lustre of spiritual knowledge. *"You are lustre, put lustre in me, in me be lustre!"* he says. This prayer he prays.

तं यद् ए॒तैर् यजु॑र्भि॒र् अरो॑चयित्वा । “रु॒चि॒तो घ॒र्म” इति॑ प्रब्रूयात् । अरो॑चुकोऽध्व॒र्युः स्यात् । अरो॑चुको॒ यज॑मानः । अथ॒ यद् ए॑नम् ए॒तैर् यजु॑र्भी रोच-यि॒त्वा । “रु॒चि॒तो घ॒र्म” इति॒ प्राह॑ । रोचु॑कोऽध्व॒र्युर् भव॑ति । रोचु॑को यज॑मानः ॥३॥

If (the Adhvaryu) would proclaim: “The Gharma is shining!” without having (first) made it shine with these yajus-formulas, then the Adhvaryu would not be shining, the sacrificer would not be shining. But if he proclaims: “The Gharma is shining!” after having (first) made it shine with these yajus-formulas, the Adhvaryu becomes shining, the sacrificer becomes shining.

Anuvāka 6

Gazing at the heated Pravargya vessel

The mantras of this anuvāka are TĀ 4, 7. For a description of the ritual actions see: *Śrautakośa* vol. 2, Sanskrit part 1:532; English part 1:169; 172; 176; 179; 182; 185; 187; van Buitenen, *Pravargya*: II, §23-§24.

शिरो वा एतद् यज्ञस्य । यत् प्रवर्ग्यः । ग्रीवा उपसदः । पुरस्ताद् उपसदां प्रवर्ग्यं प्र वृणक्ति । ग्रीवास्व् एव यज्ञस्य शिरः प्रति दधाति ।

त्रिः प्र वृणक्ति । त्रय इमे लोकाः । एभ्य एव लोकेभ्यो यज्ञस्य शिरोऽव रुन्धे । षट् सं पद्यन्ते । षड् वा ऋतवः ॥१॥ ऋतुभ्य एव यज्ञस्य शिरोऽव रुन्धे । द्वादश कृत्वः प्र वृणक्ति । द्वादश मासाः संवत्सरः । संवत्सराद् एव यज्ञस्य शिरोऽव रुन्धे । चतुर्-विꣳशतिः सं पद्यन्ते । चतुर्विꣳशतिर् अर्धमासाः । अर्धमासेभ्य एव यज्ञस्य शिरोऽव रुन्धे । अथो खलु । सकृद् एव प्रवृज्यः । एकꣳ हि शिरः ॥२॥

अग्निष्टोमे प्र वृणक्ति । एतावान् वै यज्ञः । यावान् अग्निष्टोमः । यावान् एव यज्ञः । तस्य शिरः प्रति दधाति । नोक्थ्ये प्र वृञ्ज्यात् । प्रजा वै पशव उक्थानि । यद्

(General remarks on the Pravargya ceremony:) (1) The Pravargya is actually the head of the sacrifice. The Upasad-performances are the neck.[68] Before the Upasad-performance he performs the Pravargya. He puts back the head of the sacrifice on the neck.

He performs the Pravargya three times. These worlds are three. From these very worlds he gains the head of the sacrifice. These amount to six. There are, indeed, six seasons. (2) From the seasons he gains the head of the sacrifice. He performs it twelve times. Twelve months (make a) year. From the year he gains the head of the sacrifice. These amount to twenty-four. There are twenty-four half-months. From the half-months he gains the head of the sacrifice. And then, indeed, the Pravargya is to be performed once, for the head is one.

(3) He performs it at the Agniṣṭoma.[69] The Agniṣṭoma is actually coextensive with the sacrifice. He puts back the head of that which is coextensive with the sacrifice. He should not perform it at the Ukthya

उक्थ्यें प्रवृञ्ज्यात् । प्रजां पशून् अंस्य निर् दंहेत् । विश्वजिति सर्वपृष्ठे प्र वृंणक्ति ॥३॥ पृष्ठानि वा अच्युंतं च्यावयन्ति । पृष्ठैर् एवास्मा अच्युंतं च्यावयित्वावं रुन्धे ।

"अपंश्यं गोपाम्" इत्य् आंह । प्राणो वै गोपाः । प्राणम् एव प्रजासु वि यांतयति । "अपंश्यं गोपाम्" इत्य् आंह । असौ वा आंदित्यो गोपाः । स हीमाः प्रजा गोंपायति । तम् एव प्रजानां गोप्तारं कुरुते । "अनिपद्यमानम्" इत्य् आंह ॥४॥ न ह्य् एंष निपद्यंते । "आ च परां च पथिभिश् चरंन्तम्" इत्य् आंह । आ च ह्य् एंष परां च पथिभिश् चरंति । "स सध्रीचीः स विषूंचीर् वसांन" इत्य् आंह । सध्रीचींश् च ह्य् एंष विषूंचीश् च वसांनः प्रजा अभि विपश्यंति । "आ वंरीवर्ति भुवंनेष्व् अन्तर्" इत्य् आंह । आ ह्य् एंष वंरीवर्ति भुवंनेष्व् अन्तः ।

(sacrifice). The Uktha (recitations) are actually progeny and cattle. If he would perform the Pravargya at the Ukthya, he would burn his progeny and cattle. He performs the Pravargya at the Viśvajit-sacrifice that contains all Pṛṣṭha-sāmans. (4) The Pṛṣṭhas certainly drive away (even) tenacious (impurity). Having driven away from him tenacious (impurity) with the Pṛṣṭha's he gains (the head of the sacrifice).

(The priests and the sacrificer gaze at the heated Pravargya vessel:)[70] *"I saw the herdsman,"* he says. (First interpretation:) The herdsman is actually Prāṇa. He distributes life (*prāṇá*) to all creatures. *"I saw the herdsman,"* he says. (Second interpretation:) The herdsman is actually yonder Āditya (the sun), for he protects these creatures (as his herd). This (vessel) he makes the protector of creatures.[71] *"Without lying down,"* he says, (5) for he does not lie down. *"Wandering hither and thither on his pathways,"* he says, for he wanders hither and thither on his pathways. *"Enveloping himself in those (waters) that converge, in those that spread out,"* he says, for enveloping himself in those (waters) that converge, in those that spread out, he discerns the creatures. *"He just moves and moves around in all beings (or in all worlds),"* he says, for he just moves and moves around in all beings (or in all worlds).

"अत्र प्रावीर् मधुमाध्वीभ्यां मधुमाधूचीभ्याम्" इत्य् आह ["अनु वां देववीतये"] । वासन्तिकाव् एवास्मा ऋतू कल्पयति । "सम् अग्निर् अग्निना गते"त्य् आह ["सं देवेन सवित्रा । सः सूर्येण रोचते"] ॥५॥ ग्रैष्माव् एवास्मा ऋतू कल्पयति । "सम् अग्निर् अग्निना गते"त्य् आह । अग्निर् ह्य् एवैषोऽग्निना संगच्छते । "स्वाहा सम् अग्निस् तपसा गते"त्य् आह ["सं देवेन सवित्रा । सः सूर्येणारोचिष्ट"] । पूर्वम् एवोदितम् । उत्तरेणाभि गृणाति । "धर्ता दिवो वि भासि रजसः पृथिव्या" इत्य् आह ["धर्ता । उरोर् अन्तरिक्षस्य धर्ता । धर्ता देवो देवानाम् । अमर्त्यस् तपोजाः"] । वार्षिकाव् एवास्मा ऋतू कल्पयति । "हृदे त्वा मनसे त्वे"त्य् आह ["दिवे त्वा सूर्याय त्वा । ऊर्ध्वम् इमम् अध्वरं कृधि"] । शारदाव् एवास्मा ऋतू कल्पयति ॥६॥ "दिवि देवेषु होत्रा यच्छे"त्य् आह । होत्राभिर् एवेमान् लोकान्त् सं दधाति । "विश्वासां भुवां पत" इत्य् आह ["विश्वस्य भुवनस् पते । विश्वस्य

"Here you are helpful, with Madhu and Mādhvī, with Madhu and Mādhūcī [along with both of you, for the gods to feast]," he says. He forms for him the two vernal periods. *"Agni comes together*[72] *with Agni, [with the god Savitṛ, he shines together with the sun],"* he says. (Purpose of this mantra:) (6) He forms for him the two summer-periods. *"Agni comes together with Agni,"* he says. (Interpretation of this mantra:) for this Agni (the Pravargya vessel) comes together with Agni (the sun). *"Svāhā! Agni comes together with tapas, [with the god Savitṛ; he shone together with the sun],"* he says. What has been said before he praises with this subsequent (yajus-formula). *"You shine wide, bearer of the cloud-sphere of heaven, [bearer] of the earth, [bearer of the wide firmament, the bearing god of the gods, the immortal one, born from tapas],"* he says. He forms for him the two periods of the rainy season. *"You for the heart, you for the mind, [you for heaven, you for the sun; put this sacrifice upright],"* he says. He forms for him the two autumnal periods. (7) *"Bring the sacrificial acts to the gods in heaven,"* he says. With the sacrificial acts he unites these worlds. *"Lord of all continents [lord of the whole world,*

मनसस् पते । विश्वस्य वचसस् पते । विश्वस्य तपसस् पते । विश्वस्य ब्रह्मणस् पते"] । हैमन्तिकाव् एवास्मा ऋतू कल्पयति । "देवश्रूस् त्वं देव घर्म देवान् पाही"त्य् आह । शैशिराव् एवास्मा ऋतू कल्पयति ।

"तपोजां वाचम् अस्मे नि यच्छ देवायुवम्" इत्य् आह । या वै मेध्या वाक् । सा तपोजाः[73] । ताम् एवाव रुन्धे ॥७॥ "गर्भो देवानाम्" इत्य् आह । गर्भो ह्य् एष देवानाम् । "पिता मतीनाम्" इत्य् आह । प्रजा वै मतयः । तासाम् एष एव पिता । यत् प्रवर्ग्यः । तस्माद् एवम् आह । "पतिः प्रजानाम्" इत्य् आह । पतिर् ह्य् एष प्रजानाम् । "मतिः कवीनाम्" इत्य् आह ॥८॥ मतिर् ह्य् एष कवीनाम् । "सं देवो देवेन सवित्रा यतिष्ट सः सूर्येणारुक्त"त्य् आह । अमुं चैवादित्यं प्रवर्ग्यं च सः शास्ति । "आयुर्दास् त्वम् अस्मभ्यं घर्म, वर्चोदा असी"त्य् आह । आशिषम् एवैताम् आ शास्ते । "पिता नोऽसि, पिता नो बोधे"त्य् आह । बोधयत्य् एवैनम् ।

lord of the whole mind, lord of all speech, lord of all tapas,[74] *Lord of all bráhman],"* he says. He forms for him the two winter-periods. *"You are renowned among the gods, o god Gharma, protect the gods,"* he says. He forms for him the two periods of the cool season.

"Confer on us speech, born of tapas and devoted to the gods," he says. (The speech) born of tapas is actually speech fit for sacrifice.[75] This (speech) he gains. (8) *"Germ of the gods,"*[76] he says, for he is the germ of the gods. *"Father of hymns,"*[77] he says. The hymns are actually offspring. Of these he, the Pravargya, is the father. Therefore he says so. *"The protector of offspring,"* he says, for he is the protector of offspring. *"The thought of the inspired poets,"* he says, (9) for he is the thought of the inspired poets. *"With god Savitṛ the god has striven, with the sun he shone,"* he says. Yonder Āditya (the sun) as well as the Pravargya (vessel) he calls upon. *"You are the giver of a full life-time to us, o Gharma, you are the giver of lustre,"* he says. This prayer he prays. *"You are our father, as a father awaken us,"* he says, for he awakens him.

नवैतेऽवकाशा भवन्ति[78] । पत्नियै दशमः । नव वै पुरुषे प्राणाः ॥९॥ नाभिर् दशमी । प्राणान् एव यजमाने दधाति । अथो दशाक्षरा विराट् । अन्नं विराट् । विराजैवान्नाद्यम् अव रुन्धे ।

यज्ञस्य शिरोऽच्छिद्यत । तद् देवा होत्राभिः प्रत्य् अदधुः । ऋत्विजोऽवेक्षन्ते । एता वै होत्राः । होत्राभिर् एव यज्ञस्य शिरः प्रति दधाति ॥१०॥ रुचितम् अवेक्षन्ते । रुचिताद् वै प्रजापतिः प्रजा असृजत । प्रजानाꣳ सृष्टयै । रुचितम् अवेक्षन्ते । रुचिताद् वै पर्जन्यो वर्षति । वर्षुकः पर्जन्यो भवति । सं प्रजा एधन्ते । रुचितम् अवेक्षन्ते । रुचितं वै ब्रह्मवर्चसम् । ब्रह्मवर्चसिनो भवन्ति ॥११॥ अधीयन्तोऽवेक्षन्ते । सर्वम् आयुर् यन्ति ।

न पत्न्यव् अवेक्षेत । यत् पत्न्यव् अवेक्षेत । प्र जायेत । प्रजां त्व् अस्यै निर् दहेत् । यन् नावेक्षेत । न प्र जायेत । नास्यै प्रजां निर् दहेत् । तिरस्कृत्य यजुर् वाचयति ।

These are nine Avakāśa mantras.[79] That of the wife is the tenth. Nine, indeed, are the prāṇas[80] in man. (10) The navel is the tenth. He puts the prāṇas in the sacrificer. And then: the virāj-metre is ten-syllabic. Virāj is food. With the virāj-metre he gains food.

The head of the sacrifice was cut off. That (head) the gods put back with the sacrificial acts. The priests look at (the Pravargya vessel). These are the sacrificial acts. With the sacrificial acts he puts back the head of the sacrifice. (11) They look at it when it is shining. Indeed, from what was shining Prajāpati created the creatures. (Therefore, this is) for the creation of the creatures. They look at it when it is shining. Indeed, from what is shining Pravargya rains. Pravargya becomes full of rain. Together the creatures thrive. They look at it when it is shining. The lustre of spiritual knowledge is actually what is shining. They obtain the lustre of spiritual knowledge. (12) Reciting they look at (the Pravargya vessel). They attain a full life-time.

Let the wife (of the sacrificer) not look. If the wife would look, she would bring forth, but (the Pravargya) would burn her child. If she (would be present and) would not look, she would not bring forth, (and the Pravargya) would not burn her child. (The Pratiprasthātṛ)

प्र जांयते । नास्यैं प्रजां निर् दंहति । "त्वष्टींमती ते सपेये"त्य् आंह ["सुरेता रेतो दधांना । वीरं विंदेय तवं संदृशिं । माहं रायस्पोषेंण वि योंषम्"] । सपाद् धि प्रजाः प्रजायंन्ते ॥१२॥

makes her recite the yajus-formula, while she is secluded. She brings forth. He does not burn her child. *"May I as one who is associated with Tvaṣṭṛ (the former of bodies), lie with you, [with good seed, bearing the seed; may I obtain a hero son for you to see; may I not be separated from prosperity],"* she says, for from the male organ[81] children are born.

Anuvāka 7
Milking the cow and the goat

The cow and the goat are milked, the Pravargya vessel is filled with their milk and brought to the Āhavanīya fire. At the end of this anuvāka the offering of the southern Rauhiṇa cake in the Āhavanīya is dealt with. The mantras of this anuvāka are to be found in TĀ 4, 8 and 4, 9, 1/2(1); the last mantra (to accompany the Rauhiṇa oblation) is TĀ 4, 10, 4(7). For a description of the ritual actions see: *Śrautakośa* vol 2, Sanskrit part 1:532-534 and 535; English part 1:192-210 and 229-230; van Buitenen, *Pravargya*: III, §1-IV§4.

"देवस्य त्वा सवितुः प्रसव" इति रशनाम् आ दत्ते प्रसूत्यै । "अश्विनोर् बाहुभ्याम्" इत्य् आह । अश्विनौ हि देवानाम् अध्वर्यू आस्ताम् । "पूष्णो हस्ताभ्याम्" इत्य् आह यत्यै । "आ ददे", "ऽदित्यै रास्नासी"त्य् आह यजुष्कृत्यै । "इड एह्य्, अदित एहि, सरस्वत्य् एही"त्य् आह । एतानि वा अस्यै देवनामानि । देवनामैर् एवैनाम् आ ह्वयति । "असाव् एह्य्, असाव् एह्य्, असाव् एही"त्य् आह । एतानि वा अस्यै मनुष्यनामानि ॥१॥ मनुष्यनामैर् एवैनाम् आ ह्वयति । षट् सं पद्यन्ते । षड् वा ऋतवः । ऋतुभिर् एवैनाम् आ ह्वयति । "अदित्या उष्णीषम् असी"त्य् आह । यथायजुर् एवैतत् ।

"वायुर् अस्य् ऐड" इत्य् आह । वायुदेवत्यो वै वत्सः । "पूषा त्वोपावसृजत्व्"[82]

(1) With: *"You at the impulse of the god Savitṛ"* he takes the tether, for stimulation. *"With the arms of the Aśvins,"* he says, for the two Aśvins were the Adhvaryus of the gods. *"With the hands of Pūṣan,"* he says for guidance. *"I take (you)."*[83] *"You are the girdle of Aditi,"*[84] he says for the performance with the yajus-formula. *"Iḍā come, Aditi come, Sarasvatī come,"* he says. These, indeed, are her divine names. By the divine names he calls her. *"So-and-so come, so-and-so come, so-and-so come,"* he says. These, indeed, are her human names. (2) By the human names he calls her.[85] These (names) amount to six. There are, indeed, six seasons. By the seasons he calls her. *"You are the tiara of Aditi,"* he says. This is exactly like the yajus-formula (expresses).

"You are Vāyu, the descendant of Iḍā," he says (to the calf). The calf is indeed sacred to Vāyu. *"May Pūṣan let you go (towards the cow),"* he

इत्य् आह । पौष्णा वै देवतया पशवः ॥२॥ स्वयैवैनं देवतयोपावसृजति । "अश्विभ्यां प्र दापये"त्य् आह । अश्विनौ वै देवानां भिषजौ । ताभ्याम् एवास्मै भेषजं करोति । "यस् ते स्तनः शशय" इत्य् आह ["यो मयोभूः येन विश्वा पुष्यसि वार्याणि । यो रत्नधा वसुविद् यः सुदत्रः सरस्वति तम् इह धातवे कः"] । स्तौत्य् एवैनाम् । "उस्र घर्मं शिंष्वोस्र घर्मं पाहि, घर्माय शिंष्वे"त्य् आह । यथा ब्रूयाद् "अमुष्मै देही"ति । तादृग् एव तत् ।

"बृहस्पतिस् त्वोप सीदत्व्" इत्य् आह ॥३॥ ब्रह्म वै देवानां बृहस्पतिः । ब्रह्मणैवैनाम् उप सीदति । "दानवः स्थ पेरव" इत्य् आह । मेध्यान् एवैनान् करोति । "विष्वग्वृतो लोहितेने"त्य् आह व्यावृत्यै । "अश्विभ्यां पिन्वस्व, सरस्वत्यै पिन्वस्व, पूष्णे पिन्वस्व, बृहस्पतये पिन्वस्वे"त्य् आह । एताभ्यो ह्य् एषा देवताभ्यः पिन्वते । "इन्द्राय पिन्वस्वेन्द्राय पिन्वस्वे"त्य् आह । इन्द्रम् एव भागधेयेन सम् अर्धयति ।

says. Cattle have Pūṣan as their deity. (3) He lets him (the calf) go (to the cow) by his own god. *"Make (the cow) give milk for the Aśvins,"* he says. The Aśvins are indeed the physicians of the gods. For these two she produces the healing (milk), (intended) for him (the calf). *"This teat of thine, ever flowing, [which brings refreshment, with which you make prosper all desirable things, that gives treasures, finds wealth and is liberal, Sarasvatī, make this (your teat) ready to be sucked],"*[86] he says. He praises her. *"O bull (calf), leave the Gharma (milk), o bull (calf), protect the Gharma (milk), leave (milk) for the Gharma (sacrifice),"* he says. Like if one would say: "give milk for him," exactly like that it is.[87]

"Let Bṛhaspati approach[88] *you,"* he says. (4) Bṛhaspati is actually bráhman[89] among the gods. With the bráhman-formula (the Adhvaryu priest) approaches her. *"You are swelling drops,"* he says, for he makes them fit for the sacrifice. *"Staying apart from blood,"*[90] he says, to make a distinction. *"Swell for the Aśvins, swell for Sarasvatī, swell for Pūṣan, swell for Bṛhaspati,"* he says, for she swells for these gods. *"Swell for Indra, swell for Indra,"* he says. Indra she brings to fulfilment with a

द्विर् "इन्द्रायें"त्य् आंह ॥४॥ तस्माद् इन्द्रों देवतांनां भूयिष्ठभाक्तंमः । "गायत्रोंऽसि, त्रैष्टुंभोऽसि जागंतम् असी"तिं शफोपयमान् आ दंत्ते । छन्दोंभिर् एवैनान् आ दंत्ते । "सहोर्जो भागेनोप मेही"त्य् आंह । ऊर्जं एवैनं भागम् अंकः ।

अश्विनौ वा एतद् यज्ञस्य शिरंः प्रतिदधंताव् अब्रूताम् । "आवाभ्यांम् एव पूर्वाभ्यां वषंट् क्रियाता" इतिं । "इन्द्रांश्विना मधुंनः सारघस्ये"त्य् आंह । अश्विभ्यांम् एव पूर्वाभ्यां वषंट् करोति । अथों अश्विनांव् एव भांगधेयेंन सम् अंर्धयति ॥५॥

"घर्मं पांत वसवो यजंता, वड्" इत्य् आंह । वसूंन् एव भांगधेयेंन सम् अंर्धयति । यद् वंषट्कुर्यात् । यातयांमास्य वषट्कारः स्यांत् । यन् न वंषट्कुर्यात् । रक्षांꣳसि यज्ञꣳ हंन्युः । "वड्" इत्य् आंह । परोक्षंम् एव वषंट् करोति । नास्यं यातयांमा वषट्कारो भवंति । न यज्ञꣳ रक्षांꣳसि घ्नन्ति ॥६॥

"स्वाहां त्वा सूर्यस्य रश्मयें वृष्टिवनंये जुहोमी"त्य् आंह । यो वा अंस्य पुण्यों

portion. He says twice: "for Indra." (5) Therefore, among the gods Indra is receiving most. With: *"You belong to the gāyatrī, you belong to the triṣṭubh, you belong to the jagatī,"* he takes[91] the two tongs and the supporting vessel.[92] He takes them with the metres. *"With a share of the food, come unto me,"*[93] he says. A share of the food she makes for him.

The two Aśvins, putting back that head of the sacrifice, said indeed: "Let the vaṣaṭ-cry be uttered for us at the beginning." *"O Indra, o Aśvins, (drink the Gharma) of bees' honey,"*[94] he says. He utters the vaṣaṭ-cry for the Aśvins at the beginning. And then he brings the Aśvins to fulfilment with a portion.

(6) *"Drink the Gharma, o Vasus, offer worship. Vaṭ!"* he says. The Vasus he brings to fulfilment with a portion. If he would say *"Vaṣaṭ!"* his vaṣaṭ-cry would be exhausted. If he would not utter the vaṣaṭ-cry, the Rakṣases would destroy his sacrifice. He says: *"Vaṭ!"* He utters the vaṣaṭ-cry in a veiled way. His vaṣaṭ-cry does not become exhausted. The Rakṣases do not destroy his sacrifice.

(7) *"Svāhā! I offer[95] you as an oblation for the sun's ray which gains (and gives)[96] rain,"* he says. The ray of him that is pure, that actually gains

रश्मिः । स वृष्टिवनिः । तस्मा एवैनं जुहोति । "मधु हविर् असी"त्य् आह । स्वदयत्य् एवैनम् । "सूर्यस्य तपस् तपे"त्य् आह । यथायजुर् एवैतत् । "द्यावापृथिवीभ्यां त्वा परि गृह्णामी"त्य् आह । द्यावापृथिवीभ्याम् एवैनं परि गृह्णाति ॥७॥ "अन्तरिक्षेण त्वोपयच्छामी"त्य् आह । अन्तरिक्षेणैवैनम् उप यच्छति ।

न वा एतं मनुष्यो भर्तुम् अर्हति । "देवानां त्वा पितृणाम् अनुमतो भर्तुं शकेयम्" इत्य् आह । देवैर् एवैनं पितृभिर् अनुमत आ दत्ते । वि वा एनम् एतद् अर्धयन्ति । यत् पश्चात् प्रवृज्य पुरो जुह्वति । "तेजोऽसि, तेजोऽनु प्रेही"त्य् आह । तेज एवास्मिन् दधाति । "दिविस्पृङ् मा मा हिंसीर्, अन्तरिक्षस्पृङ् मा मा हिंसीः, पृथिविस्पृङ् मा मा हिंसीर्" इत्याहाहिंसायै ॥८॥ "सुवर् असि, सुवर् मे यच्छ, दिवं यच्छ दिवो मा पाही"त्य् आह । आशिषम् एवैताम् आ शास्ते ।

शिरो वा एतद् यज्ञस्य । यत् प्रवर्ग्यः । आत्मा वायुः ।उद्यत्य वातनामान्य् आह ।

(and gives) rain. To this he offers the (cow's milk). *"You are the sweet oblation,"*[97] he says. He makes (the goat's milk) sweet (with this mantra). *"Heat the heat of the sun,"* he says. This is exactly like the yajus-formula (expresses). *"With heaven and earth I encompass you,"*[98] he says. With heaven and earth he encompasses it. (8) *"With the firmament I support you,"*[99] he says. With the firmament he supports it.

A human being certainly cannot carry it. *"With the consent of gods and fathers, may I be able to carry you,"* he says. Given leave by gods and fathers he takes it. They certainly make this (Pravargya) unsuccessful, when, after having heated it in the west, they offer the oblation in the east. (To counteract this:) *"You are brilliant energy, go along after brilliant energy,"* he says. He puts brilliant energy in it. *"Touching heaven, may you not harm me; touching the earth, may you not harm me,"* he says to prevent harm. (9) *"You are sunlight, give me sunlight; give me heaven, protect me from (danger from) heaven,"* he says. This prayer he prays.

The Pravargya is actually the head of the sacrifice. The body (of the sacrifice) is the Wind.[100] After having lifted up (the Pravargya, to bring it

आत्मन्न् एव यज्ञस्य शिरः प्रति दधाति । अनवानम् । प्राणानाꣳ संतत्यै । पञ्चाह ॥९॥ पाङ्क्तो यज्ञः । यावान् एव यज्ञः । तस्य शिरः प्रति दधाति ।

"अग्नये त्वा वसुमते स्वाहे"त्य् आह । असौ वा आदित्यो ऽग्निर् वसुमान् । तस्मा एवैनं जुहोति । "सोमाय त्वा रुद्रवते स्वाहे"त्य् आह । चन्द्रमा वै सोमो रुद्रवान् । तस्मा एवैनं जुहोति । "वरुणाय त्वादित्यवते स्वाहे"त्य् आह ॥१०॥ अप्सु वै वरुण आदित्यवान् । तस्मा एवैनं जुहोति । "बृहस्पतये त्वा विश्वदेव्यावते स्वाहे"त्य् आह । ब्रह्म वै देवानां बृहस्पतिः । ब्रह्मण एवैनं जुहोति । "सवित्रे त्वर्भुमते विभुमते प्रभुमते वाजवते स्वाहे"त्य् आह । संवत्सरो वै सवितर्भुमान् विभुमान् प्रभुमान् वाजवान् । तस्मा एवैनं जुहोति । "यमाय त्वाङ्गिरस्वते पितृमते स्वाहे"त्य् आह । प्राणो वै यमो ऽङ्गिरस्वान् पितृमान् ॥११॥ तस्मा एवैनं जुहोति । एताभ्य एवैनं

to the Āhavanīya),[101] he says the names of the Wind. On the body he puts back the head of the sacrifice. (He recites the names) without taking breath,[102] for the continuity of the prāṇas. He says five names.[103] (10) The sacrifice is fivefold. The head of that sacrifice, as big as it is, he puts back.

"You for Agni, accompanied by the Vasus, svāhā!"[104] he says. Agni, accompanied by the Vasus, is actually yonder Āditya (the sun). To him he offers[105] this. *"You for Soma, accompanied by the Rudras, svāhā!"* he says. Soma, accompanied by the Rudras, is actually the moon. To him he offers this. *"You for Varuṇa, accompanied by the Ādityas, svāhā!"* he says. (11) Varuṇa, accompanied by the Ādityas, is actually in the waters. To him he offers this. *"You for Bṛhaspati, accompanied by the All-gods, svāhā!"* he says. Bṛhaspati is bráhman among the gods. To bráhman he offers this. *"You for Savitṛ, accompanied by Ṛbhu, accompanied by Vibhu, accompanied by Prabhu, accompanied by Vāja, svāhā!"* he says. Savitṛ, accompanied by Ṛbhu, accompanied by Vibhu, accompanied by Prabhu, accompanied by Vāja is actually the year. To him he offers this. *"You for Yama, accompanied by the Angirases, accompanied by the fathers, svāhā!"* he says. Yama, accompanied by the Angirases, accompanied by the fathers, is actually the Prāṇa. (12) To him he offers

देवताभ्यो जुहोति । दश सं पद्यन्ते । दशाक्षरा विराट् । अन्नं विराट् । विराजैवान्नाद्यम् अव रुन्धे ।

रौहिणाभ्यां वै देवाः सुवर्गं लोकम् आयन्न् । तद् रौहिणयो रौहिणत्वम् । यद् रौहिणौ भवतः । रौहिणाभ्याम् एव तद् यजमानः सुवर्गं लोकम् एति ।

"अहर् ज्योतिः केतुना जुषताꣳ सुज्योतिर् ज्योतिषाꣳ स्वाहा, रात्रिर् ज्योतिः केतुना जुषताꣳ सुज्योतिर् ज्योतिषाꣳ स्वाहे"त्य् आह । आदित्यम् एव तद् अमुष्मिन् लोकेऽह्ना परस्ताद् दाधार । रात्रिया अवस्तात् । तस्माद् असाव् आदित्योऽमुष्मिन् लोकेऽहोरात्राभ्यां धृतः ॥१२॥

this. To these deities he offers this. (The mantras) amount to ten.[106] The virāj-metre is ten-syllabic. The virāj is food. With the virāj he gains food.

(Offering the southern Rauhiṇa-cake:)[107] The gods went indeed to the celestial world by the two Rauhiṇa-cakes. That is why the two Rauhiṇas are called Rauhiṇas (√*ruh-*, to ascend). When the two Rauhiṇas are there, then the sacrificer goes to the celestial world by the Rauhiṇas.

"Let day enjoy the light[108] *by brightness;*[109] *good light of lights, svāhā! Let night enjoy the light by brightness; good light of lights, svāhā!"* he says. It is the Āditya (the sun) in yonder world that he thus supports by day above (in heaven); by night below (in the netherworld). Therefore yonder Āditya (the sun) in yonder world is supported by day and night.

Anuvāka 8
The offering to the Aśvins

This is the last of the five anuvākas that describe the regular daily performances of the Pravargya. The offering to the Aśvins and other deities is described in this anuvāka. The mantras discussed in this anuvāka are to be found in TĀ 4, 9, 2(2) - end, and 4, 10. For a description of the ritual actions see: *Śrautakośa* vol. 2, Sanskrit part 1:533-534 and 535-536; English part 1:193-210, 229-230; van Buitenen, *Pravargya*: IV, §5-§15.

“विश्वा॒ आशा॑ दक्षिण॒सद्” इत्य् आ॑ह । विश्वा॑न् ए॒व दे॒वान् प्री॑णाति । अथो॒ दु॒रिष्ट्या॒ ए॒वैनं᳚ पाति । “विश्वा॑न् दे॒वान् अ॑याड् इ॒हे”त्य् आ॑ह । विश्वा॑न् ए॒व दे॒वान् भा॑ग॒धेये॑न॒ सम् अ॑र्धयति । “स्वाहा॑कृतस्य घ॒र्मस्य॒ मधोः॑ पिबतम् अश्वि॒ने”त्य् आ॑ह । अ॒श्विना॑व् ए॒व भा॑ग॒धेये॑न॒ सम् अ॑र्धयति । “स्वाहा॒ग्नये॑ य॒ज्ञिया॑य॒ शं यजु॑र्भिर्” इत्य् आ॑ह । अ॒भ्य् ए॑वैनं᳚ घारयति । अथो॑ ह॒विर् ए॒वाकः॑ ॥१॥ “अश्वि॑ना घ॒र्मं पा॑तꣳ हार्दि-वा॒नम् अह॒र्दि॒वाभि॑र् ऊ॒तिभि॒र्” इत्य् आ॑ह । अ॒श्विना॑व् ए॒व भा॑ग॒धेये॑न॒ सम् अ॑र्धयति । “अनु॑ वां॒ द्यावा॑पृथि॒वी म॑ꣳसाता॒म्” इत्य् आहा॒नु॑मत्यै । “स्वाहेन्द्रा॑य॒, स्वाहेन्द्रा॒, वड्” इत्य् आ॑ह । इन्द्रा॑य॒ हि पु॒रो हू॒यते॑ । आ॒श्राव्या॑ह “घ॒र्मस्य॑ य॒जे”ति । वष॑ट्कृते

(The offering to the Aśvins:) (1) *“All quarters (has he, the Brahmán priest) who sits in the south (worshipped),”*[110] he says. (The Brahmán priest) pleases all the gods. And he protects him (the sacrificer) from failure in sacrifice. *“He has worshipped the All-gods here,”*[111] he says. The All-gods he brings to fulfilment with a portion. *“Of the sweet Gharma, consecrated with the Svāhā, drink, o Aśvins,”* he says. The Aśvins he brings to fulfilment with a portion. *“Svāhā to Agni, worthy of sacrifice; happiness with the yajus-formulas,”* he says. He sprinkles him. And he makes an oblation. (2) *“O Aśvins, drink the Gharma that is dear to your heart,*[112] *with your favours*[113] *every day,”*[114] he says. The Aśvins he brings to fulfilment with a portion.[115] *“Let heaven and earth give you their permission,”* he says, for permission. *“Svāhā for Indra, svāhā for Indra,*[116] *Vaṭ!”* he says, because for Indra an offering is made at the beginning. After having called, he says (to the Hotṛ): *“Recite the yājyā for the Gharma-oblation.”* When the vaṣaṭ-cry is uttered (by the Hotṛ in his

जुहोति । रक्षसाम् अपहत्यै । अनु यजति स्वगाकृत्यै । "घर्मम् अपातम् अश्विने"त्य् आह ["हार्दिवानम् । अहर्दिवाभिरूतिभिः"] ॥२॥ पूर्वम् एवोदितम् । उत्तरेणाभि गृणाति ।

"अनु वां द्यावापृथिवी अमꣳसाताम्" इत्य् आहानुमत्यै । "तं प्राव्यं यथावण् णमो दिवे नमः पृथिव्या" इत्य् आह । यथायजुर् एवैतत् । "दिवि धा इमं यज्ञं, यज्ञम् इमं दिवि धा" इत्य् आह । सुवर्गम् एवैनं लोकं गमयति । "दिवं गच्छान्तरिक्षं गच्छ पृथिवीं गच्छे"त्य् आह । एष्व् एवैनं लोकेषु प्रति ष्ठापयति । "पञ्च प्रदिशो गच्छे"त्य् आह ॥३॥ दिक्ष्व् एवैनं प्रति ष्ठापयति । "देवान् घर्मपान् गच्छ, पितॄन् घर्मपान् गच्छे"त्य् आह । उभयेष्व् एवैनं प्रति ष्ठापयति ।

यत् पिन्वते । वर्षुकः पर्जन्यो भवति । तस्मात् पिन्वमानः पुण्यः। यत् प्राङ् पिन्वते । तद् देवानाम् । यद् दक्षिणा । तत् पितृणाम् ॥४॥ यत् प्रत्यक् । तन्

recitation of the yājyā), he offers the oblation (with the first *"Svāhā for Indra"*). For keeping back the Rakṣases. He offers a second time (with *"Svāhā for Indra, Vaṭ!"*), by way of *svagākṛti*.[117] *"The Aśvins have drunk the Gharma [that is dear to their heart, with favours every day],"* he says. (3) What has been said before he praises with this subsequent (yajus-formula).

"Heaven and earth have given you their permission," he says, for the permission (received). *"(Permission for) the (Gharma) to be accepted favorably, as the vaṭ-cry. Homage to heaven, homage to earth,"* he says. This is exactly like the yajus-formula (expresses). *"Place in heaven this sacrifice, place this sacrifice in heaven,"* he says. He makes it go to the celestial world. *"Go to heaven, go to the firmament, go to the earth,"* he says. He fixes it firmly in these worlds. *"Go to the five quarters,"* he says. (4) He fixes it firmly in the quarters. *"Go to the Gharma-drinking gods, go to the Gharma-drinking fathers,"* he says. He fixes it firmly among both groups.

When (the vessel) overflows,[118] Parjanya becomes rainy. Therefore, overflowing it is pure. What overflows in the eastern direction, that is for the gods. What overflows in the southern direction, that is for the

मंनुष्यांणाम् । यद् उदंङ् । तद् रुद्राणांम् । प्राञ्चम् उदंञ्चं पिन्वयति । देवत्राकः । अथो खलुं । सर्वा अनु दिशः पिन्वयति । सर्वा दिशः सम् एंधन्ते । अन्तःपरिधि पिन्वयति ॥५॥ तेजसोऽस्कंन्दाय ।

"इषे पींपिह्यू ऊर्जे पींपिही"त्य् आंह । इषंम् एवोर्जं यजंमाने दधाति । "यजंमानाय पीपिही"त्य् आंह । यजंमानायैवैताम् आशिषम् आ शांस्ते । "मह्यं ज्यैष्ठ्यांय पीपिही"त्य् आंह । आत्मनं एवैताम् आशिषम् आ शांस्ते । "त्विष्यैं त्वा. द्युम्नायं त्वेन्द्रियायं त्वा, भूत्यै त्वे"त्य् आंह । यथायजुर् एवैतत् । "धर्मासि, सुधर्मामेंन्य् अस्मे, ब्रह्मांणि धारये"त्य् आंह ॥६॥ ब्रह्मंन्न् एवैनं प्रतिं ष्ठापयति । "नेत् त्वा वातंः स्कन्दयाद्" इति

यद्य् अंभिचरेंत् । "अमुष्यं त्वा प्राणे सांदयाम्य्, अमुनां सह निरर्थं गच्छे"ति

fathers. (5) What in the western direction, that is for the human beings. What in the northern direction, that is for the Rudras. He makes it overflow in the eastern and northern direction. (Thus) he brings it among the gods. But (according to others) indeed he makes it overflow in all quarters. All quarters prosper greatly. He makes it overflow inside the *paridhi*-s (sticks enclosing the sacrificial fire). (6) To prevent spilling of brilliant energy.

"Swell for nourishment, swell for food,"[119] he says. He puts nourishment and food in the sacrificer. *"Swell for the sacrificer,"* he says. For the sacrificer he prays this prayer. *"Swell for me, for pre-eminence,"* he says. For himself he prays this prayer. *"You for energy, you for splendour, you for power, you for prosperity,"* he says. This is exactly like the yajus-formula (expresses). *"You are a support, a good support, unoffensive towards us; support the Brahmins,"*[120] he says. (7) He fixes him (the sacrificer) firmly among the Brahmins. *"Lest the wind causes you to be spilt."*

If he wants to put a spell on someone, he should say with regard to whom he hates: *"I put you down on the life-breath of so-and-so, go to uselessness together with so-and-so, [who hates us and whom we hate]."*

ब्रूयाद् यं द्विष्यात् [“योऽस्मान् द्वेष्टि । यं च वयं द्विष्मः”] । यम् एव द्वेष्टि । तेनैनं सह निरर्थं गमयति ।

“पूष्णे शरसे स्वाहे”त्य् आह । या एव देवता हुतभागाः। ताभ्य एवैनं जुहोति । “ग्रावभ्यः स्वाहे”त्य् आह । या एवान्तरिक्षे वाचः ॥७॥ ताभ्य एवैनं जुहोति । “प्रतिरेभ्यः स्वाहे”त्य् आह । प्राणा वै देवाः प्रतिराः । तेभ्य एवैनं जुहोति । “द्यावा-पृथिवीभ्यां स्वाहे”त्य् आह । द्यावापृथिवीभ्याम् एवैनं जुहोति । पितृभ्यो घर्मपेभ्यः स्वाहे”त्य् आह । ये वै यज्वानः । ते पितरो घर्मपाः । तेभ्य एवैनं जुहोति ॥८॥ “रुद्राय रुद्रहोत्रे स्वाहे”त्य् आह । रुद्रम् एव भागधेयेन सम् अर्धयति । सर्वतः सम् अनक्ति । सर्वत एव रुद्रं निरवदयते । उदङ्ङ् निर् अस्यति । एषा वै रुद्रस्य दिक् । स्वायाम् एव दिशि रुद्रं निरवदयते । अप उप स्पृशति, मेध्यत्वाय । नान्व् ईक्षेत । यद् अन्वीक्षेत ॥९॥ चक्षुर् अस्य प्रमायुकं स्यात् । तस्मान् नान्वीक्ष्यः ।

“अपीपरो माह्नो, रात्रियै मा पाह्य्, एषा ते अग्ने समित्, तया सम्

Together with this (Pravargya vessel) he makes him whom he hates go to uselessness.

“For Pūṣan Śaras,[121] *svāhā!”* he says. The deities that are entitled to the oblation, to them he offers it (sc. the woodsplinter anointed with clarified butter.). *“To the pressing stones, svāhā!”* he says. The sounds that are in the air, (8) to them he offers it. *“To the promoters,*[122] *svāhā!”* he says. The promoting gods are actually the prāṇas. To them he offers it. *“To heaven and earth, svāhā!”* he says. To heaven and earth he offers it. *“To the fathers who protect the Gharma, svāhā!”* he says. The Gharma-drinking fathers are actually those who were sacrificers. To them he offers it. (9) *“To Rudra, whose Hotṛ-s are the Rudras, svāhā!”* he says. Rudra he brings to fulfilment with a portion. He anoints (the splinter) on all sides. On all sides he satisfies[123] Rudra. He throws in the northern direction. That is indeed Rudra's direction. He satisfies Rudra in his own direction. He touches water, to acquire fitness for the sacrifice.[124] Let him not look (to the splinter that is thrown away). If he would look, (10) his eye-sight would be liable to destruction. Therefore, it should not be looked at.[125]

(In the evening performance:) *“You have brought me over the day,*

इंध्यस्वायुंर् मे दा, वर्चसा माञ्जीर्" इत्य् आंह । आयुंर् एवास्मिन् वर्चो दधाति ।

"अपीपरो मा रात्रिया, अह्नों मा पाह्य्, एषा तें अग्ने समित्, तया सम् इंध्यस्वायुंर् मे दा, वर्चसा माञ्जीर्" इत्य् आंह । आयुंर् एवास्मिन् वर्चो दधाति । "अग्निर् ज्योतिर् ज्योतिंर् अग्निः स्वाहा, सूर्यो ज्योतिर् ज्योतिः सूर्यः स्वाहे"त्य् आंह । यथायजुर् एवैतत् ।

ब्रह्मवादिनों वदन्ति । "होतव्यंम् अग्निहोत्रां३, न होंतव्या३म् ?" इतिं ॥१०॥
यद् यजुंषा जुहुयात् । अयंथापूर्वम् आहुंती[126] जुहुयात् । यन् न जुंहुयात् । अग्निः परां भवेत् । "भूः स्वाहे"त्य् एव होंतव्यंम् । यथापूर्वम् आहुंती[126] जुहोतिं । नाग्निः परां भवति ।

"हुतꣳ हविर्, मधुं हविर्" इत्य् आंह । स्वदयंत्य् एवैनंम् । "इन्द्रंतमेऽग्नाव्" इत्य् आंह ॥११॥ प्राणो वा इन्द्रंतमोऽग्निः । प्राण एवैनम् इन्द्रंतमेऽग्नौ जुंहोति ।

protect me from the night. This, o Agni, is your kindling stick, be kindled with it. Give me my full life-time, anoint me with lustre," he says. He puts the full life-time and lustre in him.

(In the morning performance:) *"You have brought me over the night, protect me from the day. This, o Agni, is your kindling stick, be kindled with it. Give me my full life-time, anoint me with lustre,"* he says. He puts the full life-time and lustre in him. *"Agni is light, light is Agni, svāhā! The sun is light, light is the sun, svāhā!"* he says. This is exactly like the yajus-formula (expresses).

The expounders of the Veda say: "Should the Agnihotra be offered, or should it not be offered?" (11) If he would offer with the yajus-formula, he would offer the two oblations not in the right succession. If he would not offer, Agni would be lost. With: *"Bhūḥ, svāhā!"* (the Agnihotra) should be offered. He offers the two oblations in the right succession. Agni is not lost.[127]

"The oblation has been offered, the sweet oblation," he says. He makes it sweet (with this mantra). *"In the most Indra-like fire,"* he says. (12) The most Indra-like fire is actually the prāṇa.[128] In prāṇa, the most

"पिता नोऽसि मा मां हिꣳसीर्" इत्य् आहाहिꣳसायै । "अश्यामं ते देव घर्म मधुमतो वाजंवतः पितुमत" इत्य् आंह ["अङ्गिरस्वतः"] । आशिषम् एवैताम् आ शांस्ते । "स्वधाविनोऽशीमहि त्वा मा मां हिꣳसीर्" इत्य् आहाहिꣳसायै । तेजंसा वा एते व्य् ऋध्यन्ते । ये प्रवर्ग्येण चरंन्ति । प्राश्नन्ति । तेजं एवात्मन् दंधते ॥१२॥

संवत्सरं न माꣳसम् अंश्नीयात् । न रामाम् उपेयात् । न मृन्मयेंन पिबेत् । नास्यं राम उच्छिष्टं पिबेत् । तेजं एव तत् सꣳ श्यति ।

देवासुराः संयंत्ता आसन् । ते देवा विजयम् उंपयन्तंः । विभ्राजि सौर्ये ब्रह्म सं न्य अंदधत । यत् किंचं दिवाकीर्त्यम् । तद् एतेनैव व्रतेनांगोपायत् । तस्मांद् एतद् व्रतं चार्यम् । तेजंसो गोपीथायं । तस्मांद् एतानि यजूꣳषि विभ्राजंः सौर्यस्ये"त्य् आंहुः ।

Indra-like fire, he offers it. *"You are our father, do not harm me,"* he says, to prevent harm. *"May we eat of you, god Gharma, full of honey, full of strength, full of nourishment, [of you who are connected with the Angirases],"* he says. This prayer he prays. *". . . of (you) full of svadhā. May we eat you. Do not harm me,"* he says, to prevent harm. They are certainly deprived of their brilliant energy, who are engaged in the Pravargya. They eat.[129] (Thus) they put brilliant energy in their body.

(The observance to be followed when the Pravargya mantras are learnt:) (13) For a year[130] he should eat no meat. He should not approach a Śūdra woman. He should not drink from a clay vessel. A Śūdra should not drink his remnants. Thus he sharpens his brilliant energy.

The gods and the Asuras had come into conflict. The gods, going to the (decisive) contest for victory, deposited the sacred text (the Pravargya mantras) with Vibhrāj, son of Sūrya. Whatever (in it) that is to be recited by day, that he protected with this very observance. Therefore, this observance should be followed, to protect the brilliant energy. Therefore, they say that these yajus-formulas belong to Vibhrāj, son of Sūrya.

"स्वाहां त्वा॒ सूर्य॑स्य र॒श्मिभ्य॒" इतिं प्रा॒तः सः सांदयति । "स्वाहां त्वा॒ नक्षं-त्रेभ्य॒" इतिं सा॒यम् । ए॒ता वा ए॒तस्यं दे॒वतांः । ताभिंर् ए॒वैन॒ः सम् अंर्धयति ॥१३॥

(The Pravargya vessel is placed back on the throne at the end of each morning- and evening-performance:) With: *"Svāhā!, you for the rays of the sun"* in the morning, he places (the vessel and the other paraphernalia on the throne). With: *"Svāhā!, you for the stars"* in the evening. These are indeed his deities. With them he brings this (Pravargya) to fulfilment.

Anuvāka 9

The disposal of the Pravargya implements

The mantras of this anuvāka are TĀ 4, 11. For a description of the ritual actions see: *Śrautakośa* vol. 2, Sanskrit part 1:537-540; English part 1:245-264; van Buitenen, *Pravargya*: V, §1-§12.

“घर्म॒ या ते॑ दि॒वि शुग्” इति॑ ति॒स्र आहु॑तीर् जुहोति [“या गाय॑त्रे॒ छन्द॑सि । या ब्रा॑ह्म॒णे । या ह॑वि॒र्धाणे॑ । ता॑ त॑ ए॒तेनाव॑ यजे॒ स्वाहा॑ ॥ घर्म॒ या ते॒ऽन्तरि॑क्षे॒ शुक् । या त्रैष्टु॑भे॒ छन्द॑सि । या रा॑ज॒न्ये॑ । याग्नी॑ध्रे । ता॑ त॑ ए॒तेनाव॑ यजे॒ स्वाहा॑ ॥ घर्म॒ या ते॑ पृ॒थिव्याः शुक् । या जाग॑ते॒ छन्द॑सि । या वैश्ये॑ । या सद॑सि । ता॑ त॑ ए॒तेनाव॑ यजे॒ स्वाहा॑”] । छन्दो॑भिर् ए॒वास्यै॒भ्यो लो॒के॒भ्यः शु॒चम् अव॑ यजते । इयत्य् अ॒ग्रे॑ जुहोति । अथे॒यत्य् अथे॑यति । त्रय॑ इ॒मे लो॒काः । ए॒भ्य ए॒व लो॒के॒भ्यः शु॒चम् अव॑ यजते ।

(1) He offers the three oblations with: “*O Gharma, the scorching heat of yours in heaven, [the one which is in the gāyatrī-metre, the one which is in the Brahmins, the one which is in the Havirdhāna shed - that (scorching heat) of you I sacrifice away, svāhā!*

O Gharma, the scorching heat of yours in the firmament, the one which is in the triṣṭubh-metre, the one which is in the Kṣatriyas, the one which is in the Āgnīdhra shed - that (scorching heat) of yours I sacrifice away, svāhā!

O Gharma, the scorching heat of yours on the earth, the one which is in the jagatī-metre, the one which is in the Vaiśyas, the one which is in the Sadas shed - that (scorching heat) of yours I sacrifice away, svāhā!]”[131]

With the metres he sacrifices his scorching heat away from these worlds. First he offers on this height (this is said with a gesture indicating the height of the mouth).[132] And then on this height (with a gesture indicating the height of the navel); and then on this height (with a gesture indicating the height of the knees). Three are these worlds. From these worlds he sacrifices his scorching heat away.

"अनुं नोऽद्यानुंमतिर्" इत्य् आहानुंमत्यै ["अन्विदंनुमते त्वम्"] । "दिवस् त्वां परस्पाया" इत्य् आंह ["अन्तरिक्षस्य तनुवंः पाहि । पृथिव्यास् त्वा धर्मणा । वयम् अनुं क्रामाम सुविताय नव्यंसे"] । दिव एवेमान् लोकान् दांधार । "ब्रह्मंणस् त्वा परस्पाया" इत्य् आंह ["क्षत्त्रस्यं तनुवंः पाहि । विशस् त्वा धर्मणा । वयम् अनुं क्रामाम सुविताय नव्यंसे"] ॥१॥ एष्व् एंव लोकेषुं प्रजा दांधार । "प्राणस्यं त्वा परस्पाया" इत्य् आंह ["चक्षुंषस् तनुवंः पाहि । श्रोत्रंस्य त्वा धर्मणा । वयम् अनुं क्रामाम सुविताय नव्यंसे"] । प्रजास्व् एव प्राणान् दांधार ।

शिरो वा एतद् यज्ञस्यं । यत् प्रंवर्ग्यः । असौ खलु वा आंदित्यः प्रंवर्ग्यः । तं यद् दंक्षिणा प्रत्यञ्चम् उदंञ्चम् उद्वासयेंत् । जिह्मं यज्ञस्य शिरों हरेत् । प्राञ्चम् उद् वांसयति । पुरस्तांद् एव यज्ञस्य शिरः प्रति दधाति ॥२॥ प्राञ्चम् उद् वांसयति । तस्मांद् असाव् आंदित्यः पुरस्ताद् उद् एंति । शफोपयमान् धवित्रांणि धृष्टी इत्य्

"May Anumati ('Permission') today for us"; ["You, o Anumati"],[133] he says, for permission. *"You for the protection*[134] *of heaven [and of the firmament - protect our bodies - you, with the supporting of the earth we will follow for a newer propitious progress],"* he says. For the sake of heaven he supports these worlds. *"You for the protection of the Brahmins [and of the Kṣatriyas - protect our bodies - you, with the supporting of the Vaiśyas we will follow for a newer propitious progress],"* he says. (2) In these worlds he supports the people. *"You for the protection of the life-breath [and of the eye-sight - protect our bodies - you, with the supporting of hearing we will follow for a newer propitious progress.],"* he says. He supports the prāṇas in the people.

That Pravargya is actually the head of the sacrifice. Indeed, the Pravargya is yonder Āditya (the sun). If he would dispose of this (Pravargya) in the south, in the west or in the north, he would take the head of the sacrifice in the wrong way.[135] (But) he disposes of it in the east. In the east he puts back the head of the sacrifice. (3) He disposes of it in the east. Therefore, yonder Āditya (the sun) rises in the east. The tongs and supporting vessel, the fans, the two pokers etc., they lay down with it. (The

अ॒न्वव॑हरन्ति । सात्मा॑नम् ए॒वै॒नꣳ स॒त॑नुं करोति । सात्मा॒मुष्मि॑न् लो॒के भ॑वति । य
ए॒वं वेद॑ । औदु॑म्बराणि भवन्ति । ऊर्ग् वा उ॑दु॒म्बर॑ः । ऊर्ज॑म् ए॒वाव॑ रुन्धे ।

वर्त्म॑ना॒ वा अ॒न्वित्य॑ ॥३॥ य॒ज्ञꣳ रक्षा॑ꣳसि जिघाꣳसन्ति । साम्ना॑

प्रस्तो॒तान्ववै॑ति । सा॒म वै र॑क्षो॒हा । रक्ष॑सा॒म् अप॑हत्यै । त्रिर् नि॒ध॒नम् उपै॑ति । त्रय॑ इ॒मे
लो॒काः । ए॒भ्य ए॒व लो॒केभ्यो॒ रक्षा॒ꣳस्य् अप॑ हन्ति । पु॑रुषःपुरुषो नि॒ध॒नम् उपै॑ति ।
पु॑रुषःपुरुषो॒ हि र॑क्ष॒स्वी । रक्ष॑सा॒म् अप॑हत्यै ॥४॥

यत् पृ॑थि॒व्याम् उ॑द्वा॒सये॑त् । पृ॒थि॒वीꣳ शु॒चार्प॑येत् । यद् अ॒प्सु । अ॒पः शु॒चार्प॑येत् ।
यद् ओष॑धीषु । ओष॑धीः शु॒चार्प॑येत् । यद् वन॒स्पति॑षु । वन॒स्पती॑ञ् छु॒चार्प॑येत् ।
हिर॑ण्यं नि॒धायोद् वा॑सयति । अ॒मृ॒तं वै हिर॑ण्यम् ॥५॥ अ॒मृत॑ ए॒वै॒नं प्रति॑ ष्ठापयति ।
"व॒ल्गुर् अ॑सि श॒ंयुधा॑या॒" इति॒ त्रिः परि॑षि॒ञ्चन् पर्य् ए॑ति ["शिशु॒र् जन॑धायाः"] ।
त्रि॒वृद् वा अ॒ग्निः । याव॑न् ए॒वाग्निः । तस्य॒ शुचꣳ शमयति । त्रिः पु॒नः पर्य् ए॑ति । षट्

Adhvaryu) supplies it with its body, with its bodily form. He who knows thus has his body[136] in yonder world. (The implements) are made of Udumbara-wood. The Udumbara is actually food. He gains food.

During its course, (4) the Rakṣases want to destroy the sacrice. The Prastotṛ follows with the sāman.[137] The sāman certainly destroys the Rakṣases. To ward off the Rakṣases. The concluding passage (of the sāman) he sings three times. These worlds are three. From these worlds they ward off the Rakṣases. Each person joins in the concluding passage, for each person has Rakṣases. (Each person sings) to ward off the Rakṣases.

(5) If he would dispose of it on the earth, he would afflict the earth with suffering. If in the waters, he would afflict the waters with suffering. If on the herbs, he would afflict the herbs with suffering. If on the trees, he would afflict the trees with suffering. He lays down a piece of gold and disposes of it (on that). Gold is actually immortal. (6) He places it on the immortal.[138] With: *"You are lovely, beneficent [young and the keeper of people],"* he circumambulates three times while sprinkling. Agni is actually threefold (as fire, lightning and sun). They soothe the scorching heat of Agni, as far as he extends. He circumambulates again three

संपद्यन्ते । षड् वा ऋतवः । ऋतुभिर् एवास्य शुचꣳ शमयति ।

"चतुःस्रक्तिर् नाभिर् ऋतस्ये"त्य् आह ।।६।। इयं वा ऋतम् । तस्यां एष एव नाभिः । यत् प्रवर्ग्यः । तस्माद् एवम् आह । "सदो विश्वायुर्" इत्य् आह ["शर्म सप्रथाः"] । सदो हीयम् । "अप द्वेषो अप ह्वर" इत्य् आह भ्रातृव्यापनुत्त्यै ["अन्यद्व्रतस्य सश्चिम"] । "घर्मैतत् तेऽन्नम् एतत् पुरीषम्" इति दध्ना मधुमिश्रेण पूरयति । ऊर्ग् वा अन्नाद्यं दधि । ऊर्जैवैनम् अन्नाद्येन सम् अर्धयति ।।७।। अनशनायुको भवति । य एवं वेद ।

"रन्तिर् नामासि दिव्यो गन्धर्व" इत्य् आह ["तस्य ते पद्वद् हविर्धानम् । अग्निर् अध्यक्षाः । रुद्रोऽधिपतिः"] । रूपम् एवास्यैतन् महिमानꣳ रन्तिं बन्धुतां व्याचष्टे । "सम् अहम् आयुषा सं प्राणेने"त्य् आह ["सं वर्चसा । सं पयसा । सं

times (but in the reverse direction). That makes six. There are, indeed, six seasons. With the seasons he soothes his scorching heat.

"(You are) the four-cornered navel of the cosmic law," he says. (7) The cosmic law is actually this (Uttraravedi). Of this (Uttaravedi) the Pravargya is the navel.[139] Therefore he says thus. *"(You are) the Sadas, having an entire life-time, [(you are) a wide shelter],"* he says, for this (part of the) earth is the Sadas. *"From the hatred, from the deceit [of him who lives a different vow we put ourselves apart],"* he says, to remove rivals. With *"O Gharma, this is your food, this is your filling* (púrīṣa)*,"*[140] he fills it up (*pūrayati*) with curds mixed with honey. Curds are actually nourishing food. With nourishing food he brings it to fulfilment. (8) He does not get hungry, who knows thus.

"You are Ranti by name, the celestial Gandharva. [The Havirdhāna is your runner, Agni your overseer, Rudra your lord],"[141] he says. He expresses here the form, the greatness, the delight, the deeper sense[142] of it (the Pravargya). *"May I be with a full lifetime, with life-breath, [with lustre, with milk, with the possession of cattle, with prosperity],"* he says.

गौपत्येन । सꣳ रायस्पोषेण"] । आशिषम् एवैताम् आ शास्ते । "व्य् असौ योऽस्मान् द्वेष्टि, यं च वयं द्विष्म" इत्य् आह । अभिचार एवास्यैषः । "अचिक्रदद् वृषा हरिर्" इत्य् आह । वृषा ह्य् एषः ॥८॥ वृषा हरिः । "महान् मित्रो न दर्शत" इत्य् आह ["सꣳ सूर्येण रोचते"] । स्तौत्य् एवैनम् एतत् । "चिद् असि, समुद्रयोनिर्" इत्य् आह । स्वाम् एवैनं योनिं गमयति । "नमस् ते अस्तु मा मा हिꣳसीर्" इत्य् आहाहिꣳसायै ।

"विश्वावसुꣳ सोम गन्धर्वम्" इत्य् आह ["आपो ददृशुषीः । तद् ऋतेना व्य् आयन् । तद् अन्ववैत् । इन्द्रो रारहाण आसाम् । परि सूर्यस्य परिधीꣳर् अपश्यत्"] । यद् एवास्य क्रियमाणस्यान्तर्यन्ति । तद् एवास्यैतेना प्याययति । "विश्वावसुर् अभि तन् नो गृणात्व्" इत्य् आह ["दिव्यो गन्धर्वो रजसो विमानः"] ॥९॥ पूर्वम् एवोदितम् । उत्तरेणाभि गृणाति । "[यद् वा घा सत्यम् उत यन् न विद्म] धियो

This prayer he prays. *"May he be without who hates us and whom we hate,"* he says. This is a spell on him (who hates us and whom we hate). *"The golden bull has roared,"* he says, for he is a bull, (9) a golden bull. *"The great one, pleasant to see like a friend; [he shines equal to the sun],"* he says. Here he praises it. *"You are Thought, with the ocean as birthplace,"*[143] he says. He makes it go to its own birthplace. *"Obeisance be to you, do not harm me,"* he says, to prevent harm.

"[When the waters spied] Viśvāvasu, the Gandharva, o Soma, [they dispersed in accordance with the cosmic law. Indra quickly followed this (track) of these. He saw the enclosures of the sun],"[144] he says. (That part) of this (Pravargya) which they omit when it is made (and lays disposed in the form of a person), that (part) of it he fills up by means of this (story of the recovering of the lost Gandharva-Sun). *"Let Viśvāvasu proclaim it to us, [the celestial Gandharva who measures the sky],"* he says. (10) What has been said before he praises with this subsequent (yajus-formula). *[Whether we know the truth already or not,] may he, who urges on the*

हिन्वानो धिय इन्नों अव्याद्" इत्य् आंह । ऋतून् एवास्मैं कल्पयति । "प्रासां गन्धर्वो अमृतांनि वोचद्" इत्य् आंह । प्राणा वा अमृतांः । प्राणान् एवास्मैं कल्पयति । "एतत् त्वं देंव घर्म देवो देवान् उपांगा" इत्य् आंह । देवो ह्य् एंष सन् देवान् उपैतिं । इदम् अहं मंनुष्यों मनुष्यांन्" इत्य् आंह ॥१०॥ मनुष्यों हि । एष सन् मंनुष्यांन् उपैतिं ।

ईश्वरो वै प्रंवर्ग्यम् उद्वासयंन् । प्रजां पशून्त् सोंमपीथम् अंनूद्वासः "सोमंपीथानु मेहि । सह प्रजयां सह रायस्पोषेणे"त्य् आंह । प्रजाम् एव पशून्त् सोंमपीथम् आत्मन् धंत्ते । "सुमित्रा न आप ओषंधयः सन्त्व्" इत्य् आंह । आशिषंम् एवैताम् आ शांस्ते । "दुर्मित्रास् तस्मैं भूयासुर् योंऽस्मान् द्वेष्टि, यं चं वयं द्विष्म" इत्य् आंह । अभिचार एवास्यैषः । प्र वा एषोंऽस्माल् लोकाच् च्यंवते । यः प्रंवर्ग्यम् उद्वासयंति । "उद् उ त्यं", "चित्रम्" इति सौरीभ्यांम् ऋग्भ्यां पुनर् एत्य गार्हपत्ये

(inspired) thoughts, further (also) these our thoughts," he says. He forms for him the seasons. *"The Gandharva proclaimed the immortal (names) of the (waters),"*[145] he says. The prāṇas are actually immortal.[146] He forms the prāṇas for him. *"Here you, o god Gharma, have gone as a god to the gods,"* he says, for he, as a god, goes to the gods. *"Here I (go) as a human being to human beings,"* he says, (11) for he is a human being. As such he goes to human beings.

He who disposes of the Pravargya, may indeed dispose of his children, cattle and Soma-drinking along with (the Pravargya vessel). *"Soma-draught, follow me, together with children and increase of wealth,"* he says. He gives children, cattle and Soma-drinking to himself. *"Good friends be to us the waters, the herbs,"*[147] he says. This prayer he prays. *"Bad friends may they be to him who hates us and whom we hate,"* he says. This is a spell on him (who hates us and whom we hate). He certainly becomes deprived of this world, who disposes of the Pravargya. With the two sun-mantras *"Upward,"* (and) *"Radiant ,"*[148] he comes back

जुहोति । अयं वै लोको गार्हपत्यः । अस्मिन्न् एव लोके प्रति तिष्ठति । असौ खलु वा आदित्यः सुवर्गो लोकः । यत् सौरी भवतः । तेनैव सुवर्गाल् लोकान् नैति ॥११॥

to the Gārhapatya and makes an oblation. The Gārhapatya is actually this world. He stands firm in this world. The celestial world is actually yonder Āditya (the sun). When the two sun-mantras are there, (the sacrificer), on account of them, is not deprived of[149] the celestial world.

Anuvāka 10

Śukriya sāmans and yajus-formulas; places for the disposal

This anuvāka deals first with the Pravargya sāmans and yajus-formulas and one of their names: Śukriya. Next, some optional places for the disposal of the Pravargya implements are mentioned. See: *Śrautakośa* vol.2, English part 1:252, 255, 257, 260; van Buitenen, *Pravargya*: V, §9 and Appendix III, §20f.

प्रजाप॑तिं वै दे॒वाः शु॒क्रं पयो॑ऽदुह्रन् । तद् ए॑भ्यो॒ न व्य् अ॑भवत् । तद् अ॒ग्निर् व्य् अ॑करोत् । तानि॒ शुक्रि॑याणि सामा॑न्य् अभवन् । तेषां॒ यो रसो॒ऽत्यक्ष॑रत् । तानि॑ शुक्रय॒जूꣳष्य् अ॑भवन् । शुक्रि॑याणां॒ वा ए॒तानि॒ शुक्रि॑याणि । सा॒म॒प॒य॒सं वा ए॒तयो॑र् अ॒न्यत् । दे॒वाना॑म् अ॒न्यत् पय॑ः । यद् गोः पय॑ः ॥१॥ तत् साम्नः॒ पय॑ः । यद् अ॒जायै॒ पय॑ः । तद् दे॒वाना॒ं पय॑ः । तस्मा॒द् यत्रै॒तैर् यजु॑र्भि॒श् चर॑न्ति । तत् पय॑सा चरन्ति । प्र॒जाप॑तिम् ए॒व तद् दे॒वान् पय॑सान्ना॒द्ये॑न॒ सम् अ॑र्धयन्ति । ए॒ष ह॒ त्वै[150] सा॒क्षात् प्र॑व॒र्ग्यं भक्षयति । यस्यै॒वं वि॒दुष॑ः प्रव॒र्ग्य॑ः प्रवृ॒ज्यते॑ ।

उ॒त्त॒र॒वे॒द्याम् उद् वा॑सये॒त् तेज॑स्कामस्य । तेजो॒ वा उ॑त्तरवे॒दिः ॥२॥ तेज॑ः

(1) The gods milked something bright (*śukrá*) as milk from Prajāpati.[151] It did not suffice for them (in its undeveloped state). Agni differentiated it.[152] The Śukriya[153] sāmans came into being. Their essence that overflowed became these Śukra-yajus-formulas. Indeed, from the Śukriya (sāmans) are these Śukriya (yajus-formulas). One of these two is actually the sāman-milk. The other milk belongs to the gods. The cow's milk (2) is the milk of the sāman. The goat's milk is the milk of the gods.[154] Therefore, when they act with these yajus-formulas, then they act with milk. Thus they bring Prajāpati and the gods to fulfilment with milk, with food. And, certainly, he actually partakes of (the fruit of) the Pravargya, for whom knowing thus the Pravargya is performed.

(Optional places for the disposal of the Pravargya implements:) Let him dispose on the Uttaravedi for a (sacrificer) who desires brilliant energy. The Uttaravedi is actually brilliant energy. (3) The Pravargya is

प्रवर्ग्यः । तेजसैव तेजः सम् अर्धयति । उत्तरवेद्याम् उद् वासयेद् अन्नकामस्य । शिरो वा एतद् यज्ञस्य । यत् प्रवर्ग्यः । मुखम् उत्तरवेदिः । शीर्ष्णैव मुखꣳ सं दधात्य्, अन्नाद्याय । अन्नाद एव भवति ।

यत्र खलु वा एतम् उद्वासितं वयाꣳसि पर्यासते । परि वै ताꣳ समां प्रजा वयाꣳस्य् आसते ॥३॥ तस्माद् उत्तरवेद्याम् एवोद् वासयेत् । प्रजानां गोपीथाय ।

पुरो वा पश्चाद् वोद् वासयेत् । पुरस्ताद् वा एतज् ज्योतिर् उद् एति । तत् पश्चान् नि म्रोचति । स्वाम् एवैनं योनिम् अनूद् वासयति ।

अपां मध्य उद् वासयेत् । अपां वा एतन् मध्याज् ज्योतिर् अजायत । ज्योतिः प्रवर्ग्यः । स्व एवैनं योनौ प्रति ष्ठापयति ॥४॥

यं द्विष्यात् । यत्र स स्यात् । तस्यां दिश्य् उद् वासयेत् । एष वा अग्निर् वैश्वानरः । यत् प्रवर्ग्यः । अग्निनैवैनं वैश्वानरेणाभि प्र वर्तयति ।

brilliant energy. With brilliant energy he brings brilliant energy to fulfilment. Let him dispose on the Uttaravedi for a (sacrificer) who desires food. That Pravargya is actually the head of the sacrifice. The Uttaravedi is the mouth. He puts the mouth together with the head for food. He becomes an eater of food.

Certainly, when birds sit around his Pravargya laying disposed,[155] in that (same) year birds sit around his children. (4) Therefore, he should dispose on the Uttaravedi, to protect his children.

Let him dispose either in front or at the rear (of the Uttaravedi). In the east, indeed, that Light rises. This goes down in the west. He disposes of it along its own source.

Let him dispose in the midst of waters. From the midst of the waters, indeed, that Light was born. The Pravargya is the Light. He fixes it firmly in its own source. (5)

Where he is whom he hates, let him dispose in that direction. That Pravargya is actually AgniVaiśvānara. Agni Vaiśvānara he throws at him.

औदुंम्बर्यां॑ शाखांयाम् उद् वांसयेत् । ऊर्ग् वा उंदुम्बरंः । अन्नं प्राणः । शुग् घर्मः ॥५॥ "इदम् अहम् अमुष्यांमुष्यायणस्यं शुचा प्राणम् अपिं दहामी"त्य् आंह । शुचैवास्यं प्राणम् अपिं दहति । ताजग् आर्तिम् आर्च्छति ।

यत्रं दर्भा उंपदीकंसन्तताः स्युः । तद् उद् वांसयेद् वृष्टिंकामस्य । एता वा अपाम् अंनूज्झावंर्यो नामं । यद् दर्भाः । असौ खलु वा आंदित्य इतो वृष्टिम् उद् ईरयति । असाव् एवास्मां आदित्यो वृष्टिं नि यंच्छति । ता आपो नियंता धन्वंना यन्ति ॥६॥

Let him dispose on a branch of the Udumbara-tree. The Udumbara is actually food. Prāṇa is food. The Gharma is scorching heat. (6) *"Here I singe the prāṇa of so-and-so, descendant of so-and-so with scorching heat,"* he says. He singes his prāṇa with scorching heat. Quickly (that enemy) falls in mischief.

Where the Darbha-grass is covered all over with white ants,[156] there he should dispose of the Pravargya for one who is desirous of rain. This Darbha-grass is actually "Discharger of the Waters"[157] by name. Yonder Āditya (the sun) actually makes the rain rise from this (earth). For him (the sacrificer) yonder Āditya (the sun) discharges the rain. These discharged waters come (together) with the dry soil.

Anuvāka 11

The different names of the Pravargya Ritual

In this anuvāka we find different names of the Pravargya, in order to praise it according to one commentator (S), for the sake of the performance of expiations (*prāyaścittārtha*) according to the other (B). The text of this anuvāka gives no indication that the different names, given to the Pravargya in the successive stages of the performance, were closely connected with expiation rites like e.g. those of ŚB 12, 6, 1 (discussed by J. Gonda in *Soma's Metamorphoses (The Identifications in the Oblatory Rites of Śatapatha-Brāhmaṇa 12, 6, 1)*, Amsterdam-Oxford-New York, 1983). It seems better to compare the identifications here with the names of the Agnihotra in its subsequent stages. There is a clear parallelism between the second series of identifications and those of the Agnihotra (see note 157 below).

प्रजापंतिः संभ्रियमांणः । संराट् संभृंतः । घर्मः प्रवृंक्तः । महावीर उद्वांसितः । असौ खलु वावैष आंदित्यः । यत् प्रंवर्ग्यः । स एतानि नामांन्य् अकुरुत । य एवं वेदं । विदुर् एंनं नाम्नां ।

ब्रह्मवादिनों वदन्ति ॥१॥ "यो वै वसींयाꣳसं यथानामम् उंपचरंति । पुण्यांर्तिं वै स तस्मैं कामयते । पुण्यांर्तिम् अस्मै कामयन्ते । य एवं वेदं" । तस्मांद् एवं विद्वान् । "घर्म" इति दिवा चंक्षीत । "संराड्" इति नक्तंम् । एते वा एतस्यं प्रिये तनुवौं । एते

(1) Prajāpati (is its name)[158] when it is being collected. Samrāṭ when collected. Gharma when placed on the fire. Mahāvīra when laying disposed.[159] This Pravargya is actually yonder Āditya (the sun). He made these names for himself. He who knows thus, him they know by (his good) name.

The expounders of the Veda say: (2) "He who pays reverence to a superior person with a suitable name, he certainly wishes him obtainment[160] of merit. People wish obtainment of merit to him who knows thus." Therefore, let him who knows thus call (the Pravargya) "Gharma" by day, "Samrāṭ" by night. These two are actually the beloved forms of this (Pravargya). These two are his beloved names. With his

अंस्य प्रिये नामंनी । प्रिययैवैनँ तनुवां ॥२॥ प्रियेण नाम्ना सम अंर्धयति । कीर्तिर् अंस्य पूर्वा गंच्छति जनतांम् आयतः ।

गायत्री देवेभ्योऽपांक्रामत् । तां देवाः प्रंवर्ग्येणैवानु व्य् अंभवन् । प्रवर्ग्येणाप्नुवन् । यच् चतुंर्विंश्शतिःकृत्वंः प्रवर्ग्यं प्रवृणक्तिं । गायत्रीम् एव तद् अनु वि भंवति । गायत्रीम् आंप्नोति । पूर्वास्य जनँ यतः कीर्तिर् गंच्छति ।

वैश्वदेवः सःसंन्नः ॥३॥ वसंवः प्रवृंक्तः । सोमोंऽभिकीर्यमांणः । आश्विनः पयंस्य् आनीयमांने । मारुतः क्वथंन् । पौष्ण उदंन्तः । सारस्वतो विष्यन्दंमानः । मैत्रः शरोंगृहीतः । तेज उद्यंतो वायुः । ह्रियमांणः प्रजापंतिः । हूयमांनो वाग् घुतः ॥४॥ असौ खलु वावैष आंदित्यः । यत् प्रंवर्ग्यः । स एतानि नामांन्य् अकुरुत । य एवं वेदं । विदुर् एंनं नाम्नां ।

ब्रह्मवादिनों वदन्ति । "यन् मृन्मयम् आहुंतिं नाश्नुतेऽथं । कस्मांद् एषोंऽश्नुत"

beloved form, (3) with his beloved name he brings him to fulfilment. Fame precedes him when he comes to people.[161]

The Gāyatrī went away from the gods. The gods followed her with the Pravargya. They reached her with the Pravargya. When he performs the Pravargya twenty-four times, then he follows the Gāyatrī, he reaches the Gāyatrī; fame precedes him when he goes to people.

Vaiśvadeva (is its name) when it is seated (on the throne). (4) Vasus when placed on the fire (on the *pravṛñjanīya*-mound). Soma when being poured over (with ghee).[162] Āśvina when the milk is poured in. Māruta when boiling.[163] Pauṣṇa when reaching to the rim of the vessel. Sārasvata when flowing over. Maitra when a film is formed (on the boiled milk). Brilliant energy when held out. Vāyu when being brought (to the Āhavanīya). Prajāpati when being offered as an oblation. Speech when offered. (5) Indeed, the Pravargya is yonder Āditya (the sun). He made these names for himself. He who knows thus, him they know by name.

The expounders of the Veda say: "If an earthenware vessel does not obtain the oblation, for what reason then does this (Pravargya vessel)

इतिं । "वाग् एष" इतिं ब्रूयात् । वाच्य् एंव वाचं दधाति ॥५॥ तस्मांद् अश्नुते ।

प्रजापंतिर् वा एष द्वांदशधा विहितः । यत् प्रंवर्ग्यः । यत् प्राग् अंवकाशेभ्यंः । तेनं प्रजा अंसृजत । अवकाशैर् देंवासुरान् अंसृजत । यद् ऊर्ध्वम् अंवकाशेभ्यंः । तेनान्नंम् असृजत । अन्नं प्रजापंतिः । प्रजापंतिर् वावैषः ॥६॥

obtain it?"[164] Let him answer: "This one is Speech." In Speech he puts Speech. (6) Therefore, (the Pravargya vessel) obtains (the oblation).

This Pravargya is actually Prajāpati divided twelve-fold.[165] With what is prior to the Avakāśa mantras,[166] with that he created the creatures. With the Avakāśa mantras he created gods and Asuras. With what is after the Avakāśa mantras he created food. Prajāpati is food. This (Pravargya) is indeed Prajāpati.

Anuvāka 12

Metamorphoses of the Pravargya

In this final anuvāka we have a series of identifications of the Pravargya performance during twelve successive days. The number twelve symbolizes the twelve-fold Year, often homologized with the sun. The last paragraph connects the Pravargya once more with the sun or Agni in the form of the sun.

सविता भूत्वा प्रंथमेऽह्न् प्र वृंज्यते । तेन कामांः एति । यद् द्वितीयेऽह्न्
प्रवृज्यतें । अग्निर् भूत्वा देंवान् एंति । यत् तृतीयेऽह्न् प्रवृज्यतें । वायुर् भूत्वा प्राणान्
एंति । यच् चंतुर्थेऽह्न् प्रवृज्यतें । आदित्यो भूत्वा रश्मीन् एंति । यत् पंञ्चमेऽह्न्
प्रवृज्यतें । चन्द्रमां भूत्वा नक्षंत्राण्य् एति ॥१॥ यत् षष्ठेऽह्न् प्रवृज्यतें । ऋतुर् भूत्वा
संवत्सरम् एंति । यत् संप्तमेऽह्न् प्रवृज्यतें । धाता भूत्वा शक्वंरीम् एति । यद्
अंष्टमेऽह्न् प्रवृज्यतें । बृहस्पतिर् भूत्वा गांयत्रीम् एंति । यन् नंवमेऽह्न् प्रवृज्यतें ।

(1) Having become Savitṛ, it is placed on the fire on the first day. Therewith, it reaches the desires (of the sacrificer).

When it is placed on the fire on the second day, having become Agni it reaches the gods.

When it is placed on the fire on the third day, having become Vāyu it reaches the breaths.

When it is placed on the fire on the fourth day, having become Āditya it reaches the rays.

When it is placed on the fire on the fifth day, having become the Moon, it reaches the stars.[167]

(2) When it is placed on the fire on the sixth day, having become the Season it reaches the year.

When it is placed on the fire on the seventh day, having become Dhātṛ it reaches the śakvarī-metre.

When it is placed on the fire on the eighth day, having become Bṛhaspati it reaches the gāyatrī-metre.

When it is placed on the fire on the ninth day, having become Mitra, it reaches these threefold worlds.

मित्रो भूत्वा त्रिवृतं इमान् लोकान् एंति । यद् दंशमेऽहंन् प्रवृज्यतें । वरुंणो भूत्वा
विराजंम् एति ॥२॥ यद् एंकादशेऽहंन् प्रवृज्यतें । इन्द्रों भूत्वा त्रिष्टुभंम् एति । यद्
द्वांदशेऽहंन् प्रवृज्यतें । सोमों भूत्वा सुत्याम् एंति ।

यत् पुरस्तांद् उपसदां प्रवृज्यतें । तस्मांद् इतः परांङ् अमून् लोकाꣳस् तपंन्न्
एति । यद् उपरिष्टाद् उपसदां प्रवृज्यतें । तस्मांद् अमुतोऽर्वाङ् इमान् लोकाꣳस्
तपंन्न् एति । य एवं वेदं । ऐव तंपति ॥३॥

"शं नस् तन् नो मा हांसीत् ।"
ॐ शान्तिः शान्तिः शान्तिः ।
हरिः ॐ ।

When it is placed on the fire on the tenth day, having become Varuṇa it reaches the virāj-metre.

(3) When it is placed on the fire on the eleventh day, having become Indra it reaches the triṣṭubh-metre.

When it is placed on the fire on the twelfth day, having become Soma it reaches the soma-pressing.[168]

Inasmuch as it is placed on the fire before the Upasads, therefore (the Pravargya/sun) goes from here directed thither, shining upon yonder worlds. Inasmuch as it is placed on the fire after the Upasads,[169] therefore (the Pravargya/sun) goes from there directed hither, shining upon these worlds. He who knows thus, he really radiates heat.[170]

"Good fortune to us . . . may it leave us not!"
Om peace, peace, peace.
Hari Om!

NOTES TO THE TEXT AND TRANSLATION

Anuvāka 1

1 *"Good fortune to us . . . may it leave us not!"* refers to the lengthy posterior śānti recitation (TĀ 4, 41; transl. van Buitenen, *Pravargya*:120-123). It is recited each day after the study of the Pravargya mantras during the Avāntaradīkṣā. The beginning of the study is marked with the recitation of the prior śānti (TĀ 4, 1; transl. van Buitenen, *Pravargya*:63-64). The two śāntis, the prior and the posterior, are also recited at the beginning and end of each performance (according to BŚS, VaikhŚS, KŚS also at the beginning and end of the collection of the materials).

2 The word *ṛ́ddhiparimitam* is explained by S on this place as *sādhanadravya-samṛddhyā parito nirmitam prauḍham*, modifying *sátram*. But his explanation in a similar phrase in TB 2, 2, 8, 4 implies a very improbable connection with *yaśas* in *yáśaskāmāḥ*: *dhānādisamṛddhyā yuktaṃ yaśaḥ kāmayamānāḥ*. My rendering of the term corresponds to B's *kālaṃ yāvat phalasiddhir bhavati tāvantaṃ kālam*. This is a very reasonable interpretation which fits TB 2, 2, 8, 4 as well.

3 Introduction, note 69.

4 *ny àkāmayata*, "desired . . . for himself." This place confirms Caland's remark that this word means "wollte . . . für sich allein behalten" (Caland, *'Wunschopfer'*, Amsterdam 1908:25, note 90).

5 (a) In the ŚB version it is Viṣṇu (and not Makha Vaiṣṇava) who simply takes his bow and three arrows. We may translate *makhó víṣṇur* in ŚB 14, 1 ,1, 1 with "Viṣṇu, the Sacrifice," instead of suggesting the presence of two different gods as in Eggeling's translation "Makha, Viṣṇu." *makhó víṣṇur* corresponds to Makha Vaiṣṇava in the TĀ-version. ŚB 14, 1, 1, 13 has that "Makha (the Sacrifice), indeed, is the same as Viṣṇu."

(b) Read *yajñájanma* instead of *yajñájanmā*? All editions have the latter form without variant readings, but *iṣudhanváṃ* (*púṇyajanma*) is neuter sg.

6 *upadī́ka* here and in TB and ŚB 14, 1, 1, 8, is a certain species of ants that is supposed to find water even in the desert. Zysk, *Religious Healing*, interprets *upajī́ka* in AV 2, 3, 4 and 6 ,100, 2 as termites or white ants that take up water, and the two words, *upadī́ka* and *upajī́ka*, probably refer to the same species of ants. Their connection with a bow may be taken as a *jeu de mots*: *dhánvan* means "bow" and "desert, dry place"; cf. AV 6, 100, 2ab: *yád vo devā́ upajī́kā́ ā́siñcan dhánvany udakám*. For the *upadī́ka/upajī́ka* see also Krick, *Feuergründung*:143, note 372. In the Kaṭha version it is Indra who in the form of the ants eats through the bowstring (KaṭhĀ 3, 207+).

7 The loss of life-energy (*vīryà*) is connected with the loss of the head. So, with the head, the life-energy flew off. Rather than: "Virile energy (or seed *vīryam*) fell from the mighty one (*mahat*)" (Muir, quoted in the inroduction of TĀ edition C, p. 27). S and Bh, commenting upon TĀ 5, 3, 4, explain that *vīryà* resides, in the context of that passage, in

the face (*múkha*): S: "in the body of a man, the *vīryà*, the ability to see, hear etc., . . . is found in the face." Bh: "the *vīryà* corresponds to the face."

8 *gráha*, "ladleful" is a technical term of the Soma sacrifice. It occurs in its proper context in the similar TS passage 6, 4, 9. It is not adapted to the new context of the Pravargya, in which no real "ladlefuls" are offered from the Gharma milk, either because the word was taken in the secondary meaning of "libation" (Renou, *Vocabulaire du Rituel Védique* (Paris 1954): 62f), or in order to create an additional connection with the Soma sacrifice, the high status of which was well established.

Anuvāka 2

9 (a) The oblation is offered by the Adhvaryu with the verse TĀ 4, 2, 1(1) on the Āhavanīya fire. The verse = TS 1, 2, 13*a* (where it forms part of the recitation at the *havirdhāna-maṇḍapa-karaṇa*, Caland-Henry, Agniṣṭoma:80-81 and comes *after* the Pravargya in case the Agniṣṭoma comprises this rite) = TS 4, 1, 1*d* (where it forms part of the recitation at the *ukhā-saṃbharaṇa* of the Agnicayana, a rite parallel in several respects to the *pravargya-saṃbharaṇa*) = ŚvetU 2, 4 = ṚV 5, 81, 1.

yuñjáte mána utá yuñjáte dhíyaḥ / víprā víprasya bṛható vípaścítaḥ / ví hótrā dadhe vayunāvíd éka ít / mahī́ devásya savitúḥ páriṣṭutiḥ,

"They yoke their minds, and yoke the visions, the inspired (priests yoke the visions) of the mighty inspired (Savitṛ). He alone, who knows the implications, establishes the sacrificial acts; great is the praise of the god Savitṛ."

For discussions and translations of the verse see especially Gonda, *Vision*:115f; and Renou, *ÉVP* 15 (1966): 24. The Kaṭhas, who have the verse too, comment at this place: "With mind verily Prajāpati performed the sacrifice, then with speech and then with action. With mind the sacrificer performs the sacrifice, then with speech, then with action."

(b) This interesting verse and its place at the beginning of this and some other rites clearly indicate the importance of bringing the mind in the right condition before or at the beginning of the performance (Cf. Gonda, *Vision*:36-40.) The verb *yuj-*, "yoke," is in its concrete sense used in connection with horses or other animals yoked to a vehicle. Here, the implication seems to be that with mind and visions or hymns (*dhíyaḥ*) as horses, the chariot of the sacrifice should traverse some space. This space is according to B. Oguibenine the space between "phénomènes de divers ordres" ("phenomena of different orders") between which connections and identifications should be established. The connections and identifications should be established "entre le microcosme et le macrocosme, entre le monde rituel et le monde mythique, entre l'ordre humain et divin." ("between the microcosm and the macrocosm, between the ritual world and the mythical world, between the human order and the divine order"; B. Oguibenine, "Sur le terme *yóga*, le verbe *yuj-* et quelques-uns de leurs dérivés dans les hymnes védiques," *IIJ* 27/2: especially p.86,87).

10 This section is also in TS 5, 1, 1. S connects the puronuvākya with the gāyatrī, the yājyā with the triṣṭubh, the devatā with the jagatī and the vaṣatkāra with the anuṣṭubh. We often find that the anuṣṭubh-metre represents a fourth, concluding element after the triad gāyatrī, triṣṭubh, jagatī. Therefore, the connection of the anuṣṭubh with the vaṣaṭkāra, the concluding part of the formulas that accompany a *juhoti*-oblation, is understandable. The place of the devatā in the triad corresponding to gāyatrī, triṣṭubh and jagatī, however, is somewhat peculiar. For, the name of the devatā, the deity to whom the oblation and the accompanying verses are directed, is uttered *before* the puronuvākya (by the Adhvaryu) and *before* the yājyā by the Hotṛ in the words *ye3 yajāmahe* (plus the name of the devatā in the accusative). It is not a separate formula that is uttered like the other three. See Caland, '*Wunschopfer*':XIII-XIV and Hillebrandt, *Ritualliteratur*:99.

11 *hotavyàṃ dīkṣitásya gṛhā́3í, ná hotavyā́3m íti*. This phrase occurs, in a different context, in TS 6, 1, 4, 5 (referring to TS 1, 2, 3*b*, whispered by the sacrificer before drinking the *vrata*-milk). The *dīkṣitá* cannot mean the one who has undergone the Dīkṣā of the normal Agniṣṭoma: the collection of the materials for the Pravargya that starts with the Savitṛ-oblation and that is discussed here, takes place at the *adhyavasānam* (Caland-Henry, *Agniṣṭoma*:§12), i.e. before the Dīkṣaṇīyeṣṭi etc. (*Agniṣṭoma*:§15ff). According to S, there are some ritualists who place the *pravargya-saṃbharaṇa* not before the Dīkṣaṇīyeṣṭi, but after the completion of the Dīkṣā. The Śrauta Sūtras mention this possibility for someone who undergoes the Dīkṣā at another place than the place of sacrifice (cf. Caland, note 1 and 2 on ĀpŚS 15, 1, 2). So our passage may refer to this probably exceptional situation.

However, there is another possibility. The word *dīkṣitá* may refer to a sacrificer who has undergone the Avāntaradīkṣā of the Pravargya and in that case the Avāntaradīkṣā is not obligatory because the sacrificer who is *dīkṣitá* at this point is mentioned as a special case. We have *dīkṣitá* referring to someone who has undergone the Avāntaradīkṣā also in KaṭhĀ 198+. This was already suggested by van Buitenen (*Pravargya*:55, note 2), who referred to BŚS 9, 1. This contains the following passage: "If the prior *śānti* has not been (already) gone through, it should be gone through at this juncture. Then the Adhvaryu should melt clarified butter over the Gārhapatya fire, purify it, take four spoonfuls of it into the ladle, and, while the sacrificer remains touching him, offer on the Āhavanīya fire an oblation to Savitṛ with '*they yoke their mind and they yoke the visions* etc.'. In the case of a sacrificer who has not been initiated, the Adhvaryu should offer an oblation with the above-mentioned verse; in the case of a sacrificer who has been initiated, he should (only) murmur that verse" (translation Dandekar, *Śrautakośa* II, Engl.part1:28-29, my translation of the *pratīka*; van Buitenen translates *anvārabdhe yajamāne* erroneously with "in case the yajamāna is only latterly initiated"). Now the *śānti* can only refer to the śānti recitation of the Pravargya. It is prescribed both in the Pravargya proper (in ĀpŚS at a later stage: ĀpŚS 15, 5, 4), and in the Avāntaradīkṣā$_p$ (BŚS 9, 19; ĀpŚS 15, 20, 2). If it has been already gone through here, at the very beginning of the Pravargya proper, before the collection of the materials, it has most probably made part of a form of the Pravargya Avāntaradīkṣā, preceding the performance and to be undergone by the sacrificer (see Introduction section 3.3 and note 130 below). But this form of the Pravargya Avāntaradīkṣā is not explicitly discussed in the Śrauta Sūtras. By the time the Pravargya was completely incorporated in the Agniṣṭoma, the Avāntaradīkṣā for the sacrificer became redundant and was eventually dropped. But there are still some reminiscences of it in this book of the Āraṇyaka.

12 *havír vaí dīkṣitáḥ*:, "the oblation is actually the initiate": nominal sentence, as in *yajñó vaí makháḥ* "Makha is actually the Sacrifice" and, in a typical anaphoric construction, *śíro vā́ etád yajñásya, yát pravargyàḥ*, lit.: "That is actually the head of the Sacrifice: the Pravargya." Many complete identifications (A=B) may actually be short expressions for: there exists a special relation (*bándhu*) between A and B (note 142 below). These identifications and connections, which may often strike us as strange and bizarre, are perhaps better appreciated when we assume that the Vedic sacrifice is a complex consisting of actions, words and thoughts, that express and explain an original experience of unity or interconnection between different spheres of existence (Cf. B. Oguibenine in IIJ 27/2:92).

13 "He should say only the yajus-formula." See Caland note 2 on ĀpŚS 15, 1, 2. Here, in the Āraṇyaka, two possibilities for a sacrificer who has already been initiated (see note 11 above), are given consideration: a) the Adhvaryu-priest performs the complete oblation (according to the Śrauta Sūtras consisting in the putting on the fire of a thorny fire-stick, followed by the four-fold butter oblation with the verse *"they yoke their mind . . .* "); b) the verse is recited without butter oblation, and probably also without putting the fire-stick on the fire. In ĀpŚS, the two possibilities that are mentioned for a sacrificer who has already been initiated, are somewhat different: a) the recitation of the verse accompanies the putting on the fire of the thorny fire-stick only; b) the recitation of the verse takes place without butter oblation and without putting the fire-stick on the fire.

14 In TS 2, 6, 2, 5, the *váṣaṭ*-call is a *vájra* (see note 16 below) that can be hurled at the foe. See also Krick, *Feuergründung*:555, note 1504.

15 This passage corresponds to TS 6, 2, 10, 1.

16 The comparison of the shovel with a *vájra* supports Rau's conclusions about the shape of a *vájra* in Vedic texts. It must have been a kind of harpoon. See Rau, *Metallgeräte*:37-46.

17 Appeasement may have been thought necessary simply because "the shovel is like a *vájra*." The author of the Āraṇyaka has probably interpreted *nā́ri* like S: "you are *na ari*, not an enemy." Otherwise there would have been no basis for him to state that the mantra produced "appeasement." *ábhri* may have been derived from the rare root *bhṝ*, "to injure," thus: "not injuring."

18 This half-verse is used by the Adhvaryu to invite the Brahmán priest to rise and to go to the clay-pit (east of the Āhavanīya). The other half of this verse (TĀ 4, 2, 1/2(4), identical with ṚV 1, 40, 1) is uttered by the Brahmán and Adhvaryu priest together, after the Brahmán priest has risen: *úpa prá yantu marútaḥ sudā́navaḥ I índra prāśū́r bhavā sácā, "Let the very liberal Maruts come here. Indra, be quickly at hand."* There is another use of this verse, according to which the Adhvaryu is addressed. See Gonda "Pravargya Mantras":259. This implies a less complete correspondence between mantra and activity.

19 The word *sūnṛ́tā* is often found in hymns to the Dawn, see Renou *ÉVP* 3:17 and 4:58. Renou arrives, on the basis of contextual reasons, at the translation "libéralité" ("generosity"), contrasting with etymologically reconstructed meanings like "virtue, quality of a great-hearted man." Here we should probably understand *sūnṛ́tā*, sc. *vā́k* ("speech"). For, not only the commentators have: *yajñātmikā satyā vāk* (Bh) and *yajña-sambandhinī mantragatapriyavākyarūpā devī* (S). But we also have the Kaṭha explanation *vā́g vaí devī́ sūnṛ́tā* (KaṭhĀ 2,6). The unselfish liberality of *vāg devī* is elsewhere often expressed by characterizing her as a milch cow (see Gonda, *Pūṣan and Sarasvatī* (Amsterdam-Oxford-New York, 1985): 44). This by no means contradicts the TĀ expression *yajñó vaí sūnṛ́tā*, because we find the close relation between sacrificial worship (*yájña*) and speech (*vā́k*) more than once expressed in the form of a complete identification (Gonda, *Pūṣan and Sarasvatī*:35-36, §23). Cf. in later Sanskrit *sūnṛtā vāk* as described in a verse of the poet Bhavabhūti. After having stated that *rākṣasī vāk*, bad speech of the arrogant and conceited, is the source of all enmity and the doom of the world, he continues: "The wise call truthful and agreeable speech [*sūnṛtā vāk*] a cow, the mother of all blessings; a cow that grants desires, removes misery, begets fame and destroys sin" (Bhavabhūti, *Uttararāmacarita*, Act V, verse 31; tr. M. R. Kane 1924, reprint Delhi-Varanasi-Patna 1982).

20 The hero (*vīrá*) is in the context of this rite the Mighty Hero (*mahāvīrá*), i.e. the vessel or the sun. S and Bh take *ácchā vīrám̐ náryam paṅktírādhasam* with *devā́ yajñám nayantu naḥ* in d. But Geldner, translating the identical ṚV 1, 40, 3 and following Uv. on VS 33, 89, takes it with b, *prá devy ètu sūnṛ́tā*.

21 With *"For Makha you,"* he carries away the clay that has been dug out and with *"For the head of Makha you"* he throws it down on the black antelope skin (*Śrautakośa* vol.II, Engl.part 1:29ff).

22 Here, the fourth shovelful corresponds to the unbounded (encompassing and going beyond the three worlds: earth, firmament and heaven) and to silence.

23 This is again followed by *"Today may I realize the head of the Sacrifice; for Makha you, for the head of Makha you."* The mantra, referring to the myth of the earth being taken up from the primeval waters by the boar, is used with the taking of earth, dug up by a boar, one of the prescribed ingredients. Cf. Krick, *Feuergründung*:145-155.

24 The material from the ant-hill is taken with: *dévīr vámrīr ásya bhūtásya prathamajā́ ṛtā́varīḥ, "Divine ants, first-born of creation, following the cosmic law"* and again

"Today, may I ...." (The Kaṭhas have *vamriyo* instead of *vámrīr*). In the ant-hill, subterranean materials (the essence of the earth) are built into a stronghold, together with pieces of wood etc. and the saliva of the ants. It stands for nutritious material. Because of its direct connection with subterrestrian regions it is the "ear of the earth." Cf. Krick, *Feuergründung*:139-144; for the "ear of the earth" note 368 on p.368.

25 (a) The *sambhārá* of the *pūtī́ka*-plants is accompanied by: *índrasyáujo'si*, *"You are Indra's power"* and *"Today, may I . . . "* (TĀ 4, 2, 4(13)). C omits the first part of the mantra; the deficient number of phrases in the daśati shows that the part, which is present in the other two editions, should be there. The Pūtīka plants appear to be grass or herbs that grow in clumps or tussocks that have some firmness. They are different from those plants referred to by the same name in later Sanskrit: Zysk, *Religious Healing*:260; Meulenbeld, *Mādhavanidana*:537. In the KaṭhĀ 2, 11+ they are a kind of *óṣadhi*, i.e. a herb or herb-like plant. "When Indra slew Vṛtra, his manly energy left him. It entered the herbs (*óṣadhīḥ*). They became the Pūtīkas. (The mantra for the Pūtīkas is therefore:) *"You are Indra's power."* If he collects the Pūtīkas as ingredients, he collects Indra's power as ingredient."

(b) The Pūtīka is here one of the ingredients of the clay for the Pravargya vessel. But elsewhere it is also considered to be a substitute for the Soma plant itself (see Introduction, note 35). In "The Mahāvīravessel and the plant Pūtika (sic)" (*JAOS* 95/2 (1975): 222-235), S. Kramrisch sought to defend the hypothesis that the Pūtīka was a mushroom, the consumption of which would bring about some psychotropic effects. This Pūtīka/Ūtīka passage of the TĀ and the passage of the KaṭhĀ translated in part (a) of this note, however, if they are looked at more carefully, clearly indicate that the Pūtīka was anything but a mushroom. Bh on TĀ 4, 2, 4 (edition M: 7, 2, 5(14a)) calls the Pūtīka "dark Durva-grass" (*śyāmā dūrvāḥ pūtīkāḥ*). Ḍārila on KauśS 22, 15 calls them *tṛṇāni prasiddhāni*, "the well-known kind of grass or herb." Cf. F. B. J. Kuiper, "Was the Pūtīka a mushroom?" in *Amṛtadhārā*:219-227. The most important cornerstone in Kramrisch's argument is the identification of the Sanskrit Pūtīka with the Santal Putka, which Kuiper shows to be unjustified on linguistic grounds (op. cit., pp. 222-225). In cases like the identification of the Vedic Pūtīka plant or the Soma plant, it seems more advisable to admit how little we know, than to build far-flying theories on the basis of hypotheses that can neither be proved nor disproved. A well-balanced approach is exemplified in R. P. Das' "On the identification of a Vedic plant" in: *Studies on Indian Medical History* (ed. by G. J. Meulenbeld and D. Wujastyk, E. Forsten, Groningen 1987): 19-42. In this article the author discusses the case of Pāṭā, another plant (again most probably not a mushroom) mentioned as substitute for the Soma plant. Useful bibliographical references to the Soma controversy can be found in a recent article by Harry Falk, in which he rejects the Soma-mushroom theory and argues (not entirely convincingly) that the Soma plant was Ephedra (Harry Falk, "Soma I and II," *Bulletin of the School of Oriental and African Studies*, Univ. of London, Vol. 52, part 1 (1989): 77-90).

26 This mantra of the fifth and last requisite is again followed by *"Today, may I . . . "*. Bh has here goat's milk as the fifth ingredient, but at TĀ 4, 2, 4(15) he mentions the mixture of the hair of a she-goat and the hair on the skin of a black antelope. S and most of the Śrauta Sūtras have this mixture of the two kinds of hair added with this mantra. Only BŚS prescribes that goat's milk should be made to trickle over the clay with this mantra, while the two kinds of hair are added (in accordance with TĀ) a little later, when the ingredients have been carried to the specially prepared and fenced in mound. See also van Buitenen, *Pravargya*:57, §15 with notes. Baudhāyana, who has given us the oldest Taittirīya Śrauta Sūtra, follows the TĀ again most closely. Also KaṭhĀ and ŚB refer to goat's milk at the corresponding places. Rau, however, interpreted this passage only in the light of the later Śrauta Sūtras (*Töpferei*:60, note 1 and 2).

27 They take the ingredients to an enclosed plot, north of the fires, in the Prācīnavaṃśa. Rau (*Töpferei*:60) inaccurately in sing.: "Eine Sühnung eben vollzieht er dabei" ("He makes a recompense at it"). Moreover, *ápaciti* had been better derived from a different root *ci*-: what is meant is that by taking it up by many people, they pay reverence to it. So also S.

28 The Kaṭhas have *mádhunā* instead of *madhulā́*: *"mádhu tvā mádhunā karotv"íty apá úpa sṛjati | mádhu vā́ etán mádhunā sáṃ yauti | madhavyò bhavati* (KaṭhĀ 2, 14). The form *madhulā́*, which is less common in later regular Sanskrit and probably original in the mantra, is also in MS 4, 9, 1; 121, 6. Cf. ṚV 1, 191, 10.

29 *armakapālā́ni*, "potsherds from an *árma*," also in TS 5, 1, 6, 2. KS 19, 5, and KapS 30, 3 have *armyaiḥ kapālaiḥ*. Burrow interpreted *árma* as a term for the ruined cities of the Indus civilization, and thus as a piece of literary evidence in regard to the overthrow of the Indus civilization by the Vedic Aryans (Burrow, "On the significance of the term *árma, ármaka* in early Sanskrit literature" in the *Journal of Indian History*, 1963:159-166). But Rau convincingly shows that *púr* and its synonyms in Vedic literature do not refer to anything like the architecturally complex Mohenjo Daro-Harappa cities (Rau, *The meaning of púr*, and *Zur vedischen Altertumskunde*:36-38). R. Gopal's "lake" for *árma* in this compound ("Refutation of T. Burrow's theory on the significance of *árma* and *ármaka*," *All-India Oriental Conference*, Poona 1978) is improbable and unattractive, because with this interpretation the opposition with *grāmyá*, "belonging to a (to a greater or lesser extent wandering) community" is lost and the whole passage becomes meaningless.

árma therefore means in this context: "deserted village (where a community was temporarily settled)" and *grāmyá*: belonging to a (semi-nomadic) community.

30 *śárkarāḥ*, according to Rau pieces of limestone ("Kalksteinbrökchen" *Töpferei*:60). Krick (*Feuergründung*:162) draws the attention to "das Wesen der Kiesel als 'Festbanner' (das Gute, Eigene herbei; das Böse hinaus)," "the nature of pebbles as 'hold-banisher' (the good, the own nature here, the evil out)."

Anuvāka 3

31 *brahma-varcas-á* has the suffix *-a-* of the "neuter determinative compound which is not-collectival, but which must originally have been intended as collectival, and in which the last member is based on a neuter in *-as, -us*" (tr. from Wackernagel-Debrunner, *Altindische Grammatik*, II (Göttingen 1957), 1:113). Scholars differ considerably in their translation of this frequently occurring word. Keith's "splendour" and Whitney's "vedic splendor" (AV 19, 71) are no doubt too flat. Translations like "the prestige of a priest or of a Brahmin" ("priesterliches Ansehen," Caland, Krick; "Brahmanenansehen," Witzel) stress the social aspect of this notion too much. The context of our rite asks for a translation that expresses some directly visible aspect of one who has *bráhman* or spiritual knowledge (cf. note 89 below), so: "glow or lustre of spiritual knowledge." The lustre of the sun is made concrete, as it were, in the glowing vessel, and should be realized in the participants of the rite as well. That *brahmavarcasá* shines or glows as it were, becomes clear also from JB 2, 130, where it is said that one whose face is besmeared with the remains of the Soma beverage becomes *brahmavarcasí-*. Cf. JUB 3, 13, 1: *bhātī̆va hi brahmavarcasam*, Oertel: "For lustre in sacred lore shines, as it were"; KS 11, 5: *śvetā́yāś śvetávatsāyā ā́jyam bhávati, śuklā́ vrī̆háya: evám iva vaí brahmavarcasám* (sc. *śvetám* and *śuklám*). Compare Weber, *IS* 10 (1868): 105, and the following passage in the well-known story of Satyakāma Jābāla in the Chāndogya-Upaniṣad: *brahmavid iva vai, saumya, bhāsi. ko nu tvānuśāseti.* "You shine, my friend, like a man who knows *bráhman*. Who instructed you?" (ChU 4, 9, 2).

32 *prāṇá* means in the first place "breath," "breathing out," but acquired in plural the meaning of "vital powers" and even "sense functions." Cf. below TĀ 5, 4, 4 and see Bodewitz, *JBtransl*:21, note 2; 47, note 9; and in *ALB* 50 (1986): 326-348.

33 Because the Pravargya vessel is connected with the sun, it will afflict the breath (*prāṇá*) with its *śúc*, which means: "the scorching heat of sun or fire," and secondarily: "suffering." During the Agnyādheya ceremony one should not come between the fire and the sun (ĀpŚS 5, 14, 10-11); Cf. Oldenberg, *Weltanschauung*: 120 "offenbar bewegen sich zwischen der Sonne und dem mit ihr identischen Agni Kräfte, die man stören oder durch die man beschädigt werden würde, käme man ihnen in den Weg." ("apparently, between the sun and Agni, who is identical with the sun, powers are travelling which one would disturb or by which one would be damaged, if one would come in their way.")

34 The yajus-formula is TĀ 4, 2, 5(21): *áditis te bílaṃ gṛhṇātu / pā́ṅktena chándasā*, "*Let Aditi take your bowl with the Paṅkti-metre.*"

35 The distinction to be established by the mantra is the distinction between vessels for daily use, and the vessels for the Pravargya ceremony.

36 "So big he makes it" has, according to S, to be accompanied by a gesture that indicates one *pradeśa* (the span from the tip of the thumb to that of the forefinger). More than once we come across indications like this, that the Vedic texts originally belonged to

an oral tradition. Cf. Bodewitz, *JBtransl*:143, note 9. According to Rau in his translation (*Töpferei*:61), the first gesture indicates a circumference of "eine Spanne" (*prādeśa*), the second "eine Elle" (approximately = yard, 0.91m) and the third "ein Klafter" (approximately = fathom, 1.75m). But S takes the second and third expression with "so big he makes it" as expressions to "praise" the same measure of one *prādeśa*. This seems more acceptable.

37 The passage in the KaṭhĀ (2, 21+) has: "(The vessel) measures one *prādeśa*. For, so big is the mouth (or face: *múkha*). The mouth of the gods is Agni. (The vessel) becomes commensurate with the mouth and gets a bowl from above; this is to satisfy the deities. One is satisfied by progeny and cattle. The Soma beverage falls to the share of him, who knows thus." Here, unlike the parallel TĀ-passage, the text can be understood without accompanying gestures.

38 *parigrīvá* indicates that it has a girdle all around the neck for holding it with the tongs (Kashikar, "Apropos":4). The vessel as it is used nowadays (see van Buitenen, *Pravargya*, picture opp. to p.52; Staal, *Agni* 1:231, plate 28D) has no girdle. It is moreover made on a potter's wheel, which would make it unfit for sacrifice according to the ancient Vedic texts.

39 Both the horse and Agni (who = the sun = the Pravargya vessel) are frequently said to be born from Prajāpati. Cf. TB 1, 1, 8 ,2-3: "Prajāpati created Agni. This one, having become a 'tail-horse' (horse with a remarkable tail), went away from him." (For *áśvo vā́ro* see Krick,*Feuergründung*:411, note 1105.) Krick drew attention to the fact that the well-known etymological connection between the horse (*áśva*) and the eye of Prajāpati that swelled (*aśvayata*) is facilitated by the identifications Horse = Horse of the sun; sun = Eye (*Feuergründung*:392).

40 Edition P has *díśo'nuvíbhāti*. One expects an accent on the last syllable of *díśo* from *ánu*, and this is what the other two editions have.

41 "He puts brilliant energy in it" (also TĀ 5, 2, 13 and 5, 4, 1): *asmin* ("it"/"him") refers to the vessel (in TĀ 5, 2, 13 to the materials for the vessel), but, because of the brahmanical identification, at the same time to the sacrificer.

42 When fire is flaring up, it is sacred to Varuṇa; when it grows less, it is sacred to Mitra (Oldenberg, *Weltanschauung*:112). The verse or verses with which appeasement of the negative aspects of the hot vessels in the fire is to be brought about, are: TĀ 4, 3, 1(3a-c) = TS 4, 1, 6*g*: *abhī́maṃ mahinā́ dívam / mitró babhūva saprátʰāḥ / utá śrávasā pṛthivī́m*, *"Mitra, spreading out, encompassed this heaven with his might, and the earth with his fame."* Instead of this verse, the next one can be used: TĀ 4, 3, 2(3d-f) = TS 4, 1, 6*h* and 3, 4, 11*p*: *mitrásya carṣaṇīdhṛ́taḥ / śrávo devásya sānasí / dyumnáṃ citrá-śravastamam*, *"The victorious fame of god Mitra, the supporter of the people, is the most brilliantly glorious lustre."* (reading, with MS and KS, *sānasí* instead of *sānasím*; see Keith (*TStransl*) on TS 3 ,4 ,11*p*). BŚS, SatyŚS, and MŚS prescribe both verses. For the positive and negative aspects of the asuric god Varuṇa, cf. Gonda, *Religionen*:76.

KaṭhĀ 3, 169+ comments on another verse that contains "Mitra" and that is recited during the disposal of the Pravargya implements (KaṭhĀ 3, 169 = TĀ 4, 11, 6(16)): "If this one in the form of Varuṇa would burn on the offspring, he would not leave anyone whosoever; having become Mitra ('a friend') he burns on the offspring."

43 Rau reads and translates *purā́ś* (Töpferei:59); the three editions (M, C and P) have the unaccented form. P has *punaś*- on p. 444, but on p. 294 twice (correctly) *puraś*.

44 S: "Because the pot is extremely terrible (*atyugra*) on account of its heat, it is fit for the Asuras, but not for the gods. Let him therefore pour (the milk) over it, for the sake of the gods. Therewith, he makes a gentle, cool vessel for the gods." Cf. above, where the vessel in the fire is said to belong to Varuṇa (who is god and Asura). Extreme things belong to the Asuras. For Varuṇa and the Asura's see also Kuiper, "Basic Concept."

45 The milk is poured with the following yajus-formula (see the corresponding Śrauta Sūtra prescriptions for details), of which only the latter part is discussed in the Brāhmaṇa:

gāyatreṇa tvā chándasā́ cchṛṇadmi, traíṣṭubhena tvā chándasā́ cchṛṇadmi, jā́gatena tvā chándasā́ cchṛṇadmi; chṛṇáttu tvā vā́k, chṛṇáttu tvórk, chṛṇáttu tvā havíḥ; chṛndhí vā́cam, chṛndhy ū́rjam, chṛndhí havíḥ,

"With the gāyatrī-metre I pour over you, with the triṣṭubh-metre I pour over you, with the jagatī-metre I pour over you; let Speech pour out on you, let food pour out on you, let the oblation pour out on you; pour out Speech, pour out food, pour out the oblation."

Anuvāka 4

46 TĀ 4, 4, has a more elaborate *praiṣa*: *"O Brahmán, we shall proceed with the Pravargya; o Hotṛ, praise the Gharma; o Agnīdh, put on the Rauhiṇa cakes; o Pratiprasthātṛ, lay out; o Prastotṛ, sing the sāmans."*

47 Since the Petersburger's Wörterbuch it is usual to translate the word *sam-ardhayati*:, if it occurs with an instrumental, with "supply with" (Keith, e.g. TS 1, 5, 1, 4; 6, 1, 9, 7), "unite" ("vereinigen," Caland, ĀpŚS 11, 20, 1). In many or all of these places a translation that does more justice to the etymology of the word would fit equally well in the context. Being the causative or tenth class conjugation of √*ṛdh*- ("grow, increase, prosper, succeed") with the prefix *sam*- "completely," translations like those of Witzel (in similar contexts as those of the above mentioned translations) are to be preferred: KaṭhĀ 3, 151+ "Damit lässt er ihn gedeihen" ("With this he makes him prosper"); 2, 23+ "mit Hilfe der Gestalt (Prajāpatis) lässt er den (Opferherrn) voll-Erfolg erlangen" ("by means of the form (of Prajāpati) he makes the (sacrificer) obtain complete success"). A translation like "to bring to complete realisation, to bring to fulfilment" fits very well in the context of the head of the Sacrifice that should be realized, or a god who receives an oblation or offering. It would also fit e.g. KaṭhĀ 3, 192+ better than Witzel's "lässt zusammenkommen mit" ("makes come together with").

48 According to Caland on ĀpŚS 15, 6, 4, the materials are sprinkled in such a way that when he sprinkles a second time, he starts again where he began, so not to and fro. With regard to the sacrificer, "in due order" means according to S *pitṛputrādikrameṇa*, which suggests that the several utensils of the Pravargya are sprinkled in order of importance: first the main pot, then the two spare ones and the other utensils.

49 The Hotṛ recites the Brahma-jajñānam hymn: ṚVkhila 3, 22, 1-4; (3 of the verses are AV 4, 1, 1; 2; 4cd, 5ab). See Introduction, section 3.1, p 14; and Gonda, "Pravargya Mantras":238 and 247-248. The wordings of this hymn, the first recitation of the Hotṛ, show that it is intimately connected with the Pravargya ceremony. It was probably already connected with the earliest forms of the Pravargya.

50 *ánavānam*, without taking breath, also TĀ 5, 7, 9. Caland, ĀpŚS 15, 10, 8 translates "ohne auszuatmen" ("without breathing out"). Because during speaking always some breath has to go out, it seems better to take it as "without breathing in" (*Śrautakośa* 2, Engl. Sect. 1:198) or "without taking breath." The Ṛgvedic ĀśvŚS explains that each verse should be recited without breathing, that the *praṇava* should be uttered at the end and that then there is a pause for breathing (ĀśvŚS 4, 6, 1).

51 Usually there are five *prāṇá*-s. The Śrauta Sūtras prescribe seven or eleven Prāṇāhutis, or *prāṇá*-oblations with clarified butter (not to be confused with the Prāṇāhutis of the Prāṇāgnihotra, for which see Bodewitz, *JBtransl*:331, note 2). The seven prāṇas of the head (*śīrṣaṇyà*, unlike *múkhya* not or rarely with a figurative sense "principal") are enumerated in TĀ 4, 5, 1(3): (1) *prāṇá*, (2) *vyāná*, (3) *apāná*, (4) *cákṣus*, (5) *śrótra*, (6) *mánas*, (7) *vā́k sárasvatī*. Note that *vyāná* and *mánas* are normally not *śīrṣaṇyà*, belonging to the head. They are respectively placed in the middle of the body (or diffused in the body) and in the heart. For the introduction of vital powers and sense-functions in the series of prāṇas, see Bodewitz, *JBtransl*:220. Four additional *prāṇāhutí*-s can be offered to (8) *dákṣa*, (9) *krátu*, (10) *ójas*, and (11) *bála*. Cf. note 79, 80 and 128.

52 (a) Read with C and P *tejasaivainam* instead of *tejasaivenam* in M.

(b) When the vessel, being held over the Āhavanīya fire, is anointed or filled with ghee (van Buitenen, *Pravargya*:72), the Prastotṛ sings the *śārga* sāman, composed on ṚV 9, 86, 43, that is, on a verse to Soma Pavamāna. In TĀ 5, 11, 4 the Pravargya's name is Soma when it is poured over (sc. with ghee).

53 See above, note 41.

54 This mantra continues with: *śócasva devavītamaḥ | ví dhūmám agne aruṣáṃ miyedhya | sṛjá praśasta darśatám*, "*Be scorchingly hot as the one who is the best inviter of the gods, o Agni, partaker of the sacrifice, send forth your reddish and beautiful smoke, you who are praised.*"

55 This passage seeks to explain why it is here not the Hotṛ who pronounces the prayers of the sacrificer, but the sacrificer himself (see below). The answer seems to be that in a sacrifice where the prayers precede the main ritual acts (like in the sacrifice under discussion), the sacrificer himself pronounces these prayers.

56 The formulas are (TĀ 4, 5, 3/4(9)):
anādhr̥ṣyā́ purástāt | agnér ā́dhipatye | ā́yur me dāḥ ||
putrávatī́ dakṣiṇatáḥ | índrasyā́dhipatye | prajā́ṃ me dāḥ ||
suṣádā paścā́t | devásya savitúr ā́dhipatye | prāṇáṃ me dāḥ ||
ā́śrutir uttaratáḥ | mitrā́váruṇayor ā́dhipatye | śrótraṃ me dāḥ ||
vídhr̥tir upáriṣṭāt | bŕ̥haspáter ā́dhipatye | bráhma me dāḥ kṣattráṃ me dāḥ | téjo me dhā várco me dhāḥ | yáśo me dhās tápo me dhāḥ | máno me dhāḥ,
"(You, the eastern quarter, are) invincible in the east, under Agni's overlordship; grant me long life.
(You are) rich in sons in the south, under Indra's overlordship; grant me progeny.
(You are) good to dwell in in the west, under the overlordship of the god Savitr̥; grant me prāṇa.
(You are) hearing in the north, under the overlordship of Mitra-Varuṇa; grant me the faculty of hearing.
(You are) separated maintenance (of high and low) above, under the overlordship of Br̥haspati; grant me spiritual knowledge (bráhman), grant me lordly power, grant me brilliant energy, grant me lustre, grant me fame, grant me tapas, grant me mind."
The sacrificer pronounces these respective mantras while he holds the span of his hand over the vessel, first on the east side of the vessel, then on the south, the west, the north and lastly in the middle above the vessel. (Caland on ĀpŚS 15, 7, 6.) Cf. the mythical passage that precedes these mantras in the KaṭhĀ: "The quarters feared the Mahāvīra vessel, which had been put on the fire: 'He will burn us all away with his glow!' They ran towards Prajāpati (for help). Prajāpati said: 'He burns you on every span. I will hide you with the deities.' Therefore, (the sacrificer) metes out the quarters with the span of his hand." (KaṭhĀ 2, 79+)

57 The following passage shows that according to the author of this text, the sacrificer turns in all directions, while pronouncing the above mentioned formules (note 56). This seems to be incompatible with the prescription in some Śrauta Sūtras (BhŚS, ĀpŚS and HirŚS), that the fingers should always be pointing towards the east.

58 The Maruts are usually atmospheric, very tempestuous powers of storm (Gonda, *Religionen* 1:61). But the R̥gvedic adjectives used to describe their outlook are words like: *viśvábhānu, svábhānu, hiraṇyáya, sū́ryatvac,* expressing a sunlike character. In R̥V 5, 55, 3 they are *sū́ryasyeva raśmáyaḥ*. The sunlike outlook of the Maruts should originally perhaps not be connected with rays of the sun, but rather with their celestial, divine character and possibly with the lightning of their storms.

59 This passage of Agni and the Vikaṅkata wood is approximately TB 1, 1, 3, 12.

60 The additional thirteenth month is sometimes identified with the year itself. An additional element often comprises and synthesizes the other elements, e.g. when a fourth item is added to a three-fold totality. The year is often identified with the sun and JB 1, 50 connects the thirteenth month directly with the sun: *eṣa trayodaśo ya eṣa tapati.* ("The

thirteenth month is he who burns yonder (the sun).") See Gonda, *Prajāpati and the Year*:23; Bodewitz, "The Waters in Vedic Cosmic Classifications," *Indologica Taurinensia* 10 (1982), especially p. 47; Bodewitz, *JBtransl*:59-60, note 4.

61 This mantra should accompany the placing of the thirteenth enclosing stick. The corresponding Kaṭha-fragment has: "With: '*You are the concealment of the firmament*', he puts the fuel-stick on top. With wood he conceals it from above." The Adhvaryu and the Pratiprasthātṛ place the twelve sticks around the pot in three layers, with the formulas "*You are measure,*" etc. (van Buitenen, *Pravargya*:§17). They are placed at four sides; for Caland's remark (on ĀpŚS 15, 8, 3) that the east remains free, I cannot find any support. Now the thirteenth stick is put down, according to all Sūtras of the Taittirīyas, to the south. Most Sūtras have the stick laid down, but Baudhāyana prescribes it should be fixed up, with its tip pointing upward (*ūrdhvāgram niminoti*). The Sūtra of the Maitrāyaṇīyas, Mānava Śrauta Sūtra, differs from all Taittirīya Sūtras in that it prescribes the placing of the thirteenth stick (together with the gold plate) on top of the Pravargya vessel as a covering. In this way the agreement between action and mantra seems more complete than in the other Sūtras: the *antardhí* is here a real *antar-dhí* (from *antar-dhā*, to conceal), and not, like the other twelve sticks, a *pari-dhí*. The KaṭhĀ also speaks of putting the thirteenth stick on top, which according to the context must mean: on top of the vessel. The problem with this interpretation is, however, that the placing of the *antardhí* is *followed* by the placing of the gold plate on top. If the fuel stick should have been placed there before, ashes would fall into the hot milk vessel during or after burning. Possibly, we are to assume that in the KaṭhĀ and Mānava version of this element of the rite, the thirteenth stick is placed on or near the top but not over the opening. The TĀ, however, gives no indication where the stick should be placed and most Taittirīya Sūtras treat the thirteenth stick as an additional enclosing stick, without giving a special meaning to the word *antardhí* in the mantra. The discrepancy was felt by S who explained - inconvincingly - that the stick was to be laid down "with the concealment of the upper region in mind" (*ūrdhvalokadigvyavadhānabuddhyā*).

62 This mantra (TĀ 4, 5, 7(17)) is approximately ṚV 2, 33, 10. There: *ábhva*, instead of here: *ábbhuva. viśvárūpa* is not "many-coloured" but "brilliant as the sun, fire or gold" (Bodewitz, *WZKS* 1985:15-19). This Rudra mantra, used as a verse of praise of the Pravargya vessel, is better at its place in the "Rudra-oriented" Kaṭha version than here and in the MS (the mantra is not in the VS).

63 For Ugradeva Rājani see Caland, *JB in Auswahl*:300.

64 Compare above TĀ 5, 3, 1, where the same ailment was predicted for one who comes between the Pravargya vessel, while it is being prepared, and the sun. "Having a bad skin": according to the Indian commentators the skin-disease is *kuṣṭha*. This name refers to a class of diseases which comprises leprosy. Cf. Zysk, *Religious Healing*:20. A disease called *kuṣṭha* is described by Suśruta at Nidāna Sthāna 5, 23, 7.

65 See Staal, *Agni* 1:370-371, plate 57.

Anuvāka 5

66 TS 5, 5, 9, 4 also connects "Dyutāna Māruta, together with the Maruts" with the north. Dyutāna, son of the Maruts, is not a very frequently occurring character. TS 1, 3, 1, 2 has a mantra for him. His name is also found in KS 35, 16; VS 5, 17; ŚB 3, 6, 1, 16 and TS 6, 2, 10, 4.

67 *ási*, the finite verb in the first of two antithetical clauses, is accented (MacDonell, *Vedic Grammar for Students*:468). In the immediately following pair of antithetical clauses, one expects the accented *ási* too, but the unaccented form is actually found.

Notes to anuvāka 6

68 The Upasads are called the neck (*grīvā́s*, feminine plural, like *upasádas*) in AiB 1, 25 too, but there the Guest Reception (*ātithyeṣṭhi*) is the head of the Sacrifice.

69 KaṭhĀ 3, 207+ is somewhat more elaborate: "The Jyotiṣṭoma (the Soma sacrifice, of which the Agniṣṭoma is the basic form) was in that time the sacrifice. Just like here (in the sacrifice) from fire, when it is born, the other fires are taken, like that the other sacrifices are born from this (Jyotiṣṭoma). Therefore, he should perform the Pravargya at the Jyotiṣṭoma, for elevation (of the Pravargya)."

70 This and the following sections of this anuvāka would have fitted well in Gonda's enumeration of Vedic texts prescribing "ritual acts performed to derive some advantage from looking on a mighty being or event, to participate in its nature and essence, to be purified or raised to a higher level of existence by being vis-à-vis with such a man or deity or by witnessing such an event" (Gonda, *Eye and Gaze*:55; at other places the author frequently refers to the numerous other instances in this rite where "looking" has some dangerous or beneficial effects). Thus, the priest and the sacrificer get a share in the sunlike power and lustre of the heated vessel. Note that the accompanying mantras aim at establishing a connection between the Pravargya vessel and the sun.

Cf. finally KaṭhĀ on the importance of gazing only with the Avakāśa mantras (see note 79 below): "The gods and the Asuras [did in the Pravargya ceremony] the same. [What the gods did, that the Asuras did.] The gods saw these [mantras for] gazing. With these [mantras they gazed at the Pravargya vessel on the fire. The gods] prospered, the Asuras perished. If one [gazes] at the Pravargya vessel with these [Avakāśa mantras], one prospers and becomes fit [for the sweet beverage]" (KaṭhĀ 3, 226+, text completed by Witzel).

71 While this Āraṇyaka interprets the first words of this well-known verse (TĀ 4, 7, 1(1) = ṚV 1, 164, 31 = ṚV 10, 177, 3) in two ways, these two interpretations are not worked out in relation to the rest of the verse. The Kaṭha-fragment on this mantra clearly

takes only the interpretation of *gopā́m* as the sun into consideration: "'*Wandering hither and thither on his pathways.*' Therefore he follows all pathways, the southern and northern ones. '*Enveloping himself in those (quarters) that converge, in those that spread out.*' Four indeed are his converging (or: main?) quarters. Four his diverging (or: secondary?) [quarters]. Enveloping himself in these, he covers these worlds with brilliant energy" (KaṭhĀ 2, 102-103+).

72 Edition C reads *gataḥ* in Pravargya mantra TĀ 4, 7, 1(3), with an incorrect visarga. Van Buitenen seems to follow this reading (*Pravargya*:93). The pratīka here and in the KaṭhĀ, as well as the accentuation, show that we have to read (*a-*)*gata*, either root-aorist or injunctive If we assume an augmented form, the past-tense meaning is incidental or absent, like e.g. in *havír evā́kaḥ* in anuvāka 3, daśati 9 and *arociṣṭa* in the next mantra. For the difference between the injunctive and the corresponding augmented forms, and their relative interchangebility, see K. Hoffmann, *Der Injunktiv im Veda*, Heidelberg 1967.

73 C: *tapojā́* (without visarga).

74 Tapas is "the generation of creative internal glow, belonging to the brahman methods of rising above normal human conditions and possibilities, of obtaining revelations of secret wisdom and contact with the divine powers" (Gonda, *Change and Continuity*:294). Tapas also means heat (cf. the mantras discussed above in this anuvāka). The root *tap-* is connected with the subjective but concrete physical feeling of heat, contrasting with *dah-* ("burn") that always has objective, visible effects (Blair, *Heat in the Rig Veda and Atharva Veda*, (New Haven 1969): 89). For the connection between tapas and the gaining of insight and wisdom see Hauwer, *Yogapraxis*:67; Gonda, *Change and Continuity*:342; and W. O. Kaelber, "Tapas, Birth and Spiritual Rebirth in the Veda," *History of Religions* 15 (1975):343-386.

75 S interprets the "speech, born of tapas" as "speech fit for the sacrifice and in the form of mantras." The tapas may refer to the Avāntaradīkṣā, the period of "tapas" in which the mantras are studied and certain vows are undertaken.

76 "*Germ of the gods*": Agni/Pravargya is here called the *gárbha* (germ or embryo) of the gods. S: *devair apekṣitasya haviṣo'tra garbharūpeṇāvasthānāt.* "because the offering, to which the gods look forward, is here in the form of a *garbha*." The *gárbha* is the subject to be fostered, growing fast or about to undergo a total transformation. This term should be understood in the light of the symbolism of the initiated sacrificer (*dīkṣitá*) as *gárbha*. Cf. Krick, *Feuergründung*:96. The sacrificer who is consecrated for the sacrifice (*dīkṣitá*), will come out reborn from the final bath. The *gárbha* of the armies, who should come out of the bàttle reborn (as the victor), is the King (Krick, *Feuergründung*:113, note 291). ŚB explains differently: he is the *gárbha* of the gods because he holds (*grabh-*) everything.

77 *matí*, here meaning thoughts that acquired the shape of hymns and formulas. *matí, dhī́, manīṣā́* are words belonging to the same semantic field. All these words can have a concrete and a more abstract sense (Cf. Gonda, *Vision*:7-13). Here the concrete

manifestations of the "inspired thought" are meant. Below, *máti* (note the accent) is used in its more abstract sense: "(inspired) thought of the poets."

78 C and P have the svarita accent on the first syllable, which is what one expects.

79 The nine Avakāśa mantras (TĀ 4, 7, 1(1)ff) are according to S: 1. *"I saw the herdsman . . . "*; 2-7: the mantras relating to the six seasons; 8 and 9: the non-metrical rest of TĀ 4, 7, up to *"May I as one who is associated with Tvaṣṭṛ . . . "* The words *ava-kāśá* and *ā-kāśá* may mean "the place where (the sense-function or vital power) manifests itself." See Bodewitz, *JBtransl*:56, note 5: "Here the *prāṇāḥ* are not lifebreaths or vital powers, but the organs of sense, or rather the orifices through which the gods (= vital powers, sense-functions) enter. . . . The *ākāśāḥ* are in fact every kind of opening." But the root *kāś-* has not only the meaning of "to be visible," but also of "to see or survey," e.g. in the intensive *cākaśīti*. Thus, *avakāśa* is the technical name of "certain mantras during the recitation of which the eyes must be fixed on a particular object" (Gonda, *Eye and Gaze*:22; and see KaṭhĀ 3, 226+ in note 70). These Avakāśa mantras are here connected with the nine apertures of the human body and the prāṇas that manifest themselves there. The Avakāśa mantras and the prāṇas are also connected in ŚB 14, 1, 4, 1 and 2, 2, 51.

80 Cf. the seven prāṇas in anuvāka 4 and note 51 Here the two organs of secretion are probably added to this series of seven prāṇas. Cf. the Bhagavad Gītā, 5, 13, where the body is called a nine-gated stronghold.

81 *sápa* is in all texts interpreted as *śepha*, "male organ," although an etymological connection between the two does not exist (Mayrhofer, *Concise Etymological Sanskrit Dictionary*, vol. 3 (Heidelberg 1976), s.v.). It should be connected with the root *sap-*, "to adore, honour (gods); to love (also sexually)." Cf. Caland on ĀpŚS 10, 23, 8.

Notes to anuvāka 7

82 The verb, itself unaccented, is compounded with two verbal prepositions, like in the TS. See Weber, *IS* 13(1873): 62-63.

83 *I take (you)"* belongs to the former mantra *"You, at the impulse of the god Savitṛ, etc."* S: "because its sense is clear, the citation is its explanation."

84 The Adhvaryu has taken the thether for the cow with the former mantra and speaks now this mantra over it.

85 The Adhvaryu pronounces the divine names softly. Then he goes out through the southern door and pronounces the cow's own name in a loud voice. Thus, BŚS, BhŚS and ĀpŚS have the Adhvaryu first go out through the eastern door; then, they have him call the cow softly by her divine names. Then he is to return, go out through the southern door and call the cow in a loud voice by her own name. HirŚS, KŚS and MŚS are slightly different (*Śrautakośa*, Engl. part 1:192-207). "Southern gate" is to be read instead of "eastern gate" in the last section on p. 95 of van Buitenen's description.

86 For a different application of this verse see Bṛhad-Āraṇyaka-Upaniṣad (BĀU) 6, 4, 27: "Then (the father) hands the (new born babe) to his mother and gives him her breast, saying '*This breast of thine, ever flowing etc.*'"; cf. also Pāraskara Gṛhya Sūtra 1, 16, 21.

87 S explains: "For in everyday life (*loke*) the mother of a child asks the master of the house: 'give milk for the child'; that is how it should be understood."

88 *upasīdatu*: the verb is used in the sense of "to approach (respectfully) in order to milk," cf. Bodewitz, *Agnihotra*, Leiden 1978:56 note 3: "In connection with cattle it seems to denote careful attention and waiting upon them (cf. AV 3, 14, 6) perhaps especially by milking them."

89 Bṛhaspati is connected with the *brahmán*-priest in the ritual and with *bráhman* (neuter), "spiritual knowledge," or, more specific, "le pouvoir formulateur" (Renou, "Les Pouvoirs de la Parole dans le Ṛgveda" in *ÉVP* 1 (1955): 12), so "the power to formulate," i.e. the power to express spiritual knowledge in *bráhmans:* hymns, formulas or enigmatic cosmic equations.

90 Van Buitenen translates *viṣv-ag --vṛ́t* with "surrounded by (blood)," possibly connecting or confusing it with *viṣv-ag--vṛ-ta* that occurs in this meaning in later Sanskrit. But *vṛt* cannot be pressed into the meaning "surround." The context suggests a meaning like Caland's "(von dem Blute) euch abwendend" ("turning away (from the blood)"). This translation is not without problems either, because *viṣu* does not usually mean "away from." The word *viṣv-añc* however appears to have in some cases the meaning "separated or different from," if construed with instrumental or ablative (Petersburger Wörterbuch vol. 6 :665, referring among other places to TS 1, 5, 9, 7 and 2, 3, 2, 6). In our case we have the instrumental *lóhitena*. Moreover, there is a word *viṣū-vṛ́t*. This probably means "indifferent to, not partaking of" in ṚV 10, 43, 3, where it is connected with two ablatives (thus PW, 6:1258; different: Grassman and Geldner). Although the meaning cannot be ascertained beyond any doubt in this way, Caland's translation is still the most acceptable one.

91 The Adhvaryu and his assistant have now finished milking and given the pails with the milk to the Āgnīdhra. They have gone to the Vedi, where they take the tongs and the supporting vessel (van Buitenen, *Pravargya*:100).

92 The *upayama* or *upayamana* is according to S a wooden vessel (*kāṣṭhāviśeṣa, pātraviśeṣa, kāṣṭhāpātra:* S on TĀ 4, 8, 4(13); (20); 11, 3(6)), but van Buitenen's picture (*Pravargya*, plate 3-3, facing p.52) shows a ladle. The *Śrautakośa* has "supporting ladle."

93 This verse is pronounced by the Adhvaryu when looking upon the milk that is now being brought in by the Āgnīdhra (who also comes to the Vedi; van Buitenen, *Pravargya*:100).

94 The verse accompanies the pouring of the cow's milk into the hot vessel (van Buitenen, *Pravargya*:101-102).

95 *juhomi*: in this anuvāka this verb signifies the pouring into the hot vessel of the cow's milk and the goat's milk. The actual offering is the subject of the next anuvāka.

96 *vani* is an action noun from √*van*-. This verb is often used in connection with a god who wins something for his worshipper, e.g. ṚV 1, 36, 17bc; 1, 162, 22d; 7, 15, 4c. What is said by Grassmann on the root *san*- (Wörterbuch zum Rigveda, p.1465) applies here too: the notion splits in two: "to obtain" and "to give," and often it is difficult to decide between the two, because according to the Vedic point of view "obtaining" on the part of the gods results in "giving." Here, the sun's ray gains rain in order to give it. It contains a reference to the well-known idea that water is sucked up by a sun-ray, so that it can pour it down in the form of rain (See TĀ 5, 10, 6 below, and e.g. Lüders, *Varuṇa* 1:308ff: "Die Sonne als Spenderin des Regens").

97 With this and/or the following phrase, the Adhvaryu should gaze at the glow from the milk in the hot vessel. There are several differences in the details between the Śrauta Sūtras; see van Buitenen, *Pravargya*:102; *Śrautakośa*, 2 Engl. 1:192 and 198.

98 *"With heaven and earth I encompass you"*: the Pratiprasthātṛ takes hold of the Pravargya vessel by means of the tongs. The vessel now contains the milk of the cow and the goat (van Buitenen, *Pravargya*:103).

99 He supports it by means of the supporting vessel.

100 The space between the western or Gārhapatya fire (representing this world or the earth) and the eastern or Āhavanīya fire (representing yonder world or heaven) is connected with the firmament and the Wind. Compare TĀ 5, 11, 4, where the Pravargya is sacred to Vāyu, the Wind, when being brought (sc. to the Āhavanīya).

101 The Pravargya, filled with the milk-mixture, is lifted up and taken to the Āhavanīya fire for the offering.

102 *ánavānam*: see above, note 50.

103 The five names are taken from the following seven formulas (the last two are optional according to S): *samudrā́ya tvā vā́tāya svā́hā / salilā́ya tvā vā́tāya svā́hā / anādhṛṣyā́ya tvā vā́tāya svā́hā / apratidhṛṣyā́ya tvā vā́tāya svā́hā / avasyáve tvā vā́tāya svā́hā / dúvasvate tvā vā́tāya svā́hā / śímidvate tvā vā́tāya svā́hā,* (1) *"You to the ocean (of air or atmospheric waters), to the Wind, svāhā!"* (2) *"You to what is waving (salila), to the Wind, svāhā!"* (3) *"You to the unassailable, to the Wind, svāhā!"* (4) *"You to the irresistible, to the Wind, svāhā!"* (5) *"You to him who desires to help, to the Wind, svāhā!"* (6) *"You to the favourable, to the Wind, svāhā!"* (7) *"You to Śimidvat, to the Wind, svāhā!"*

(For (2), *salilá*, see Gonda, *Sel. Studies* 3:432, and 419 note 41; the name *śímidvat* (7) is unclear; it also occurs at MS 4, 9, 8.)

104 Cf. KaṭhĀ 2, 129. The mantras of the Vājasaneyins are slightly different (VS 38, 8, 9; ŚB 14, 2, 2, 6ff).

105 *havis-prakṣepābhāve'pi svāhā-śabda-prayoga-mātreṇa juhotīti* (S): "although there is no pouring of the oblation from one vessel to the other, he still pours in (*juhoti*) merely by using the word 'svāhā!'"

106 Of the six mantras referred to here (TĀ 4, 9, 1/2(1)), only five are used. Together with the first five names of the Wind this makes ten. The ŚB prescribes 12 names of the Wind.

107 The southern Rauhiṇa-cake is offered by the Pratiprasthātṛ, before the milk-offering, with "Let day etc." in the morning and with "Let night etc." in the evening. These two mantras also belong to the offering of the northern Rauhiṇa-cake (e.g. ĀpŚS 15, 11, 5 and 8). In TĀ 4 these mantras are not found after 4, 9, 1/2(1) (which would be expected on the basis of the sequence in this chapter), but at the point where the northern Rauhiṇa-cake is offered, i.e. after the milk-offering, and mostly also after the offering of the six woodsplinters (TĀ 4, 10, 4(7); ĀpŚS and BhŚS: before the offering of the six woodsplinters).

108 In Caland's translation of this verse (TĀ 4, 10, 4(7), in ĀpŚS 15, 10, 10), followed by van Buitenen (*Pravargya*:107), *jyótis-* is in apposition with the subject, while the verb *juṣ-* is construed with an instrumental instead of the usual accusative. It is better to take *jyótis-* as the object. In that way, the appositional relation of *jyótis-* with *rā́tri-* in the latter part, being hardly acceptable, is avoided, and √*juṣ-* is regularly construed with the accusative.

109 The *ketú-*, "banner, torch, brightness," is the Rauhiṇa-cake that is being offered in the Āhavanīya fire (Caland, ĀpŚS 15, 9, 2 and 10, 10). Being saturated with ghee, it flares up. For *jótiṣām* in M read *jyótiṣām*.

Notes to anuvāka 8

110 While pronouncing this verse-quarter, the Adhvaryu looks at the Brahmán priest. "And he protects him from failure in sacrifice" refers to the expiatory function of this priest who is the generalist, not specialized in one of the three Vedas. The knowledge of the expiations for different mistakes and calamities during the sacrifice arises from his more general knowledge of the cosmic background of the rite. This general, universal knowledge expresses itself both in his silence and in his power to put this knowledge into formulas (bráhmans, see note 89). He is connected with the south, probably because he is the one who protects against dangerous aspects of this quarter that belongs to Death (cf. below: "what (overflows) in the south, that is for the fathers") and the Asuras. According to Bodewitz, the south should be considered to represent originally that which encompasses and transcends the differentiated creation (i.e. the undifferentiated totality), rather than that which is in opposition to this creation (Bodewitz, "The Fourth Priest (Brahmán) in Vedic Ritual," *Studies in the History of Religions (Supplements to NUMEN)*, 45 (1983): 43-45) Cf. Krick, *Feuergründung*:245, note 599, who mentions in the context of the southern fire (*dakṣināgni*) "die - ursprünglich positive - Asura-Natur dieses Feuers . . . , das als Manenfeuer den Gegenpol zum Āhavanīya der Götter bildet"

("the - originally positive - asuric nature of this fire . . . , that formed, as the fire of the forefathers, the counterpole to the Āhavanīya of the gods").

111 The Adhvaryu looks at the Hotṛ.

112 *hārdi-vānám* means "having the heart," "dear to the heart." The Vājasaneyins have *hārdvānám*, a term which the author of the ŚB seems to consider as obscure: according to him it stands, together with the next word, for "not distinctly expressed," *ániruktam* (ŚB 14, 2, 2, 21).

113 *ūtí-* from √*av-*. Note that forms of this root have often *dhì-* or cognate terms as their object (Gonda, *Vision*:127ff). If we take "to favour" as the central meaning, this "favouring" may consist either of giving help or promotion, or of accepting an offer or song or *dhí-* favourably. This last mentioned meaning I take to be applicable in *ūtí-* in our mantra also. "To accept favourably" is one of the meanings of √*av-* according to Monier-Williams' Dictionary, p. 96. So it means "(your, the Aśvins') favour to accept and enjoy the oblation." Van Buitenen's "help" (*Pravargya*:109: "Drink, o Aśvins, . . . with your help") does not seem to make much sense (but compare ṚV 1, 46, 15, recited by the Hotṛ just before).

114 *áhar-divábhir*. The texts have an anomalous double accentuation of this word (also VS 38, 12b; but ŚB 14, 2, 2, 21: *ahardivábhir*, cf. MS 4, 9, 134).

115 For a picture of the offerings from the Pravargya vessel, held with the two tongs in the Āhavanīya fire, see Staal, *Agni* 1:372-373. The sequence of the formulas and offerings in this section, exactly correspond to Baudhāyana's description. Other Śrauta Sūtras have *"O Aśvins, drink . . ." after* the Adhvaryu's request to the Hotṛ to recite the yājyā (for the yājyā see ĀpŚS 4, 7, 4 and ṚV 1, 46, 15; AV 7, 73, 4 and 5).

116 *"Svāhā, ye two Indras, vaṭ!"* (van Buitenen, *Pravargya*:109), though grammatically correct, makes no sense. The form *índrā* probably stands for *índrāya* (cf. Bh ad loc. and Caland on ĀpŚS 15, 10, 11, note 9).

117 *svagákṛtyai* literally means "for the exclamation 'svagā!'" But the exclamation "svagā!" is not uttered at these oblations. This exclamation, far less frequently used than e.g. "svāhā!" and "vaṣaṭ/vaṭ!" probably originally meant "good speed" or "safe journey." Cf. e.g. TB 3, 3, 8, 11: "'Svagā to the divine priests!' he says. Therewith he renders the sacrifice *svagā* (having a good speed or safe journey towards the gods)." See also Gonda, *Pūṣan and Sarasvatī* (Amsterdam-Oxford-New York, 1984):130 (§110 and for references note 58). Here, *svagákṛtyai* probably means: "for the wish for a good journey, normally expressed by the exclamation 'svagā!'" After one offering to Indra, that was meant "for keeping back the Rakṣases," the second offering can now have "good speed" or a "safe journey" (towards the gods).

118 After the oblation to the Aśvins, the vessel is again filled, either with milk (according to BŚS and MŚS), or with cooked curds that have been prepared before (according to ĀpŚS and others). See Caland note 4 on ĀpŚS 15, 10, 12.

119 TĀ 4, 10, 1(1ab). The formula continues (TĀ 4, 10, 1(1c-j): *bráhmaṇe pīpihi* / *kṣattrā́ya pīpihi* / *adbhyáḥ pīpihi* / *óṣadhībhyaḥ pīpihi* / *vánaspátibhyaḥ pīpihi* / *dyā́vāpṛthivī́bhyām pīpihi* / *subhūtā́ya pīpihi* / *brahmavarcasā́ya pīpihi*, *"Swell for the Brahmins, swell for the Kṣatriyas, swell for the waters, swell for the lords of the forest (the trees), swell for heaven and earth, swell for well-being, swell for the lustre of spiritual knowledge."* And finally (TĀ 4, 10, 2(1kl)): *"swell for the sacrificer; swell for me, for pre-eminence"* (see text).

120 Between this part and the following "*Lest the wind . . .*," the full mantra (TĀ 4, 10, 2(3)) has moreover: *kṣattrā́ṇi dhāraya* / *víśaṃ dhāraya*, *"support the Kṣatriyas, support the Vaiśyas."* I prefer to divide: *dhárma-asi sudhárma-ámeny asmé* / *bráhmāṇi dhāraya kṣattrā́ṇi dhāraya víśaṃ dhā́raya*. S and van Buitenen, however, read: *dhármā-asi sudhármā́ me ny asmé* / *bráhmāṇi dhāraya*. etc. The double accent of *sudhármā́* is suspicious; *ā́* as preposition or from a compound verb **ā́-ni-dhṛ* is unlikely. Bh reads *dhármā* and *sudhármā*, and has to explain *ámeny* as *ámenī* (from *ámeni* + *in*). This seems rather far-fetched. Moreover, VS 38,14fg has: (f) *dhármāsi sudhárma* / (g) *ámeny asmé nṛmṇā́ni dhāraya bráhma dhāraya kṣattrám dhāraya víśam dhāraya.*

Another difficulty in the TĀ mantra is *bráhmāṇi*. The parallelism with *kṣattrā́ṇi* and *víśam* in the same mantra suggest the interpretation "class of Brahmins," but this is usually expressed by the neuter singular (as in VS 38, 14fg). S explains *bráhmāṇi*. and *kṣattrā́ṇi* as the works to be done by the class of Brahmins and the class of the Kṣatriyas respectively. The KaṭhĀ has: *dhármāsi sudhármemā́ny asmai bráhmāṇi dhāraya*. This looks like a linguistic simplification. The difficulties of *ámeni* and *bráhmāṇi* are avoided. *bráhmāṇi* may refer in this mantra simply to the bráhman-formulas, to be supported for the sake of the sacrificer.

121 Below, anuvāka 11 daśati 4, the Pravargya ceremony is sacred to Pūṣan in the stage where the milk reaches the rim of the vessel, but sacred to Mitra when a film has been formed on the boiled milk (*śáro-gṛhītaḥ*; also MS 1,8,10). *śáras*, the cream or film on boiled milk may express Pūṣan's connection with thriving and prosperity.

122 *pratirá*, "promoting, promoter." The Āraṇyaka takes the word in this abstract sense. Caland (ĀpŚS 15, 11, 6) thinks that it refers to the "sound-holes." He adds in a note: "unsicher!" ("uncertain!") He probably assumed that it is a short form of the infrequent *pratiravá*, that may stand for *uparava* ("sound-hole").

123 For the accentuation of *nir-áva-dayati*, see note 82. The verb is often used to denote a sacrifice to Rudra. To eliminate the inauspicious and dangerous aspects of Rudra, this god must be satisfied and appeased. Cf. Arbman, *Rudra. Untersuchungen zum altindischen Glauben und Kultus* (Uppsala, 1922): 55.

124 Because the Adhvaryu has touched the woodsplinter for Rudra, he has lost his sacrificial purity. He regains it by touching water.

125 Cf. Gonda, *Eye and Gaze*:28.

126 C: *ā́hutīr* instead of *ā́hutī*.

127 This passage is the same as TB 1, 1, 6, 9. The meaning in the context of the Pravargya is that the first mantra of the Agnihotra, intended for its evening performance, would be applied at the first performance of the Pravargya, which takes place in the morning. If at the first occasion the formula "Bhūḥ svāhā!" is used instead, the two mantras ("Agni is light, light is Agni, svāhā!" and "The sun is light, light is the sun, svāhā!") will be regularly used in the next evening and morning performances of the Agnihotra. Cf. Bodewitz, *Agnihotra*, Leiden 1976:172.

128 Prāṇa is the most important one in the five-fold series of vital powers. This series includes at least some powers that also belong to the series of five senses (*indriyā́ṇi*). See Bodewitz in *ALB* 50 (1986):343. This equation of prāṇa with the fire in which the oblation is offered, seems to foreshadow the identifications underlying the Prāṇāgnihotra, in which the daily oblations in the fire are replaced by daily offerings of food in the prāṇas. This amounts to the ceremonial consummation of food by the sacrificer. See Bodewitz, "Agnihotra and Prāṇāgnihotra" in *JBtransl*:213-343; and cf. note 51 above.

129 See Staal, *Agni* 1:376-377, plate 60A. Either they all drink the milk (or eat the curds, see note 118 above), or only the sacrificer drinks (or eats) while the priests just smell at it (van Buitenen, *Pravargya*:117).

130 (a) This passage (the first part of TĀ 5, 8, 13) relates to the period of study before the actual performance of the Pravargya ceremony. By following the observances the pupil "sharpens his brilliant energy" or, more generally, he increases his sacrificial purity and mental power. The observances mentioned here are less severe than those that are found in the Avāntaradīkṣā$_p$ prescriptions of the Pravargya portions of the Śrauta Sūtras. While in the latter the pupil should not even speak to a woman or a Śūdra, we have in our passage the prohibition to approach a Śūdra woman (*rāmā́*, but Keith: "woman of pleasure", *TStransl*: 462, n. 1) sexually. Whether *rāmá* should be interpreted as *ramaṇīyaḥ putraḥ* (S; cf. Weber, *IS* 10 (1868): 74, n. 1), or, more likely, as "Śūdra" (Bh) or "servant," the subject of these observances must be someone in the householder stage of life (*gṛhastha*). Therefore, it was certainly not the Veda student who followed these observances, but rather the sacrificer. Now, the immediately following mythical passage on Vibhrāj Saurya connects these observances with the Pravargya mantras "to be recited by day" (*divākīrtyà*). If they are connected with recitation, they must be connected with a period of study before the actual performance. Perhaps BŚS 9,1 also refers to such a period of study by the sacrificer before the Pravargya performance (note 11 above). It is not very likely that a year of study had to precede each performance or continuous series of performances of the Pravargya. It was possibly permitted to represent the year by a few days, as seems to be suggested by ŚB 14, 1, 1, 28. In our passage the term Avāntaradīkṣā is not used, but if it was considered to be a special form of the Avāntaradīkṣā$_p$, adapted for the sacrificer, the difference of this Avāntaradīkṣā with the initiation rites of the Soma sacrifice, the Dīkṣā and Avāntaradīkṣā$_s$, would have become

very small. For the way in which this passage of the Āraṇyaka is used and reinterpreted in the Śrauta Sūtras see Introduction section 3.3, p. 24.

(b) Although not all rules in this passage are completely clear as far as their significance is concerned, it seems that in general their observance was believed to preserve and increase the potency of the subject. For the purpose of abstinence from sexual intercourse before the performance of a sacrifice see Gonda's article "Ascetics and Courtesans" (*ALB* 25 (1961): 78-102 = *Select.* 4:223-247; especially pp. 93-95 (238-240)): "In a considerable number of cases we read also in the Vedic texts that the intending sacrificer must not only fast, sleep on the ground etc., but also abstain from sexual intercourse. It is undesirable that the consecrated man should lose any potency" (95). A person who studied the sacred knowledge had to apply his whole person and all his energy. See also Gonda, *Change and Continuity*, Chapt. 9 on Brahmacarya and Chapt. 10 on Dīkṣā; and W. Kaelber, "Tapas, Birth and Spiritual Rebirth in the Veda," *History of Religions* 15 (1975): 343-386. For the prohibition to drink from a clay or earthenware vessel, see note 164.

Notes to anuvāka 9

131 KaṭhĀ 3,174-176 has the metres in reverse order; it connects jagatī with heaven, triṣṭubh with the firmament and gāyatrī with the earth.

132 The need for gestures to make the information complete again shows that these texts were meant for "live" recitation.

133 With these verses they all leave the Prācīnavaṃśa, taking the Pravargya implements with them. They will bring the implements to the place of disposal. TĀ 4, 11, 2(3) has only the two *pratīkas*. The complete verses are in TS 3, 3, 11, *l* and *m*: *ánu no 'dyā́numatir yajñáṃ devéṣu manyatām | agníśca havyavā́hano bhávatāṃ dāśúṣe máyaḥ, "May Anumatī today for us favour our sacrifice among the gods. May she and Agni, the bearer of the oblation, be a joy to the giver"* and *ánv íd anumate tvám mányāsai śáṃ ca naḥ kṛdhi | krátve dákṣāya no hinu | prá ṇa ā́yūṃṣi tāriṣaḥ, "You, o Anumati, should favour us and give us well-being. Impel us for intelligence and skill, lengthen our life-time."*

134 (a) I follow Calland and van Buitenen in translating "for protection," although one would expect in that case the dative *paraspā́yai* in all three mantras. But only TĀ 4, 11, 3(6) has the dative, the other two, TĀ 4, 11, 2/3(4) and TĀ 4, 11, 3(5) have the gen./abl. *paraspā́yāḥ*. KaṭhĀ has in this series of three mantras *paraspā́m* instead of the genetive and dative, which may be considered a simplification.

(b) The first mantra is recited by the Adhvaryu after the first chanting of the *tyagnāyiḥ* sāman, the second mantra after the second chanting and the third mantra after the third chanting, when they have arrived at the place of disposal (see below, note 137).

135 Compare for *jihmā́ṃ yajñásya śíro haret* AiĀ 3, 2, 4: *jihmaśiras*, "with a crooked head," which is an inauspicious omen.

136 Here *sā́tman* is used to express a bodily rebirth in heaven. Normally we find *sátanu* and *sā́ṅga* "with a body" and "with limbs." Because in the previous sentence the "bodily form" of the disposed Pravargya is emphasized (with the words *sā́tman* and *sátanu*) a translation like "pourvu d'un ātman" ("endowed with an ātman"), that is elsewhere defensible (Minard, *Énigmes* 2:171), is here impossible. The same can be said of the translation "of the same essence" Gonda, *Prajāpati and the Year*:25 note 33; and Minard, loc. cit.

137 All the priests and the sacrificer and his wife are going from the Prācīnavaṃśa to the place where the Pravargya implements will be disposed. The Prastotṛ starts the *tyagnāyiḥ* sāman three times (van Buitenen, *Pravargya*:126): when they depart, when they arrive and when they are halfway.

138 *amṛ́ta evaínam práti ṣṭhāpayati*, "he (the Adhvaryu) places it on the immortal" refers to the vessel that is being placed on the plate of gold, but, because of the identification of the Pravargya vessel with the sacrificer, also to the sacrificer. From this second point of view we might translate: "he (the Adhvaryu) fixes him (the sacrificer) firmly in the world of immortality." Cf. ŚB 12, 8, 1, 22: "Gold is non-dying (*amṛtam*), in non-dying ('immortality') they thus finally establish themselves" (tr. Gonda in the article "Pratiṣṭhā" in *Select.Studies* 2:363).

139 Most Śrauta Sūtras prescribe that the mantra *"(You are) the four-cornered navel of the cosmic law"* (TĀ 4, 11, 4(9)), should accompany the touching of the Uttaravedi with the hand. Such an act would leave the identification of the navel with the Pravargya baseless. The act prescribed by the Śrauta Sūtra of the Vājasaneyins, Kātyāyana, fits in better with this (Taittirīya) identification. It prescribes that the Pravargya vessel should be placed on the Uttaravedi in such a way that it touches its navel. (Cf. van Buitenen, Pravargya:129, note 1 on §8, where L. should be read as K(ātyāyana).) "The four-cornered" of the mantra, in the TĀ Pravargya Brāhmaṇa explanation interpreted as *iyám* (S: *uttaravedi* or *bhūmi*), is interpreted as "he who shines yonder (the sun); for the quarters are his corners" in the ŚB (ŚB 14, 3, 1, 17). The Kaṭha-fragments we have, contain nothing about this mantra.

140 The rest of the mantra that accompanies the filling of the main Pravargya vessel with curds mixed with honey is (TĀ 4, 11, 4(12b-d)): *téna várdhasva cā́ ca pyāyasva / vardhiṣīmáhi ca vayám ā́ ca pyāsiṣīmáhi, "O Gharma, this is your food, this is your filling; through it, grow and swell. May we also grow and may we swell."*

141 This (TĀ 4, 11, 5(13)) and the following seven mantras are called Gandharva mantras. They are recited when the Pravargya lies disposed. According to Baudhāyana, the Adhvaryu has the sacrificer recite these mantras. Other Śrauta Sūtras have the mantras recited by all participants. The Gandharva is in Vedic texts the protector of Soma, of divine secrets and of the place of conception (Gonda, *Religionen* 1:100ff). He

may have a solar character and be favourable to men, promulgating divine secrets and stimulating "visions" (ṚV 10, 177, 2; 10, 123; and below, 10, 139, 5; Gonda, *Vision*:91). "The Gandharva no doubt is the archetype of the poet who attempts to reveal the mystery" (Gonda, *Vision*:357). The Gandharva in the Ṛgveda often means the sun (ṚV 8, 77, 5; 9, 85, 12; 10, 123, 7), not only the physical sun, but also the spiritual sun that brings enlightenment and is situated or perceived in the heart (cf. ṚV 10, 177, 1-2). Besides these eight Gandharva mantras, there are several other Pravargya mantras in which this name occurs, e.g. in ṚV 10, 123, 4; 5; 7 in the Hotṛ's recitation during fanning; and in ṚV 9, 83, 4 in the Hotṛ's recitation during the milk-offering.

142 *bándhu* or, with the suffix *-tā* creating abstract nouns, *bandhútā*, means "connection," "relation," "relative." In Brahmanical thought it may have the specialized meaning of the cosmic connection of some ritual element, or its "deeper sense." It is one of the central notions in Brahmanical thought and is basic for many identifications. In fact many complete identifications (A=B) may actually be short expressions for: "there exists a *bándhu* (connection, relationship) between A and B." If some sacrificial element or act is considered to have a special connection with some macrocosmic aspect or event, then this connection in the macrocosmic sphere may be called its *bándhu* or deeper sense. See Oldenberg, *Weltanschauung*:4, 110-123; S. Schayer, "Struktur der magischen Weltanschauung" in *Zeitschrift für Buddhismus*, 1925:259ff.; Renou in *JA* 1953:171-175; Gonda, "Bandhu in the Brāhmaṇas," *ALB* 29 (1965):1-29; more recently Oguibenine: "*Bandhu* et *Dakṣinā*. Deux termes védiques illustrant le rapport entre le signifiant et le signifié" in *JA* 1983:263-275.

143 This mantra (TĀ 4, 11, 6(17a-d)) occurs also in TS 4, 7, 13, 1 and TB 3, 10, 4, 2: *cíd asi samudráyoniḥ / índur dákṣaḥ śyená ṛtā́vā / híraṇyapakṣaḥ śakunó bhuraṇyúḥ / mahā́nt sadhásthe dhruvá ā́ níṣattaḥ*, *"You are Thought, with the ocean as birthplace. You are the skilful drop, the hawk that is in season, the golden-winged quivering bird, sitting large and firm in the assembly."* The accent shows that *samudrá-yoniḥ* is a bahuvrīhi. Van Buitenen's "thought, source of the floods" is therefore incorrect. The ocean is the heart as the seat of thoughts (Introduction §3.1, p. 14; and Geldner *ṚVübers* 1, note on ṚV 1, 159, 4; F. B. J. Kuiper, "The Bliss of Aša":125; Gonda, *Vision*:281). The terminology of this mantra (occurring only in YV texts) is close to that of the Soma-hymns of the ṚV.

144 This and the following two mantras (TĀ 4, 11, 7/8(18-20)), are with slight differences ṚV 10, 139, 4-6. While these mantras were often interpreted in the light of the mythical theft of the Soma by the Gandharva Viśvāvasu (e.g. K. Rönnow, *Trita Āptya*, Uppsala 1927:89; Geldner, *ṚVübers*, ad loc.), there is a lot to say for Lüders' hypothesis that they rather refer to the discovery of the sun by Indra (Lüders, *Varuṇa* 2:540; Renou, *ÉVP* 15:32, appears to prefer Lüders' interpretation). Soma is invoked in verse 4, but there is no reference to his being taken away. The whole sūkta ṚV 10, 139 is a hymn to the rising sun (Lüders, *Varuṇa* 2:538). This was probably also the way these verses were inter-

preted by those who introduced them into this rite, because this interpretation fits the general character of the Pravargya and the use of the verses at this place in the rite much better than the Soma-theft interpretation advocated here by S. So, we may assume that these verses originally referred to the discovery of the sun by Indra, and were as such introduced in the rite. According to Lüders the Gandharva helps Indra in this matter. But it is very well possible that the sun was in this hymn actually identified with the Gandharva (ṚV 8, 77, 5 is also best interpreted in that way). Such an interpretation, at least, seems to have formed the reason for employing this verse as a mantra at this place of the rite. What remains a difficulty in the first verse, also in this interpretation, is *tát* and *āsām* in pāda c, metrically superfluous in the Ṛgveda. Did Indra follow the Ṛta (cosmic law) of the waters (Lüders)? Did he follow their track *from* the sun, or rather *towards* the sun?

145 (a) The complete verse is (TĀ 4, 11, 8(20)): *sásnim avindac cáraṇe nadī́nām / ápāvṛṇod dúro áśmavrajānām / prā́sāṃ gandharvó amṛ́tāni vocat / índro dákṣaṃ pári jānād ahī́nam, "He found the Winner (the sun) in the course of the (heavenly) rivers. He opened the gates for (the waters) that were enclosed in rock. The Gandharva proclaimed the immortal (names) of the (waters). Indra became fully acquainted with (his) perfect skill."* TĀ 4, 11 has *ahī́nam*, easily construable with *dákṣam*, instead of *ahī́nām* in ṚV 10, 139, 6, (genitive plural of the difficult *ahí*, for which see Lüders, *Varuṇa* 2:535).

(b) *āsām* (feminine genitive plural) are female entities enclosed in rock: either the cows (*gā́vas*) or the waters (*ā́pas*).

146 In the context of the mantras it seems most logical to interpret *amṛ́tāni* (neuter plural) as "immortal names." On the basis of *prāṇā́ vā́ amṛ́tāḥ* it is not clear whether the author of the TĀ did the same.

147 The same formulas are employed in BŚS 2,5 (Krick, *Feuergründung*:72, note 185).

148 TĀ 4, 11, 8(24) has only the two *pratīkas*. The complete verses are TS 1, 4, 43*a* (ṚV 1, 50, 1): *úd u tyáṃ jātávedasaṃ deváṃ vahanti ketávaḥ / dṛśé víśvāya sū́ryam, "His rays bear upward the god Jātavedas, that all may see the sun,"* and TS 1, 4, 43*b* (ṚV 1, 115, 1):*citráṃ devā́nām úd agād ánīkaṃ cákṣur mitrásya váruṇasyāgnéḥ / ā́prā dyā́vāpṛthivī́ antárikṣaṃ sū́rya ātmā́ jágatas tasthúṣaśca., "Radiant has risen the countenance of the gods, the eye of Mitra, Varuṇa and Agni. He has filled heaven and earth and the firmament. The sun is the self of all that moves and stays."*

149 √*i*- with ablative with the meaning of √*cyu*- with ablative: "to be deprived of, lose."

Notes to anuvāka 10

150 C: *vaí* instead of *tvaí*.

151 The different layers of imagery that are interwoven in this mythical passage may be distinguished as follows. To the usual identification of Prajāpati with the sun, a second identification with a cow is added. This cow is the genetrix or depositary of sacred

knowledge in the form of speech and chant. Thus we have Prajāpati/sun/cow/depositary-of-sacred-knowledge. From him/it is obtained light (*śukra*)/milk/sacred-knowledge-in-the-form-of-speech-and-chant. For the identification of Prajāpati with a cow cf. Gonda, *Prajāpati's rise to higher rank* (Leiden, 1986): 10-11. For the remarkable metaphor of the mantras and sāmans that are "milked" from a divine place or person, compare the following places in the ṚV. In ṚV 5, 44, 13 the seer Sutambhara is said to milk the udder of all *dhī́*-s, *dhī́* meaning vision or thought, but also its concrete manifestation in the form of mantra and song (cf. note 77 above). In ṚV 3, 57, 2 Indra and Pūṣan milk the everflowing (*śaśayā́*) [udder] of heaven. The preceding stanza makes it clear that the "everflowing [udder]" which is milked, is the vision (*manīṣā́*) of the poet. In ṚV 3, 1, 9, Agni is said to have found the udder of the Father, and to have let flow from it *dhā́rā dhénā*, nourishing streams of speech.

In our passage, the streams of inspired speech and songs, the Śukriya sāmans and yajus-formulas, are first conceived in the form of undifferentiated *śukrám páyas*, "bright milk" or "something bright in the form of milk." The brightness no doubt emphasizes the visionary character of this undifferentiated "stream" of sacred knowledge. In the ṚV, the word *śukrá* is more than once found to characterize a word like *dhī́*: a bright or pure shape or form (*śukró várṇaḥ*) "belonged to the *dhī́ḥ* because of its very character as a vision, obtained by an extraordinary faculty of seeing and given to man by those gods who are particularly characterized by their relations to 'light'" (Gonda, *Vision*:167).

152 *tád agnír vy àkarot*: the activity in relation to the undifferentiated "sāman- and yajus-milk," here expressed by the verb *vi-kṛ*, is very similar to the activity in relation to undifferentiated speech, expressed by *vy-ā-kṛ*, e.g. in TS 6, 4, 7, 3. See Thieme, "Meaning and form of the 'grammar' of Pāṇini," *Studien zur Indologie und Iranistik*, 8/9 (1982/3):23-28 for several examples with *vy-ā-kṛ* in the context of speech. Thieme (loc. cit.) states the meaning of *vy-ā-kṛ* to be among other things "to distinguish [by separating similar objects from one another or by separating a seeming whole into its parts]" and "to form in different ways." Whether or not these meanings are acceptable as the basis of the etymology of *vyākaraṇa*, they quite agree with the use of *vy-ā-kṛ* in the context of speech, and with the use of *vi-kṛ* here in the context of the undifferentiated "sāman- and yajus-milk."

153 Śukriya is an old name for the Pravargya. In the so-called Ārṣeyapāṭha of the Taittirīyas, the *śukriyāṇi*, i.e. the Pravargya mantras and Brāhmaṇa, formed part of the second or Saumya kāṇḍa of this division of the Taittirīya Yajurveda (see Introduction section 5, p. 34f). While the study of these *śukriyāṇi* is connected with the Avāntaradīkṣā, the study of the Saumya kāṇḍa as a whole is connected with what is called the *śukriyavrata*. In the KaṭhĀ-manuscripts the term *śukriya* is rather frequent (in its narrower sense of "Pravargya"): the śānti recitation begins with *oṃ, śukriyaṃ rudrasya*; the mantras are the *śukriya-mantrāḥ* and the Pravargya Brāhmaṇa is called *śukriya-brāhmaṇam*.

154 The imagery of Prajāpati/sun/cow/depositary-of-sacred-knowledge from whom/which light/milk/a-stream-of-sacred-knowledge is being obtained, is now connected with the ritual: the cow's and goat's milk are identified with the stream of sacred knowledge that is differentiated into the yajus-formulas and sāmans. Although this has not been explicitly stated, Prajāpati/sun/etc. is here no doubt identified with the Pravargya vessel.

155 Birds should not be allowed to sit around the disposed Pravargya until the next rite in the Agniṣṭoma: the carrying forth of the sacred fire. See Caland on ĀpŚS 15, 16, 7, where this passage of the TĀ has been translated. He adds: "Die Absicht ist nicht ganz klar" ("The intention is not completely clear"). One should compare KaṭhĀ 3, 186 and 239a. This last passage shows that "birds sitting around his children" means that the children have died: "Death aims at the children of him, at whose Mahāvīra, in the course of the Pravargya ceremony, birds or beasts of prey come running along. He should [in that case] offer two oblations with 'bloody-mouthed' and 'Go asunder (?)'." If the latter *pratīka* should be read as *ví gā́ indra* (Witzel, *KaṭhĀtransl*:138, note 186.2), the two verses occur also in TĀ 4, 29, 1(1) and 4, 28 ,1(1) (see van Buitenen, *Pravargya*, Appendix III, the Rites of Reparation, §20f.)

156 *upadī́ka-santatāḥ*, not: "eaten up by white ants" (Rudradatta on ĀpŚS 15, 16, 5 and *Śrautakośa*) but "covered all over with white ants." For the connection of the upadīka ants with water see above note 6.

157 *anūjjhā́varī* may be derived from *anu + ud + hā*, with the suffix *-varī*. Caland (on ĀpŚS 15, 16, 5) hesitatingly: "'pflegt nach Wasser auszugehen', "ist wasserhaft'?" ("'is in the habit of going out towards water', 'is watery'?"). He apparently had *hā, jihīte* in mind. The other root, *hā, jahāti*, would result in a translation like "giving up, discharging water"; but it is the sun that is explained by the author as the collector and discharger of rain (cf. TĀ 5, 7, 7 and note 96 above). This sun is represented here by the Pravargya vessel, and the Darbha-grass is the place from which water is collected.

Notes to anuvāka 11

158 This series of identifications concerns the preparation, use and disposal of the vessel. The second series below shows the heating of the vessel and the offering of milk in its various stages.

159 The Mahāvīra is here the name of the last stage of the Pravargya. In the TĀ this name is not as frequent as in other texts (ŚB, KaṭhĀ) where it is often given to the Pravargya vessel. In the KaṭhĀ the sun is called Rudra Mahāvīra. Cf. note 52 of the Introduction.

160 *púṇyārtiṃ tásmai kāmayate*: cf. TB 3, 2, 3, 7 *pradātré púṇyam āśāste*. The accentuation of *púṇyārtiṃ* (on the first member of the compound) is in accordance with the regular accentuation in the older language of a compound with an action noun on *-ti* as the second member (Wackernagel-Debrunner, *Altindische Grammatik*, II (Göttingen 1957), 1:214 (§90a)). The usual translations of *ā́rti* are "painful occurrence, pain, injury, mischief; sickness" (e.g. Monier-Williams, *Sanskrit-English Dictionary*, P. 149; delete "for 2.*ārti* see s.v."). S and Bh interpret *ā́rti* in this way (explaining *púṇyārtiṃ* as *bhāgyahānim* (S) and *puṇyanāśam* (Bh)), and this creates two problems. First, the context forces them to attribute a special connotation to *yathānāmám*. S: "(merely) with his own given name" (*tadīyaṃ nāmānatikramya nāmakaraṇakāle saṃpāditenaiva nāmnā*); Bh: "with a name not made for the (special) purpose" (*anarthakṛtena nāmnā*). More serious is the second problem: the person "who knows thus" (*yá eváṃ véda*) obtains something undesirable ("mischief or damage to his merit"), whereas the one "who knows thus" is elsewhere always rewarded with something desirable. Bh sensed the problem, and gave an alternative interpretation of *ārti* as *vyasana*. He probably had in mind "arduous devotion to", one of the meanings of the latter word; but *ā́rti* itself is nowhere else attested in that meaning. The solution proposed here is the following. The Vedic verb *ār* (*ā* + *ṛ*) means "to reach, obtain", and is usually pregnant with a negative connotation ("to reach mischief"), but not always. Cf. for the latter case Grassmann, Wörterbuch zum Rig-Veda:99, under *ar* + *ā*; and Suryakanta, A Practical Vedic Dictionary:145, under *ār*. The derivative action noun *ā́rti* may have been used here in the neutral sense of "obtainment." In the dictionaries it has been recorded only in the negative sense, which it has, it is true, in almost all cases: "obtainment of mischief: painful occurrence etc." If *púṇya* in *púṇyārtim* is adjectival, the translation is: "good, pure or meritorious obtainment."

161 *jána* and *janátā*, collectiva in singular, may refer, according to Rau, *Staat*:64, to foreign, distant regions, to which one goes in order to obtain fame and wealth. Indian commentators, however, take the words in the meaning of "assembly" or "court-room" (*janasamūha*, *sabhā*) here and elsewhere; cf. Caland, *'Wunschopfer'*, 6 note 36.

162 See note 52 above.

163 Compare this and the following three identifications of the series, with the identifications of the Vaiśvadeva Agnihotra in JB 1, 21 and parallel passages (Bodewitz, *JBtransl*:66ff.). We have here the same chronological order as in TB 2, 1, 7,1 (and VādhS 3, 37) with *mārutā́ḥ kváthan* instead of *vaiśvadevā́ bhindávaḥ* (cf. MS 1, 8, 10: *mārutám bindumát*) and *maitrā́ḥ śárogṛhītaḥ* instead of *maitrā́ṃ śáraḥ*.

164 The earth is connected with the dead and with Untruth (*ánṛta*) and therefore clay as such would not be suitable for an oblation to the gods (see TB 3, 2, 3, 11 and Oldenberg, *Die Religion*:419). This is also the reason why one should not drink from a clay vessel during the study of the Pravargya mantras (TĀ 5, 8, 13), because the entire rite is

directed towards the sun. The solution given here is that the vessel is "Speech," i.e. "it is of the nature of Speech because it is produced with mantras (and thus it is not an ordinary clay vessel)" (S). ŚB 14, 2, 2, 54 motivates the use of clay for the Pravargya vessel in a more down-to-earth way as follows: "But if it were made of wood, it would be burnt; and if of gold, it would dissolve; and if of copper, it would melt; and if of stone, it would burn the two handling sticks; and that (Gharma) itself submitted to that (earthen vessel): therefore, it is by means of an earthen (vessel) that he offers it."

165 The basic identification underlying this rite is that of the Pravargya vessel/ceremony and the sun. Here the line of identifications continues in the well-known identifications of the sun, the Year and Prajāpati (See Gonda, *Prajāpati and the Year*:16, 90, 91).

166 For the Avakāśa mantras see note 79 above.

Notes to anuvāka 12

167 The identifications during the first five days can be commented upon as follows: at the beginning of sacrificial acts we usually find Savitṛ. Agni, Vāyu and Āditya (the sun) correspond to the three worlds: earth, firmament and heaven. The moon and the stars represent the fourth world. Cf. Bodewitz, "The Waters in Vedic Cosmic Classifications," *Indologica Taurinensia*, 10 (1982): 45-54.

168 Cf. TS 5, 7, 21 (on the Aśvamedha), where the sixth offering is for the Year, the seventh for the Maruts, the eighth for Bṛhaspati, the ninth for Mitra, the tenth for Varuṇa, the eleventh for Indra, the twelfth for the All-gods. Elsewhere (TS 1, 7, 11) the seven-footed śakvarī-metre is connected with the Maruts; Bṛhaspati and the gāyatrī-metre are on the eighth place; Mitra and the threefold stoma (consisting of nine verses) are on the ninth place; Varuṇa (in the ṚV also called *samrā́j*, Emperor) and the ten-syllabic virāj-metre on the tenth place; Indra and the triṣṭubh on the eleventh place; and the All-gods and the jagatī-metre on the twelfth place.

169 The Pravargya in the Agniṣṭoma is usually performed before the Upasad (Caland-Henry, *Agniṣṭoma*: §50-51, §56-57 etc.). Some Śrauta Sūtras mention as an alternative that the Upasad can be performed first (ĀpŚS 11, 2, 5, HirŚS 7, 4, VaikhŚS 13, 7). The author possibly refers to these two alternatives. However, the two properties "shining from here" and "shining from there" seem to belong to the Pravargya simultaneously. Does the author refer to two ways of looking at the same series of performances: Pravargya-Upasad, Pravargya-Upasad, Pravargya-Upasad, . . . can be taken as (Pravargya), Upasad-Pravargya, Upasad-Pravargya, Upasad- . . . ?

170 The radiation of heat (*aívá tapati*) by him "who knows thus" should of course be interpreted in the light of the concept of *tápas* (note 74). Bh comments on this final word of the Taittirīya Pravargya section: "The meaning is: he (i.e. the performer of the Pravargya who knows the implications) becomes the sun."

APPENDIX 1

The Place of Sacrifice for a Pravargya that forms part of a Soma Sacrifice

The regular performances of the Pravargya (TĀ 5, anuvāka 4-8) take all place in the Prācīnavaṃśa, except that the Adhvaryu and his assistant leave the hut through one of the doors, in order to milk the cow and goat (see anuvāka 7, and note 81). The twice daily heating of the Pravargya vessel takes place on the western or *pravṛñjanīya* mound. At the end of each performance, except at the time of the final disposal, the implements are put on the Saṃrāḍ-āsandī or Emperor's Throne. The Patnī-śālā (Wife's Hall) is at the west of the Prācīna-vaṃśa.

The previously prepared clay-pit, from which the clay is procured for the preparation of the implements, is at a certain distance east of the Āhavanīya. To the north of this place is the black antelope skin, spread out with its neck towards the east and the hairy side upwards (anuvāka 2). At the time of the preparation of the implements, the Mahāvedi (Great Altar Space), the Uttaravedi, the Sadas (Hall of Recitation) and Havirdhāna (Soma Hall) are not yet meted out and put up. The ingredients are mixed and the implements are formed out of the clay-mixture on a mound to the north or north-east of the place of sacrifice.The implements are baked in a fire-pit, dug to the east of the Gārhapatya fire (BŚS: to the north of the hut).

The disposal of the implements after the last performance (anuvāka 9 and 10) normally takes place at the by now constructed Uttaravedi. The Sadas and the Havirdhāna are put up afterwards.

The plan shows the Prācīnavaṃśa where the main actions of the Pravargya take place, and some places that will play a role in the Soma sacrifice to which the Pravargya is the introductory part.

The Saṃrāḍ-āsandī, the Emperor's Throne for the Pravargya vessels, is according to some not east but west (HirŚS) or north (KātyāyanaŚS; optional in VaikhŚS) of the King's Throne or Rājāsandī.

The peg for the cow is south of the middle of the southern door, according to the Sūtras within the sight of the Hotṛ. The pin for the calf is south of the eastern door post of the southern door, so towards the east of the cow's peg. The pin for the she-goat is towards the south of the western door post of the southern door, so towards the west of the cow's peg. The one for the lamb is north of the peg for the she-goat. According to ĀpŚS, the pin for the she-goat is closer to the southern door than the cow's peg and the calf's pin.

The western or *pravṛñjanīya* mound is north of the Gārhapatya; the eastern or *udvāsanīya* mound is north of the Āhavanīya; the *ucchiṣṭa* or cleaning-up mound, is in the north-eastern region (according to BŚS in the northern section of the sacrificial hall), and has an outlet on the outside.

Gārh. Gārhapatya or Domestic Fire.
Āhav. Āhavanīya or Offering Fire.
Dakṣiṇ. Dakṣiṇāgni or Southern Fire.
R. Rājāsandī, the King's Throne for the Soma stalks.
S. Saṃrāḍ-āsandī, the Emperor's Throne for the Pravargya vessels.
m. *methī* and *mayūkha*-s, the peg and pins for the cow, the calf, the she-goat, and the lamb.
kh. *khara*-s, the mounds.
Utt. v. Uttaravedi.
n. nābhi.

(The plan and the additional information are mainly based on: Planche IV of Caland-Henry, *Agniṣṭoma* (at the end of vol.1); BŚS 11, 6, 8-16; ĀpŚS 15, 6, 10-22; HirŚS 24, 2, 10-11; van Buitenen, *Pravargya*, Plate 2 (opp. to p. 12); Staal, *Agni* 1:376-377, Plate 60B.)

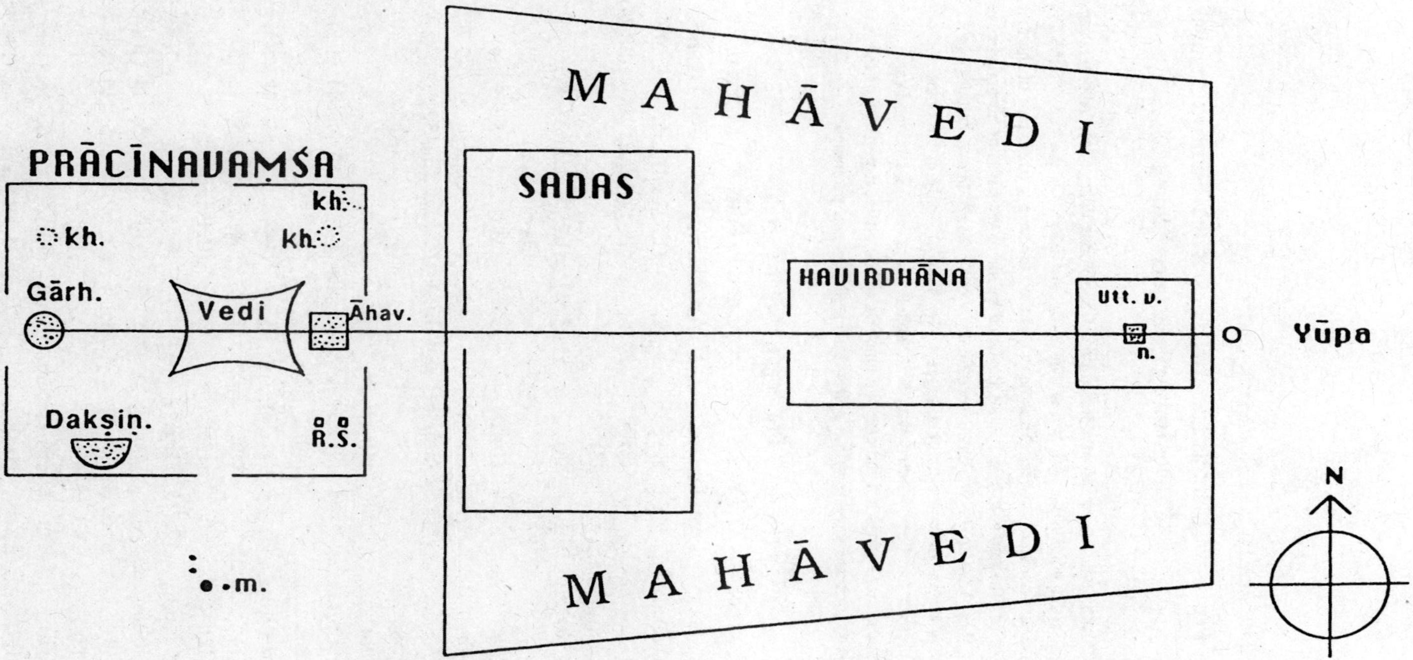

PRĀCĪNAVAṂŚA
kh.
kh.
kh.
Gārh.
Vedi
Āhav.
Dakṣiṇ.
R.S.
m.
MAHĀVEDI
SADAS
HAVIRDHĀNA
Utt. v.
n.
Yūpa
MAHĀVEDI
N

APPENDIX 2

The Pravargya Mantras and Brāhmaṇa of the Taittirīya Āraṇyaka

Concordance of the three editions

C is the Calcutta edition, M the Mysore edition, P the Poona edition (see Abbreviations under TĀ). Prap. is the prapāṭhaka, An. the anuvāka, Da. the daśati; in the case of the Pravargya mantras, the last number (between parentheses), is the number a specific part of the text has in edition C or M. The letters a, b, c . . . are attributed by me to the pādas or portions between two daṇḍas, if they have to be indicated specifically. "om" means that a certain part has been omitted or is absent. In case a number appears - by mistake - only in the notes and not in the text, the number has been marked with *. C and P (both with S's commentary) are almost similar, except that P does not indicate the numbers of the different portions of the text. Other differences (which are very few) have been indicated between parentheses.

Pravargya Mantras

C and P, Prap. 4			M, Prap. 7		
An.	Da.	no.	An.	Da.	no.
1,	1	(1-2)	1,	1	(1)
		(3)			(2)
		(4-6)			(3)
		(7-8)			(4)
2,	1	(1-4a)	2,	2	(1-4a)
2,	2	(4b-d)	2,	3	(4b-d)
		(5-6)			(5-6)
		(7a)			(7)
		(7b)			(8)
2,	3	(8a)	2,	4	(9)
		(8b)			(10)
		(9-10)			(11-12)
		(11)			(13a)
		(12)			(13bc)
2,	4	(C: om)	2,	5	(13de)
		(C: om)			(14a)
		(13)			(14b-e)
		(14a-c)			(15a-c)
2,	5	(14de)	2,	6	(15de)
		(15-17)			(16-18)

C and P, Prap. 4			M, Prap. 7		
An.	Da.	no.	An.	Da.	no.
2,	6	(18)	2,	7	(19)
		(19-23)			(20-24)
3,	1	(1-2)	3,	8	(1-2)
		(3a-c)			(3)
3,	2	(3d-f)	3,	9	(4)
		(4-6c)			(5-7c)
3,	3	(6d)	3,	10	(7d)
		(8-11)			(7-10)
4,	1	(1-2)	4,	11	(1-2)
5,	1	(1-4)	5,	12	(1-4)
5,	2	(5)	5,	13	(5)
		(C, P: om)			(6*)
		(6-8)			(7, 8*, 9)
5,	3	(9a-j)	5,	14	(10a-j)
5,	4	(9k-r)	5,	15	(10k-r)
		(10ab)			(11ab)
5,	5	(10c)	5,	16	(11c)
		(11-13c)			(12-14c)

C and P, Prap. 4 An. Da.	no.	M, Prap. 7 An. Da.	no.
5, 6	(13d-16a)	5, 17	(14d-17a)
5, 7	(16b-19)	5, 18	(17b-20)
6, 1	(1)	6, 19	(1a-d)
	(2)		(1e-f)
	(3a-d)		(1g-j)
6, 2	(3e-h)	6, 20	(1k-n)
	(4)		(2*)
	(5)		(3ab)
	(6ab)		(3cd)
(P:6, 3)	(6c)	6, 21	(3e)
	(7)		(4)
7, 1	(1)	7, 22	(1)
	(2a)		(2)
	(2cd)		(3)
	(3)		(4)
7, 2	(4-6b)	7, 23	(5-7)
7, 3	(6cd)	7, 24	(7cd)
	(7)		(8a-f)
	(8)		(8g)
	(9)		(8h)
7, 4	(10)	7, 25	(9a)
	(11)		(9b)
	(12)		(9c)
	(13)		(9d)
	(14)		(10)
	(15)		(11a)
	(16)		(11b)
	(17ab)		(11cd)
7, 5	(17cd)	7, 26	(11ef)
	(18-19)		(12-13)
8, 1	(1-4)	8, 27	(1-4)
8, 2	(5-9b)	8, 28	(5-9b)
8, 3	(9c-12)	8, 29	(9c-12)
8, 4	(13-19)	8, 30	(13-19)

C and P, Prap. 4 An. Da.	no.	M, Prap. 7 An. Da.	no.
(P:8, 5)	(20-22)	8, 31	(20-22)
9, 1	(1a-j)	9, 32	(1a-j)
9, 2	(1k-5a)	9, 33	(1k-5a)
9, 3	(5b-7f)	9, 34	(5b-7f)
(P:9, 4)	(7g-n)	9, 35	(7g-n)
10, 1	(1a-j)	10, 36	(1a-j)
10, 2	(1k-3)	10, 37	(1k-3)
10, 3	(4-6)	10, 38	(4-6)
10, 4	(7)	10, 39	(7)
	(8a-f)		(8-9a)
10, 5	(8g-j)	10, 40	(9b-d)
	(9a)		(10)
	(9b)		(11)
	(10)		(12)
	(11)		(13)
	(12a)		(14)
	(12b)		(15)
11, 1	(1)	11, 41	(1a-e)
	(2a-e)		(1f-j)
11, 2	(2f-j)	11, 42	(1k-o)
	(3a)		(2)
	(3b)		(3)
	(4a-c)		(4a-c)
11, 3	(4d-7a)	11, 43	(4d-7a)
11, 4	(7b-12)	11, 44	(7b-12)
11, 5	(13)	11, 45	(13a-d)
	(14)		(13e-j)
11, 6	(15)	11, 46	(13k-m)
	(16-17d)		(14-15d)
11, 7	(17e-19c)	11, 47	(15e-17c)
11, 8	(19d)	11, 48	(17d)
	(20a-c)		(18)
	(20d)		(19)
	(21-23a)		(20-22a)

C and P, Prap. 4 An. Da.	no.	M, Prap. 7 An. Da.	no.
	(23b-d)	11, 49	(22b-d)
	(24a)		(23)
	(24b)		(24-25)
	(25)		(26)
12, --	(1-3)	12, 50	(1-3)
13, --	(1-2)	13, 51	(1-2)
14, --		14, 52	(1)
|		| |	
16, --		16, 54	(1)
17, --		17, 55	(1-5)
18, --		18, 56	(1)
19, --		19, 57	(1a-j)
		19, 58	(1k-q)
20, 1	(1)	20, 59	(1)
	(2a)		(2)
	(2b)		(3)
	(3-4c)		(4-5c)
20, 2	(4d)	20, 60	(5d)
	(5)		(6-7)
	(6-7)		(8-9)
20, 3	(8)	20, 61	(10)
	(9)		(11-15)
	(10)		(16-19)
21, 1	(1)	21, 62	(1-3)
22, --	(1)	22, 63	(1)
|		| |	
|		| |	
27, --	(1)	27, 68	(1)
28, 1	(1-3)...	28, 69	(1-3)
29, --	(1)	29, 70	(1)
|		| |	
|		| |	
40, --	(1)	40, 81	(1)
41, 1	(1-2a)	41, 82	(1-2a)
41, 2	(2b-3b)	41, 83	(2b-3b)
41, 3	(3c-5a)	41, 84	(3c-5a)
41, 4	(5b-e)	41, 85	(5b-8)
	(6a-f)		(9a-f)
41, 5	(6g-p)	41, 86	(9g-10g)
41, 6	(6q-z)	41, 87	(10h-11h)
	(6aa-hh)	41, 88	(11i-16)
42, 1	(1)	42, 89	(1ab)
	(2a)		(1c)
	(2bc)		(2)
	(3-6a)		(3-6a)
42, 2	(6b)	42, 90	(6b)
	(7ab)		(7)
	(7c-8)		(8)
	(9-13)		(9-13)
42, 3	(14-18)	42, 91	(14-18)
42, 4	(19-24a)	42, 92	(19-24a)
42, 5	(24b-25)	42, 93	(24b-25a)
	(26-27)		(25bc)
	(28-37)		(26-35)

Pravargya Brāhmaṇa

C and P, Prap. 5 An. Da.	M, Prap. 8 An. Da.	C and P, Prap. 5 An. Da.	M, Prap. 8 An. Da.
1, 1-7	1, 1-7	7, 1-12	7, 58-69
2, 1-13	2, 8-20	8, 1-13	8, 70-82
3, 1-9	3, 21-29	9, 1-11	9, 83-93
4, 1-13	4, 30-42	10, 1-6	10, 94-99
5, 1-3	5, 43-45	11, 1-6	11, 100-105
6, 1-12	6, 46-57	12, 1-3	12, 106-108

General index

The numbers refer to the pages. If the number appears in italics, this means that the word or text-place occurs only in a footnote starting on that page. Numbers in bold face refer to the translation. Only relatively important places have been indexed.

Index of Textplaces

ERRATUM

on p. 5, line 13, read "over the Āhavanīya (some sources: Gārhapatya) fire" instead of "over the Āhavanīya fire".